# Ethiopian Yearbook of International Law 2017

**Editor-in-Chief**

Dr. Zeray Yihdego

**Editors**

Prof. Dr. Melaku Geboye Desta
Martha Belete Hailu
Dr. Fikremarkos Merso

**Assistant Editors**

Jasmin Hansohm
Emily Hirst
Abubakri Yekini

**Editorial Advisory Boards**

Prof. Dr. Daniel Abebe, University of Chicago Law School, Chicago, CA, USA
Dr. Musa Abseno, Independent Consultancy and Law Practice, Addis Ababa, Ethiopia
Prof. Dr. Jean Allain, Monash University, Clayton, VIC, Australia
Prof. Dapo Akande, University of Oxford Faculty of Law, Oxford, UK
Dr. Yacob Arsano, Addis Ababa University, Addis Ababa, Ethiopia
Dr. Mulugeta Mengist Ayalew, Prime Minister's Office, Addis Ababa, Ethiopia
Dr. Mohamed Abdelsalam Babiker, University of Khartoum Faculty of Law, Khartoum, Sudan
Dr. Assefa Fiseha, Addis Ababa University, Addis Ababa, Ethiopia
Prof. Dr. James Thuo Gathii, Loyola School of Law, Chicago, IL, USA
Ambassador Minelik Alemu Getahun, World Intellectual Property Organisation (WIPO), Geneva, Switzerland
Prof. Dr. L. van den Herik, Leiden University, Leiden, The Netherlands
Ambassador Ibrahim Idris, Addis Ababa University, Addis Ababa, Ethiopia and Ethiopian Ministry of Foreign Affairs, Addis Ababa, Ethiopia
Prof. Dr. Jeremy Levitt, Florida A & M University College of Law, Orlando, FL, USA
Prof. Dr. Makane Moïse Mbengue, University of Geneva, Geneva, Switzerland
Dr. Benyam Dawit Mezmur, Dullah Omar Institute of the University of the Western Cape, Western Cape, South Africa and UN Committee on the Rights of the Child, Geneva, Switzerland
Prof. Sean Murphy, George Washington School of Law, Washington, DC, USA and International Law Commission (ILC), Washington, DC, USA
Prof. Dr. Makau Mutua, The State University of New York (SUNY) Buffalo Law School, Buffalo, NY, USA
Prof. Dr. John Paterson, University of Aberdeen Law School, Aberdeen, UK
Prof. Chris Maina Peter, International Law Commission (ILC), Washington, DC, USA and University of Dar es Salaam, Dar es Salaam, Tanzania
Dr. Salman Salman, International Water Resources Association (IWRA), Khartoum, Sudan
Prof. Dr. Wenhua Shan, Xi'an Jiaotong University, Shaanxi Sheng, China
Judge Abdulqawi A. Yusuf, International Court of Justice, The Hague, Netherlands and Institut de Droit International, Geneva, Switzerland

The Ethiopian Yearbook of International Law (EtYIL) is a peer-reviewed academic journal that publishes scholarly works of the highest standard in the field of international law broadly defined, but with a focus on Ethiopia and the Horn of Africa region. International law presents both opportunities and challenges to developing countries; however, their role in the making of the law and the scholarly analysis and debate that informs and underpins its evolution remains marginal. By choosing Ethiopia as its geographical focus, this Yearbook aims to contribute towards filling this gap and the long-term goal of rebalancing the narrative of international law in a manner that better reflects the diversity of its actors and subjects. With this in mind, EtYIL welcomes contributions in all areas of international law and relations. Particular issues of interest to the Yearbook include sustainable development law, the law of international trade and investment, the peaceful settlement of disputes, the sharing and preservation of transboundary resources, regional integration, peace and security, humanitarian law and human rights, and regional and international institutions.

More information about this series at http://www.springer.com/series/15093

Zeray Yihdego • Melaku Geboye Desta •
Martha Belete Hailu • Fikremarkos Merso
Editors

# Ethiopian Yearbook of International Law 2017

*Editors*
Zeray Yihdego
School of Law
University of Aberdeen
Aberdeen, United Kingdom

Melaku Geboye Desta
Leicester De Montfort School of Law
Faculty of Business and Law
De Montfort University
Leicester, UK

United Nations Economic Commission for
Africa, Addis Ababa, Ethiopia

Martha Belete Hailu
Addis Ababa University
Addis Ababa, Ethiopia

Fikremarkos Merso
College of Law and Governance Studies
Addis Ababa University
Addis Ababa, Ethiopia

ISSN 2522-5286     ISSN 2522-5294 (electronic)
Ethiopian Yearbook of International Law
ISBN 978-3-319-90886-1     ISBN 978-3-319-90887-8 (eBook)
https://doi.org/10.1007/978-3-319-90887-8

Library of Congress Control Number: 2018950231

© Springer International Publishing AG, part of Springer Nature 2018
This work is subject to copyright. All rights are reserved by the Publisher, whether the whole or part of the material is concerned, specifically the rights of translation, reprinting, reuse of illustrations, recitation, broadcasting, reproduction on microfilms or in any other physical way, and transmission or information storage and retrieval, electronic adaptation, computer software, or by similar or dissimilar methodology now known or hereafter developed.
The use of general descriptive names, registered names, trademarks, service marks, etc. in this publication does not imply, even in the absence of a specific statement, that such names are exempt from the relevant protective laws and regulations and therefore free for general use.
The publisher, the authors and the editors are safe to assume that the advice and information in this book are believed to be true and accurate at the date of publication. Neither the publisher nor the authors or the editors give a warranty, express or implied, with respect to the material contained herein or for any errors or omissions that may have been made. The publisher remains neutral with regard to jurisdictional claims in published maps and institutional affiliations.

Printed on acid-free paper

This Springer imprint is published by the registered company Springer Nature Switzerland AG.
The registered company address is: Gewerbestrasse 11, 6330 Cham, Switzerland

# Contents

**Part I Introduction**

Towards Resolving Our Development, Integration and Security
Challenges Through International Law ........................... 3
Zeray Yihdego, Melaku Geboye Desta, Fikremarkos Merso,
and Martha Belete Hailu

**Part II Articles**

The Law and Policy of Foreign Investment Promotion and Protection
in Ethiopia: An Appraisal of Theories, Practices and Challenges ....... 13
Martha Belete Hailu and Zeray Yihdego

Comparative Perspective on Exhaustible Resource Development
in Ethiopia: Lessons from the Norwegian Legal Framework
and Experience .................................................. 49
Tina Hunter

The GERD and the Revival of the Egyptian–Sudanese Dispute over
the Nile Waters ................................................. 79
Salman M. A. Salman

The Challenge of Overlapping Regional Economic Communities
in Africa: Lessons for the Continental Free Trade Area from
the Failures of the Tripartite Free Trade Area...................... 111
Melaku Geboye Desta and Guillaume Gérout

Like Fish in a Stream? Considering the Agency of the UN
Peacekeepers of the Global South: Rwanda and India as Case Studies.... 143
Philip Roberts

**Part III Current Development**

The Kenya/Somalia Maritime Boundary Delimitation Dispute ......... 173
Fayokemi Olorundami

**The ICC and Africa: Should the Latter Remain Engaged?** ............ 187
Makane Moïse Mbengue and Kirsten McClellan

**Part IV  Case Report**

**Case Note on *PetroTrans Company Ltd. v. Ministry of Mines
of the Federal Democratic Republic of Ethiopia*** ..................... 207
Thomas R. Snider and Jackson Shaw Kern

**Part V  Book Review**

**Zeray Yihdego, Alistair Rieu-Clarke and Ana Elisa Cascão (eds.):
The Grand Ethiopian Renaissance Dam and the Nile
Basin—Implications for Transboundary Water Cooperation** .......... 215
Götz Reichert

**Won L. Kidane: The Culture of International Arbitration** ............. 221
Makane Moïse Mbengue and Elise Ruggeri Abonnat

**Part VI  UN Document with Commentary**

**UN Security Council Resolution 2378 (2017) and the Progressive
Peacekeeping Agenda: A Commentary** ............................. 229
Christian Henderson

# Part I
# Introduction

# Towards Resolving Our Development, Integration and Security Challenges Through International Law

Zeray Yihdego, Melaku Geboye Desta, Fikremarkos Merso, and Martha Belete Hailu

As editors of the *Ethiopian Yearbook of International Law* (EtYIL), we are pleased to offer to our readers the 2017 issue of the Yearbook—the second in our series.

Feedback from our readers and the publisher about the reception of the maiden issue is encouraging. In the editorial to that volume, we set out EtYIL's purpose and mission as follows:

> EtYIL is dedicated to those issues of international law that are of particular interest to the African continent in general and Ethiopia and the Horn in particular. EtYIL's point of departure is the fact that these countries do not just lack adequate representation at the table where international law is made and interpreted; their ability to contribute to the evolution of international law is also severely constrained owing, in part, to their absence from the scholarly debate in the field. A key mission of EtYIL is therefore to provide a platform for purpose-oriented scholarly analysis and debate on issues of particular significance for these countries so as to enhance their capacity to contribute to this evolution. More generally, the Yearbook aims to contribute towards the long-term goal of rebalancing the narrative of international law in a manner that better reflects the diversity of its actors and subjects.

This mission and purpose remains at the heart of EtYIL and dictated our choice of topics for this volume. The warm reception of the maiden issue by the international

---

Z. Yihdego (✉)
School of Law, University of Aberdeen, Aberdeen, UK
e-mail: zeray.yihdego@abdn.ac.uk

M. G. Desta
Leicester De Montfort School of Law, Faculty of Business and Law, De Montfort University, Leicester, UK

United Nations Economic Commission for Africa, Addis Ababa, Ethiopia
e-mail: melaku.desta@dmu.ac.uk

F. Merso
College of Law and Governance Studies, Addis Ababa University, Addis Ababa, Ethiopia

M. B. Hailu
Addis Ababa University, Addis Ababa, Ethiopia

law and policy community shows that we probably set the bar quite high for ourselves, but we are confident that we have brought together, once again, scholarly works of the highest intellectual rigour that meet this bar.

Like in the inaugural issue, this edition also contains articles of varying sizes on a range of international law issues, but all of them focusing on issues of particular interest to Ethiopia, Africa and developing countries at large. Put together, each of these pieces of scholarship shares one key feature in common—they make a significant contribution towards EtYIL's primary goal of 'rebalancing the narrative of international law'; they give centre stage to issues of special interest to developing countries that would otherwise be relegated, if at all, to the back pages of the mainstream international law scholarship; in a word, they give voice to the voiceless.

Of the 11 scholarly pieces, both long and short, contained in this volume, three are specific to Ethiopia, addressing the legal aspects of some of the most critical areas of national policy and practice. Another set of three contributions falling in the second category deals with issues of specific concern to the sub-region around Ethiopia. A third category of contributions contains two articles that address issues of concern to the African continent as a whole. Finally, we have three contributions that fall in the fourth category that discuss issues of yet broader significance to developing countries in general. While this introduction will be structured on the basis of this geographical sequencing—from Ethiopia to the world—in the Yearbook, the contributions are arranged in accordance with the traditional approach of articles, current developments, case reports, book reviews and documents.

To start with the first category, in their article on *The Law and Policy of Foreign Investment Promotion and Protection in Ethiopia: An Appraisal of Theories, Practices and Challenges*, Martha Hailu and Zeray Yihdego, both of them members of the EtYIL editorial team, offer a comprehensive overview of Ethiopia's approach to the promotion, protection and regulation of foreign and domestic investment, which is at the top of the government's economic priority list under its Growth and Transformation Plan II (2016–2020). According to government sources, Ethiopia attracted over USD 7 billion worth of foreign direct investment during the GTP I period (2011–2015), which GTP II vowed to sustain as a matter of priority. Belete and Yihdego assess Ethiopia's policy approaches to the promotion of FDI, the municipal and international/bilateral legal instruments it employed, as well as the actual performance of the regulatory institutions, and conclude by painting a broadly encouraging picture of an economy that has registered record growth over the years. The authors, however, also identify a number of areas of concern where the government could—and indeed should—do more, including the efficiency of its institutions, protection of human rights and the environment and a rule-based and sensitive handling of the issue of land dispossession for investment purposes.

The second article in this volume that is exclusively focused on Ethiopia relates to the country's regulatory approaches to the development and exploitation of its exhaustible natural resources. In her article on *Comparative Perspective on Exhaustible Resource Development in Ethiopia: Lessons from the Norwegian Legal Framework and Experience*, Tina Hunter introduces the Ethiopian legislative framework within which the exploration, development and extraction of petroleum resources take place and asks a pertinent question of whether this framework supports Ethiopia's goals of developing its resources sustainably for the benefit of its people. Hunter's analysis is not limited to Ethiopian law in and of itself; she also examines it in comparison to Norway's highly advanced petroleum legislative framework that has been perfected over more than four decades of successful operation. Hunter concludes by drawing some lessons that Ethiopia might wish to learn in order to better support its sustainable development goals through the well-articulated policies and requirements for field development planning and depletion policy as practised in such jurisdictions as Norway and others.

The third and final piece in this issue that focuses exclusively on Ethiopia is a case comment written by Thomas R. Snider and Jackson Shaw Kern on an international arbitration award issued under the auspices of the International Chamber of Commerce (ICC) Court of Arbitration in *PetroTrans Company Ltd. v. Ministry of Mines of the Federal Democratic Republic of Ethiopia*. Unfortunately, the final decision remains confidential—a typical problem associated with international arbitration generally—but the authors tell us, on the basis of publicly available information, that the case concerned a claim for alleged unlawful termination by the Ethiopian Government of a set of five production sharing agreements (PSAs). The Geneva-based tribunal issued its final award on 31 December 2015 rejecting all of PetroTrans' claims against Ethiopia and upholding the latter's contention that it terminated the PSAs because of claimant's failure of performance. Importantly, the authors take this opportunity to also reflect on the only other petroleum-related arbitration case that Ethiopia had to defend, before a three-person panel of arbitrators that was also based in Geneva, in which Baruch-Foster Corporation, an American company, brought a case against the then Imperial Government of Ethiopia, also for premature termination of a concession contract. We learn that, just as in the PetroTrans case now, the arbitrators dismissed that claim in an award dated 15 February 1974.

This then takes us to the second category, which is a set of three contributions—one major article, a case comment and a book review—that focus on the region around Ethiopia. In a seminal article on *The Grand Ethiopian Renaissance Dam (GERD) and the Revival of the Egyptian-Sudanese Dispute over the Nile Waters*, Salman M. A. Salman uses the ongoing controversy among the three Nile riparian countries of Ethiopia, Sudan and Egypt to reflect back specifically on the colonial and post-colonial history of bilateral relations between Egypt and Sudan around the sharing of the Nile waters between them. Using the difficult negotiations among the three countries relating to the GERD today as his point of departure, Salman takes us deep into the historical politico-legal context within which previous water-sharing arrangements between the two countries were concluded and the potential for them to unravel their long-established alliance against the other Nile riparian countries upstream. Salman concludes his article with a call for genuine adherence to the established principles for sustainable, reasonable and equitable sharing of the Nile waters and for good faith negotiations and cooperation to bring peace and prosperity to the peoples of the river basin.

The second piece under this category is closely linked to Salman's article, a review of the book entitled *The Grand Ethiopian Renaissance Dam and the Nile*

*Basin—Implications for Transboundary Water Cooperation* (Earthscan, 2018), edited by Zeray Yihdego, Alistair Rieu-Clarke and Ana Elisa Cascão. The book, just like Salman's article in this issue (and, indeed, Salman himself wrote two of the chapters in the book), is highly topical in itself and, of course, highly relevant to the unfolding political and diplomatic developments in the region surrounding the GERD project. In his review of the book, Götz Reichert welcomes the timing of this publication and particularly its multidisciplinary approach bringing to bear different and complementary perspectives from leading experts in law, political science, economics and hydrology. While the reviewer regrets the absence of more Egyptian voices in the book to represent what he calls Egypt's 'persistent claim of historic rights to the Nile waters', he also praises the book for the delicate and fair balance it has managed to strike in reflecting the at times competing interests of Ethiopia, Sudan and Egypt.

The last piece in this volume that falls within the regional category of issues is a comment prepared by Fayokemi Olorundami on *The Kenya/Somalia Maritime Boundary Delimitation Dispute* case, which is currently before the International Court of Justice (ICJ). While the case is still pending, the Court has already issued its judgment on a preliminary objection raised by Kenya on two grounds: (i) the Court lacked jurisdiction because Kenya had signed a Memorandum of Understanding with Somalia, which provided for settlement of disputes through the Commission on the Limits of the Continental Shelf (CLCS), and, in the alternative, (ii) considering that both parties to the dispute are also parties to UNCLOS, the appropriate method for the settlement of any dispute on this subject would be through arbitration, the default method provided under Article 287(3) of UNCLOS. The ICJ rejected both grounds and assumed jurisdiction; the hearing on the merits is expected to commence early in 2018. Using the established jurisprudence in this area, Olorundami concludes that while the Court is likely to stay faithful to established jurisprudence, she also cautions us that trying to predict how the case is likely to end is a hazardous game worth avoiding.

This then takes us to two articles falling under a third category of contributions that address issues of relevance to the whole of Africa. In 'The Challenge of Overlapping Regional Economic Communities in Africa: What Can the Continental Free Trade Area Learn from the Failures of the Tripartite Free Trade Area?', Melaku Geboye Desta (one of our editors) and Guillaume Gérout discuss an issue that is at the top of the continental integration agenda today—the ongoing negotiations for the conclusion of the Continental Free Trade Area (CFTA). While the CFTA negotiations are at an advanced stage, there is little information that is public at this stage. However, Desta and Gérout also argue that since a block of countries that make up nearly half of the 55 African Union member states engaged in the CFTA negotiations have recently concluded the Tripartite Free Trade Area (TFTA), which aimed to bring 26 countries in the eastern half of the continent under one umbrella, there is much we can learn by closely examining the latter agreement that could be of benefit to the CFTA negotiation process. Accordingly, Desta and Gérout examine the text of the TFTA, the process through which it was negotiated, the sticking points that arose, as well as the manner in which they were resolved. Desta and

Gérout argue that the same people who negotiated the TFTA are likely to be involved in the CFTA; as a result, the same issues that came up during the TFTA are likely to emerge in the context of the CFTA, thus providing important learning opportunities that the CFTA negotiators would be well advised to heed. The manner in which the CFTA negotiators deal with the most favoured nation principle, whether or not the principle of variable geometry should have a place after the conclusion of the CFTA and the future relationships between the CFTA on the one hand and the regional economic communities (RECs) on the other, are some of the areas identified for lesson learning.

The second piece in this category takes up yet another sensitive subject for the continent—the relationship between Africa and the International Criminal Court (ICC). In their current development piece entitled 'The ICC and Africa: Should the Latter Remain Engaged?', Makane Moise Mbengue and Kirsten McClellan delve straight into what they call the 'tumultuous relationship' between Africa and the Court since the latter's establishment in 2002. Mbengue and McClellan argue that, while African states were instrumental in the establishment of the Court and the development of international criminal law more generally, the relationship between the Court and the African Union has faced a number of ups and downs over the years. Mbengue and McClellan identify the reasons behind this deterioration in the relationship, the proposals that were made by individual African countries, as well as the continental bodies, and their implications for justice in the continent. Mbengue and McClellan conclude with the wise counsel that, in order for the relationship between Africa and the ICC to continue to evolve in a positive direction, there needs to be more effective, systematised and institutionalised discourse between African states and the ICC. The authors are clear that the best way forward is to continue to engage with the ICC but also for African states to strengthen their own national judiciaries and consider expanding the jurisdiction of the African Court of Justice and Human Rights to cover international crimes.

Finally, the fourth category of contributions deals with issues of yet broader relevance to all developing countries and not just to Africa. Three pieces fall under this category—a full article; a recent UN Security Council Resolution, along with a commentary; and a book review. The major article in this group is a contribution by Philip Roberts, entitled *Like Fish in a Stream? Considering the Agency of the UN Peacekeepers of the Global South: Rwanda and India as Case Studies*. Peacekeeping operations have come to characterise the UN's response to armed conflict for several decades now, but they have also evolved during this period. In this article, Roberts argues that the evolution of peacekeeping operations is also reflected in significant changes in the composition of peacekeeping forces whereby the previously predominant troops from the developed states have given way to peacekeepers coming predominantly from the Global South. Roberts then asks the provocative question of whether this change and enhanced contribution to UN peacekeeping by countries in the Global South is motivated by self-interest, or is it the reincarnation of the hegemonic interests of the Global North through the instrumentality of the UN? Acknowledging the facts on the ground could be interpreted in different ways; Roberts reaches the nuanced conclusion that while northern hegemony remains important in UN peacekeeping operations, southern states take an active part in these operations largely for their own carefully considered, often disparate, reasons.

The second piece falling under this category is a reprint of UN Security Council Resolution 2378 (2017) on Peacekeeping Reform, which was unanimously adopted on 20 September 2017. In an accompanying note entitled *UN Security Council Resolution 2378 (2017) and the Progressive Peacekeeping Agenda: A Commentary*, Christian Henderson describes it as a notable resolution that brought together various ideas and reform proposals that have emerged over the years in connection with United Nations peacekeeping operations. As one of the leading troop-contributing countries to peacekeeping operations going back to the days of Congo and Korea, it is also notable that the Resolution was debated at the Council's special meeting in Addis Ababa in September 2017 and passed while Ethiopia was serving as President of the Council.

Finally, Elise Ruggeri Abonnat and Makane Moïse Mbengue review a book written by a prominent Ethiopian academic and practitioner, Prof. Won L. Kidane, entitled *The Culture of International Arbitration* (Oxford University Press, 2017, 336 pages). Abonnat and Mbengue welcome *The Culture of International Arbitration* as a contribution that breaks old taboos, raises difficult questions, challenges the 'establishment' and calls for the epistemic community of international arbitration to better reflect the cultural diversity of the parties that stand before it. Abonnat and Mbengue praise Kidane's analysis as a timely reminder that the status quo is not only an option but also a call for a restatement of the well-known legal maxim 'Not only must Justice be done; it must also be seen to be done'.

This is a rich collection; many of the issues covered here are so topical that EtYIL's third issue is likely to look very much a continuation of this issue. To cite just a few examples, as we are preparing to submit this edition to our publisher, Ethiopia is working hard to maintain its current status as the fastest-growing economy in the world[1] while restoring its internal stability that has been shaken by widespread popular uprising against the ruling party. International law might look like the most remote subject to Ethiopia and Ethiopians in this situation, but, in reality, international law serves, inter alia, (i) as an enabling tool with which Ethiopia can attract investors and/or access foreign markets for its products, settle international disputes (including the contentious issues surrounding the Grand Ethiopian Renaissance Dam project) and pursue any other complementary policy objectives and (ii) as a guiding force that sets limits to what the government and others may or may not do in the way they deal with internal matters or in their relations with external powers. Likewise, we are finalising this edition at a time when Africa is busy negotiating new international treaties and protocols in a broad range of subject areas—from the all-encompassing and challenging task of establishing the continental free trade area to the creation of a single African air transport market to the

---

[1] See World Bank (2018).

free movement of persons across the continent, to mention only the major ones. Indeed, it feels as though we are at a special moment in the history of international law in Ethiopia, the sub-region and the continent at large; for us, the editors, it is both a duty and a privilege to follow these developments and use the EtYIL as the platform through which to bring them out for objective, dispassionate, rigorous and purposeful analyses, debates and discussions. It is for that reason that we once again wish to seize this opportunity to invite international law scholars and practitioners in all fields to consider the EtYIL for publishing their research work of general or specific relevance to the aims and scope of the Yearbook.

The completion of this issue within schedule was possible only because of the unreserved support, guidance and encouragement we received from members of the EtYIL Advisory Board. The contributors to this volume deserve our special thanks particularly for the professional manner in which they handled the comments—at times quite critical but always constructive—from our anonymous peer reviewers, as well as from the editors. We also extend our appreciation to the external reviewers who did an excellent job and yet have to remain anonymous for obvious reasons. Our assistant editors—Jasmin Hansohm and Emily Hirst, who have been with us since the first issue, and Abubakri Yekini, who joined us for this volume—have been tireless and meticulous; we are grateful. Finally, the professional support we receive from our colleagues at Springer is second to none; we thank you.

# Reference

World Bank (2018) Global economic prospects. Washington, DC

# Part II
# Articles

# The Law and Policy of Foreign Investment Promotion and Protection in Ethiopia: An Appraisal of Theories, Practices and Challenges

Martha Belete Hailu and Zeray Yihdego

**Abstract** This article explores selected and topical features of Ethiopian foreign direct investment (FDI) law and practice in light of the laissez-faire (or liberal) and statist approaches to promoting and governing inward foreign investment. It particularly focuses on entry and operational requirements, including the extent to which some economic sectors are restricted to foreign investors, the rules of local content with emphasis on local employment, protection offered to investors and their investment, the aggressive state intervention in facilitating and attracting FDI and some of the challenges affecting FDI such as the controversial large-scale land deals between the government and foreign investors. By applying general doctrines and approaches of FDI law, it argues that the Ethiopian FDI legal framework is consistent with the trends and foundational standards of international investment law (IIL); it further finds that Ethiopian FDI law and practice are predominantly statist. While this approach to FDI can be acclaimed for attracting foreign investment and helping economic growth in developing countries like Ethiopia, lack of transparency, accountability and lack of strict adherence to local content rules and policies raise concerns. Addressing the various governance and other interpretive and technical challenges would be vital to building a healthy, sustainable and fair (foreign) investment regime to those who invest, to communities and to the country at large.

## 1 Introduction

With the change of government in Ethiopia in the early 1990s came a change of economic policy. The country declared that its long-term objective was to enhance the welfare of the people through ensuring sustainable growth with a free market

M. B. Hailu (✉)
Addis Ababa University, Addis Ababa, Ethiopia

Z. Yihdego
School of Law, University of Aberdeen, Aberdeen, UK
e-mail: zeray.yihdego@abdn.ac.uk

economic system.¹ Since then, Ethiopia has made tangible progress in attracting, promoting and benefiting from foreign and domestic investment. The latter is largely, but not exclusively, state-sponsored investment on mega projects such as hydro-power dams and other renewable sources of energy, railway networks, major roads, telecommunications, air transport services, etc. Significant inward FDI flow has also been attracted from countries such as China, India, Saudi Arabia, Turkey, the UK and the Netherlands because of a favourable foreign investment climate, including relatively cheap labour and electricity; suitable climate; attractive laws, policies and incentives; infrastructure provision; a large market, vast land resources; regional significance; and the inducements that foreign investors are afforded.² It is reported that Ethiopia 'rose to…the Top-10 investment destinations in Africa'³ in the year 2014–2015, which appears to be a result of a build-up of several years of incoming investment, including the boom between the years 2006 and 2011.

The top-performing sectors of foreign investment between 1992 and 2016 include manufacturing (over 62 billion birr or roughly equivalent to $2.7 billion), construction and water well drilling (about 10 billion birr), agriculture (about 8 billion birr) and real estate, machinery, equipment rentals and consultancy services (about 6 billion birr).⁴ Health, education and other sectors such as electricity have attracted FDI, although on a relatively smaller scale than in the above sectors.⁵

To meet the investment flow and the developmental ambition set to make the country a middle-income economy by 2025, the necessary FDI laws, regulations, policies and institutions have been evolving over the last decade.⁶ Despite this and the achievements in attracting foreign investment, Ethiopia's average double-digit GDP growth for some years now and the grand economic transformation plans⁷ that are being aggressively implemented by the government, the manner in which the government implements its foreign investment laws and policies has adversely affected the interests of certain communities. This is due, in part, to dispossession

---

[1] For an insightful historical overview see Porter (1999), pp. 362–280. See also Memorandum on the Foreign Trade Regime (MFTR): Ethiopia Ministry of Trade and Industry December 2006 http://www.ethdiaspora.org.et/phocadownloadpap/Publications/moti-memorandumonthe-ftr.pdf.

[2] Addis and Zuping (August 2016), p. 226. Ethiopian Investment Commission Guide (2014). http://www.ethiopianembassy.org/PDF/Ethiopia_Investment_Guide_2014.pdf.

[3] 'Ethiopia dethrones Ivory Coast as Africa's fastest growing economy to top the world' Business Insider, 11 June, 2017 http://www.pulse.ng/bi/strategy/strategy-ethiopia-dethrones-ivory-coast-as-africas-fastest-growing-economy-to-top-the-world-id6973194.html. See also Ethiopian Investment Commission Indicators at http://www.investethiopia.gov.et/why-ethiopia/economic-indicators. For the overall economic performance of the country see World Bank (2017), pp. 17–18, 107–108.

[4] Data obtained from Ethiopian Investment Commission (EIC), January 2017, information on file with authors.

[5] Ibid.

[6] For the main laws and regulations relevant to FDI and their amendments see http://www.investethiopia.gov.et/information-center/publications.

[7] See e.g. National Planning Commission, Addis Ababa, Growth and Transformation Plan II (GTP II), (2015/16-2019/20), May, 2016.

of land without adequate compensation and with little regard to land owners' property interests. Such behaviour has ultimately contributed to citizens' political and economic discontent, which resulted in clashes and eventually culminated in the declaration of a state of emergency in 2016. This instability threatens existing and future foreign and domestic investment in the country.[8] According to the Ethiopian Investment Commission, FDI continued to rise even during the state of emergency,[9] which lasted for 10 months before it was finally lifted in August 2017.[10]

In light of this background, and without dwelling too much on non-legal aspects of the subject under consideration, this article enquires into (1) the extent to which aspects of Ethiopian FDI law are evolving in the right direction and reflect relevant international standards and good practices, (2) whether the laws and practices are inspired by a *laissez-faire* or a statist approach to foreign investment regulation and their implications for the first question asked, (3) whether or not FDI law and relevant institutions in general have evolved to support the achievements attained in attracting foreign investors and the mounting local employment needs and, (4) assuming that the Ethiopian FDI regime is evolving in the right direction, the successes and challenges of the regime and the lessons that may be learnt by Ethiopia and other developing countries from them.

At the same time, it is notable that the scope of this article is limited as it does not purport to deal with all aspects of Ethiopian FDI law, policy and practice. Instead, the article reflects on the above questions using selected investment issues and current developments from legal and relevant policy perspectives.

To that end, the rest of this article is structured in five substantive sections: Sect. 2 sets the conceptual framework; Sect. 3, which contains the core of the article, reviews FDI laws and regulations at various levels of the investment value chain – entry and operational requirements, investor protection and local content requirements. Section 4 deals with recent developments and legal and institutional reforms; Sect. 5 articulates some of the challenges encountered over the years and the manner in which the government responded, while Sect. 6 provides concluding remarks.

---

[8] 'Ethiopia: State of emergency declared', The Economist (13 October, 2016). The newspaper predicted that: 'The declaration of a six-month state of emergency could further weaken political and, increasingly, economic stability, with a negative knock-on impact on investment and tourism. Relations with donors—which have long considered Ethiopia a beacon of relative stability in the Horn of Africa—could also be hit, given the wider use of repressive tactics'.

[9] Derso (21 February 2017). It must be noted that Ethiopian inward FDI flow was relatively low compared to the previous years. Equally, as per a recent report global FDI declined due to global economic slowdown and is predicted to pick up in 2017 see UNCTAD (Investment Report 2017b), pp. 4–6.

[10] John Aglionby, 'Ethiopia lifts 10-month state of emergency', Financial Times (4 August, 2017).

## 2 Conceptual Underpinnings

International investment law (IIL) is by now an established branch of public international law (PIL).[11] Its sources include the international law of alien protection,[12] bilateral and multilateral investment agreements, investment contracts and national investment laws.[13] Indeed, it is common to find articles, sections and chapters in international agreements that deal with foreign direct investment (FDI) as part of broader interstate trade and economic arrangements.[14]

IIL primarily, but not exclusively, aims to protect foreign nationals who are engaged in investment undertakings outside their home countries. IIL encompasses non-discrimination against foreign nationals, providing them with fair and equitable treatment and protecting their property rights.[15] However, the standard of treatment foreign investors are entitled to enjoy has been subject to debate. Developed countries, which are often, but not always, on the investing side in the territories of developing countries, have long maintained that foreign investors must be afforded protection based upon the international minimum standard, which includes full protection to their assets. This approach advocates that host states not only should treat foreign investors the same as their own citizens (the national treatment standard) but also in accordance with established standards defined by international law independently of the relevant domestic law.[16]

In contrast, developing countries traditionally maintained that foreign investors be subjected to the national treatment standard as determined by domestic law and interpreted by domestic tribunals of the host state.[17] This would also include the right of state authorities to expropriate the assets of foreign investors in accordance with their domestic laws and subject to compensation determined under those laws.[18] As Mexico put it in 1938:

> The foreigner who voluntarily moves to a country which is not his own, in search of a personal benefit, accepts in advance, together with the advantages he is going to enjoy, the risks to which he may find himself exposed. It would be unjust that he should aspire to a privileged position.[19]

---

[11] Brungenberg et al. (2015), p. 1. While these authors trace it to the 1950s (in its modern form) and to the nineteenth century as part of friendship, commerce and navigations agreements, others take it back to the eighteenth century. See e.g. Dolzer and Schreuer (2012), p. 1.

[12] Hobe (2015), pp. 6–22.

[13] Brungenberg et al. (2015), p. 1. It has been recorded that more than 3200 bilateral and multilateral investment agreements exist to date. For a detailed discussion on sources of IIL see Dolzer and Schreuer (2012), pp. 12–19.

[14] Brungenberg et al. (2015), p. 3.

[15] Dolzer and Schreuer (2012), pp. 1–3. McLachln et al. (2007), pp. 3–8.

[16] Brown (2015), p. 158. Dolzer and Schreuer (2012), p. 2.

[17] Brown (2015), pp. 158–159. Dolzer and Schreuer (2012), p. 4.

[18] Ibid.

[19] 'Official Documents' (1938) 32 AJIL Sup. 181, 188.

The conceptual distinction and doctrinal controversy between developed and developing countries did not stop the latter countries from succumbing to pressure from the former. This led to the signing of thousands of bilateral agreements, and other instruments, that are designed to give effect to the position of capital-exporting developed countries, with the international minimum standard as the rule. The various (BITs)[20] signed between host and home states and (emerging) multilateral investment (or trade) treaties[21] such as the draft 1957 International Convention for the Mutual Protection of Private Property Rights in Foreign Countries proposed by a group of experts[22] promote international minimum standards based upon the concept of fair and equitable treatment to assets of foreign investors. In fact, IIL has gone to the extent of recognising the foreign investor as a legal person with the right to sue a state before an international tribunal, notably before ICSID tribunals.[23] Nevertheless, the North–South division around IIL remains one of the most controversial subjects of international law.

As Professor Melaku Desta articulates in his work published in the 2016 volume of the Ethiopian Yearbook of International Law, the nature and evolution of IIL is

> the direct or indirect product of competing claims and counterclaims…The story of this evolution can be told as a process of fine-tuning the point of equilibrium between the claim for the fullest possible measure of sovereignty in traditionally capital-importing (host) states and the desire for the fullest possible protection of foreign investment by capital-exporting (home) states.[24]

The competition over attracting FDI by developing countries and the economic rise of some developing countries such as China,[25] which led them to be capital importers from, and capital exporters to, both developing and developed countries, has not eliminated the competing claims and standards proposed by host and home states. Nevertheless, even if foreign investors may not necessarily be given equal treatment as nationals of a state at the point of entry into the economy and market of a foreign state, IIL advocates the respect of their personal and property rights based on the international minimum standard, rather than the national treatment standard, once they have invested in those countries; the national treatment standard applies only to the extent that it does not descend below the international minimum standard.

In contemporary IIL, however, the protection of foreign investors is only one side of the equation, the other vital side being that FDI must positively contribute to the sustainable development of host countries and communities.[26] This is why

---

[20] Brown (2015), pp. 177–185.

[21] Ibid, pp. 162–175.

[22] For detail discussion on the Convention see Miller (Apr., 1959), pp. 371–378. See also *Abs-Shawcross Draft Convention on Investment Abroad 1959*, Art 1.

[23] *Convention on the Settlement of Investment Disputes between States and Nationals of other States* 1965, 18 March 1965, 575 UNTS 159 (entered into force 14 Oct 1966). Art 1 (2).

[24] Desta (2016), p. 124.

[25] Sauvant and Nolan (2015), pp. 893–934.

[26] Ward (2008), pp. 1–9. See also Zarsky (2008), pp. 17–28.

developing countries in particular began to focus on quality FDI that can contribute to their export-led growth strategies with the purpose of gaining access to foreign markets and to the transfer of knowledge, skills and technology.[27] Responsibilities towards the natural environment and labour have also become hot issues in IIL.[28] As McLachlan et al rightly observe, 'host States have a responsibility to govern in the interests of all of those within their jurisdiction, and to promote many other public objectives as well as investment'.[29] There is no doubt that protecting labour rights and the environment is among the key public policy objectives that a state ought to pursue.

As a matter of principle and to promote a freer flow of capital across borders and to protect basic human rights, including the right to property, foreign investors and their wealth must be protected under international and domestic laws. Equally important is that multinational companies and the people who run them abroad and their home states have a responsibility to contribute to the host state's sustainable development and must comply with its domestic laws and standards.

Despite the consensus on treating foreign investors fairly and equitably, different countries follow different models in their approach to FDI regulation. This may fall between two ends of a spectrum—a statist (or a developmental state[30]) end, where state intervention is the principle, and a *laissez-faire* end, where state intervention is broadly seen as the exception. Most countries in the Global North adopted a *laissez-faire* (or liberal) approach to trade, investment and economic policy—which is very much a private-enterprise-led and a minimal state activist approach to investment.[31] This does not mean that free market economies do not regulate economic activities, including inward FDI; in fact, they can be heavy handed in protecting their economic, financial and security interests. For instance, in September 2017, the president of the European Commission, Jean-Claude Juncker, unveiled:

> We are not naïve free traders. Europe must always defend its strategic interests. This is why today we are proposing a new EU framework for investment screening. If a foreign, state-owned, company wants to purchase a European harbour, part of our energy infrastructure or a defence technology firm, this should only happen in transparency, with scrutiny and debate. It is a political responsibility to know what is going on in our own backyard so that we can protect our collective security if needed.[32]

---

[27] Kumar (2002), pp. 3–9. Wang et al. (2009), pp. 1181–1206.

[28] Footer (2009), pp. 33–64.

[29] McLachlan et al. (2007), p. 21.

[30] We use developmental state in this article to refer to a governance model in which the government closely and directly controls access to key economic assets such as land, finances and crucial infrastructural facilities, actively sets development objectives and programmes and strictly regulates all economic activities by asserting effective control over all activities and actors within its territory.

[31] Hahn (2015), pp. 671–699.

[32] 'State of the Union 2017 - Trade Package: European Commission proposes framework for screening of foreign direct investments', Brussels, 14 September 2017, http://europa.eu/rapid/press-release_IP-17-3183_en.htm.

However, liberal economies protect their interests by using robust regulatory frameworks without intervening too heavily in the operations of the market.

Some, if not most, in the Global South, even those that have accepted liberal economic values, on the other hand, have opted for a statist approach to FDI and economic development. The developmental state[33] approach to economic development is a good example of a statist approach to economic regulation in general and FDI specifically. There is no single model of a statist (or developmental statist) system of economic regulation; some tend to have a preference for state-run business enterprises[34]; others focus on regulatory interventions,[35] while most fall somewhere between these two. However, they all share the same goal—advancing their economic and social development opportunities through active state involvement. While a developmental state comes with transformative ambitions, its activism also poses significant risks to good governance and the rule of law, as well as other cardinal values of a democratic and accountable system of public administration. It is argued that while aggressive state activism may well matter in effectively promoting and managing FDI and capital accumulation, there are often institutional and governance challenges, including susceptibility to corrupt practices and lack of transparency,[36] in statist economies probably more so than in *laissez-faire* systems; of course, the latter are not in any way immune from such malpractices.

In sum, all countries, whether developed or developing, statist or liberal, use different tools to realise their inward FDI attraction ambitions. Some are in favour of a multilateral approach, while others prefer bilateralism in the form of BITs. It is common practice nowadays that countries use a mix of both approaches. The next section, building on this and the other concepts and approaches considered earlier, examines some selected but crucial aspects of Ethiopian FDI law.

## 3 Ethiopian FDI Law and Regulation

FDI law regulates, inter alia, the entry, establishment and operation of foreign investment and the protection accorded to investors and their investments.

---

[33] This includes the ideology of 'developmental state' which 'refers to a state that intervenes and guides the direction and pace of economic development' (p. 28). Caldentey (2008), p. 27. The author further articulates both the history and nature of the concept as follows: 'The developmental state is associated with the leading role played by the government in promoting industrialization in Japan and East Asia in the post–World War II era. Their respective governments pursued a series of policies, including tariff protection, subsidies, and other types of controls aimed at developing selected productive sectors of economic activity. Fundamental to the design of the developmental state for these countries was the creation of an alliance between politics and the economy, which materialized in the establishment of a specialized bureaucratic apparatus that had ample powers and coordinated the developmental efforts, at least in their initial stages' (p. 27).

[34] Girma et al. (2009), pp. 866–873.

[35] Caldentey (2008), p. 40.

[36] Knutsen et al. (2011), Article 2 doi: 10.2202/1469-3569.1314.

## 3.1 Entry, Establishment and Operation of Foreign Investment

Some indicators of a state's approach to FDI regulation, and its position on the activist/*laissez-faire* spectrum, are (1) whether or not foreign investors can invest in all economic sectors in a country; (2) the ease with which they can receive investment permits, business licences or other operational requirements; and (3) the extent to which they can bring workers from their own home states.

The Ethiopian investment legal regime comprises the 1994 Constitution, international commitments such as BITs and MITs to which Ethiopia is a party, Investment Proclamation No 769/2012[37] as amended by Proclamation 849/2014,[38] the 1960 Civil Code, Regulation 270/2012[39] as amended by Regulation 312/2014,[40] as well as other directives adopted by appropriate state organs.

One of the matters covered by these investment proclamations and regulations is entry of foreign investment. Ethiopian law provides for a schedule containing a list of investment activities that are open for foreign participation while we find sectors from which foreign participation is excluded in the substantive part of the laws. For example, article 3/1 of the Regulation contains a list of economic sectors that are exclusively reserved for investors with Ethiopian nationality,[41] which includes banking, insurance and micro-credit and saving services, packaging, forwarding and shipping agency services, broadcasting services, mass media services, attorney and legal consultancy services, preparation of traditional indigenous medicines, advertisement, promotion and translation works, and air transport services using aircraft with a seating capacity of up to 50 passengers.[42] For this purpose, the nationality of business organisations is determined on the basis of 'ownership'. Article 3/2 of the Regulation requires that for any business engaged in any of the above fields to be defined as an Ethiopian business, the total capital of that organisation must be owned by Ethiopian nationals. It is notable that there are also certain sectors and forms of activities that are reserved exclusively to the government, which include the transmission and distribution of electrical energy through the integrated national grid system, postal services except courier services and air transport services using aircraft with a seating capacity of more than 50 passengers. On the other hand, such

---

[37] *Investment Proclamation* No 769/2012, Federal Negarit Gazette, 18th Year, No. 63, 17 September, 2012.

[38] *Investment Amendment Proclamation* 849/2014, Federal Negarit Gazette, 20th year, no.52, 22 July, 2014.

[39] *Investment Incentives and Investment Areas Reserved for Domestic Investors Council of Ministers Regulation*, Federal Negarit Gazette, 19th year, No. 4, 29 November, 2012.

[40] *Investment Incentives…Council of Ministers (Amendment) Regulation* 312/2014, Federal Negarit Gazette, 20th Year, No.62., 13 August, 2014.

[41] Ibid. The title of Article 3 of the Regulation says: 'Investment areas reserved for domestic investors.' However, the text provides for areas reserved for investors with Ethiopian nationality. While an investor of Ethiopian nationality is a domestic investor, a domestic investor does not always have Ethiopian nationality.

[42] Ibid.

activities as the generation, transmission and distribution of electric energy for commercial purposes using a system other than the integrated national grid are open for any person, whether of foreign or Ethiopian nationality.[43] The 2013 energy proclamation contemplates the possibility of allowing private entities to use the national electricity grid; however, this has not yet occurred.

The second exclusion under article 4/2 of the Regulation relates to those areas reserved exclusively for the government or those that the government may undertake jointly with the private sector. Two areas, telecom services and manufacturing of weapons and ammunition, are open for joint investment with the government. The cumulative reading of articles 6/2 of the Proclamation and 4/2 of the Regulation indicates that the investment areas of telecom and manufacturing of weapons and ammunition are open for joint investment with the government; nonetheless, the private partner can only be an Ethiopian national.

All foreign investors in Ethiopia and domestic investors operating jointly with foreigners are required to have an investment permit.[44] The investment permit will be issued once the investor opens a bank account at the National Bank of Ethiopia and has deposited the required minimum capital, which is USD 200,000 for a single investment.[45] The investors are also required to acquire commercial registration certificates, as well as business licences.[46]

Investment under Ethiopian law is defined using the enterprise model.[47] The enterprise to be established can take four forms,[48] an important one being the business organisation, of which there are six different types.[49] While these different forms of business organisations and other forms of investment have their own peculiar features, all of them need to be registered. Furthermore, any person engaged in a commercial activity in Ethiopia is required to have a business licence, a requirement that applies to the investor as soon as it commences commercialisation of its goods or services. This is subject, inter alia, to the operational requirement to meet local employment conditions. Considering that one potential benefit of foreign investment for a host state relates to the job opportunities that will be created, Ethiopian law allows the employment of expatriates only in cases of lack of skilled manpower locally. Furthermore, article 37/1 of the Investment Proclamation requires that expatriate workers be replaced with Ethiopian nationals within a

---

[43] See Article 4 and 6 of Energy Proclamation 810/2013, Federal Negarit Gazette 20th year No 12, 27th January 2014.

[44] See article 12 of the Investment Proclamation 769/2012.

[45] The amount of minimum capital required can be less depending on the area of investment and when the investment is made jointly with domestic investors. See article 11 of the Investment Proclamation.

[46] A business licence is required for all businesses operating in the country and is to be renewed annually. It contains information such as trade name, address of the entity and area of business.

[47] See article 2/1 together with 2/2 of Investment Proclamation 769/2012 (as amended).

[48] The four investment forms recognised are sole proprietorship, business organisations incorporated in Ethiopia or abroad, public enterprises and cooperative society.

[49] The commercial code classifies business organisations as: general partnership, limited partnership, ordinary partnership, joint venture, private limited company and Share Company.

limited period by arranging for and/or providing necessary training to Ethiopian nationals. This is enforced through work permits that are issued to expatriates only for a limited duration, normally for an initial period of 3 years, after which they need to be renewed every year. Indeed, under a more detailed directive issued by the Ministry of Labour and Social Affairs (MoLSA) in 2010,[50] employers need to prove that a person of Ethiopian nationality has been assigned or employed as a replacement for the foreigner upon completion of the latter's permit. The employer is also expected to provide training to Ethiopian nationals and submit reports, while the Ministry of Labour is charged with following up on the transfer of skills to, and the general working conditions of, Ethiopian nationals.[51]

Analysis of these and other regulatory requirements suggests that Ethiopia exhibits the protectionist or interventionist features typical of a developmental statist approach to managing FDI. Some even argue, after looking at Ethiopia's level of intervention into the private sector, that the government 'appears to be pursuing a centrally planned economic model'.[52] It should be noted, however, that many countries, including those considered the most liberal economies, impose strict measures to control or restrict foreign investment in areas that they consider are of special national interest.[53] Sectors like defence, transport, media and tourism often fall into this category.[54] The general rule is that 'no state grants unlimited access'[55] to foreign investors. Furthermore, the various entry and operational requirements, such as the investment permit, the business licence and local content requirements, are broadly present in all legal systems, irrespective of their level of development or attitude towards inward FDI. The only difference is one of degree, where countries such as the Czech Republic, the UK and Peru are often placed on the more liberal end of the spectrum, while countries such as China, Greece and Canada fall on the more interventionist end. Ethiopia is certainly closer to the latter category of countries[56]; whether or not this is in accord with the internationally recognised standards of treatment to investment and investors is considered next.

## 3.2 Treatment and Protection of Investors

The following section deals with two of these protections: protection with regard to expropriation and standard of treatment.

---

[50] Directive to Determine the Conditions for issuing Expatriate Work permit, January 2010.
[51] Ibid, article 8.
[52] Aseffa (2014).
[53] Gómez-Palacio and Muchlinski (2008), p. 236.
[54] Ibid.
[55] Shan (2012), p. 32.
[56] Ibid, p. 31.

### 3.2.1 Standards of Treatment of Investment and Investors

The national treatment principle whereby a host state extends to foreign investors and their investments treatment at least as favourable as that of national investors and investments in like circumstances is incorporated in almost all BITs signed by Ethiopia.[57] The BITs, however, exhibit some variation. For example, article 3 (2) of the BIT with the Republic of South Africa[58] provides:

> Each Party shall in its territory accord to investments and returns of investors of the other Party treatment *as favourable as* that which it accords to investments and returns of its own investors or to investments and returns of investors of any third State [italics added].

This BIT clearly requires a strict standard of equality of treatment between investments of national origin and investments from the other party. Conversely, other BITs provide a more flexible option in which the host state may treat the foreign investment more favourably than it does its own investments through a 'no less favourable treatment' standard. Chinese law and practice are a good example of providing 'superior national treatment' for foreign investors in some sectors while giving them 'inferior national treatment' in other sectors.[59]

Moreover, the most favoured nation (MFN) treatment is also contained in the BITs signed and ratified by Ethiopia. The MFN treatment is one of the pillars of IIL. It can be defined relating to the subject under consideration as an obligation to extend treatment to investment and investors in a determined relationship with that state no less favourable than the treatment extended by the granting state to investors and investments, in similar circumstances, from a third state.[60] Indeed, the second part of article 3 (2) of the BIT with the Republic of South Africa quoted above—'as favourable as that which it accords ... *to investments and returns of investors of any third State*'—is a classic expression of the MFN principle.

One of the issues that have been a subject of dispute in various investor–state arbitration cases is whether MFN clauses cover dispute settlement mechanisms. Many of the MFN clauses contained in the BITs signed by Ethiopia are designed in a general manner. These MFN provisions simply require both contracting parties to accord to investments of nationals of the other contracting party no less favourable treatment than that accorded to nationals of third states. In such situations, it is not clear if the MFN treatment applies to dispute settlement mechanisms or is limited to substantive rules only.[61]

---

[57] While the BIT signed with the People's Republic of China [signed on May 11, 1998, entered into force in May 1, 2000 contained no national treatment obligation, the BITs signed with the Republic of Sudan [signed on March 7, 2000, entered into force in 15 May 2001, and the Russian Federation, signed on February 10, 2000 entered into force in June 6, 2000, contain the national treatment standard.

[58] Agreement between Ethiopia and the Republic of South Africa signed on January 1, 2008.

[59] Shan (2012), p. 26.

[60] Rodriguez (2008), p. 90.

[61] Freyer and Herlihy (2005), p. 60.

Some BITs like the Ethiopia–UK BIT implicitly indicate that the MFN clause applies to dispute resolution,[62] while others adopt a standard MFN clause combining it with national treatment.[63] As a final example, the BIT signed between Ethiopia and China merges the MFN treatment clause with the fair and equitable treatment (FET) clause.[64]

### 3.2.2 Protection of Investment from Expropriation

A country's domestic laws, as well as the international investment agreements it enters into, provide protection for foreign investors and their investment in that country. Such laws and regulations are designed not only to protect foreign investors but also to boost their confidence in the host country. Ethiopia has signed 31 bilateral investment treaties (BITs), 21 of which are in force. Ethiopia is also a party to six other international investment agreements (IIAs).[65] These international agreements, coupled with the 1994 Constitution, investment laws and other relevant legislation, guarantee protection of foreign investment, including repatriation of profits.

The right to private ownership of property is recognised under article 40 of the Constitution. This right, however, does not extend to land as it is under the common ownership of the nations, nationalities and peoples of Ethiopia.[66] Investors, both foreign and domestic, are allowed to possess and use land for investment purposes in accordance with the land policy of the country. Recognition of private ownership sets implied limits on the power of the state to interfere in its enjoyment. In this regard, article 40/8 of the Constitution contains two conditions for the government to expropriate private property: public purpose and payment of compensation. Article 25 of the Investment Proclamation reinforces these two conditions by setting a requirement of 'due process'. All three, along with the 'non-discrimination' clause, are included in all the BITs that Ethiopia has signed and/or ratified. While this suggests

---

[62] Article 3/3 of the BIT signed between Ethiopia and the United Kingdom of Great Britain and Northern Ireland, signed on November 19, 2009, states: '… for the avoidance of doubt it is confirmed that the treatment [MFN treatment] provided for in paragraphs (1) and (2) above shall apply to the provisions of Articles 1 to 10 of this Agreement'. Article 8 of the agreement deals with dispute settlement between an investor and a state; hence, the MFN clause is applicable for the settlement of investment disputes between host state and investor.

[63] Dolzer and Schreuer (2008), p. 187.

[64] Article 3/1 of the BIT signed between Ethiopia and China states 'Investments and activities associated with investments of investors of either Contracting Party shall be accorded fair and equitable treatment and shall enjoy protection in the territory of the other Contracting Party'.

Article 3/2: The treatment and protection referred to in paragraph 1 of this article shall not be less favorable than that accorded to investments and activities associated with such investments of investors of any third state.' Yihdego (2012), p. 342.

[65] UNCTAD, (Investment Policy 2017a).

[66] Proclamation of the Constitution of the Federal Democratic Republic of Ethiopia, Proclamation No 1/1995, 1st Year No 1, 21 August 1995, Article 40/3.

that a sufficient legal framework exists for the protection of foreign investment in the country that is consistent with international standards and practices,[67] the strength of the actual protection afforded needs further examination.

The first relates to the nature of expropriation against which guarantee is provided. All the BITs that Ethiopia has signed guarantee against both direct and indirect expropriation except under the conditions specified by law. While direct expropriation is understood to occur where a state through a decree or other means expressly acknowledges that it takes or will take the property, indirect expropriation[68] consists in different acts by the state that, cumulatively, deprive the owner of the benefits from their assets.[69] What is considered as a factor in determining the existence of expropriation in the absence of a formal decree is interference by the state in the ownership right of the investor through a single or a series of measures. Government measures like deprivation of profits, exorbitant taxation or arbitrary taxation, measures substantially interfering with the management or control of a business enterprise, harassment of employees, annulment and cancellation of property rights, contractual rights, debts and licences, etc. have been considered as constituting indirect expropriation by international tribunals in appropriate circumstances and different cases.[70] Hence, when a BIT signed by a state guarantees against indirect expropriation except under the specified conditions, it is guaranteeing against interference in the enjoyment of property rights through the types of activities illustrated above.

Ethiopian law deals with matters of expropriation in the Expropriation Proclamation,[71] the Payment of Compensation Regulation,[72] the Land Lease Proclamation,[73] as well as the 1960 Civil Code.[74] The concept of expropriation is defined in article 1460 of the Civil Code as 'proceedings whereby the competent authorities compel an owner to surrender the ownership of an immovable required by such authorities for public purpose'.[75] The Investment Proclamation, unlike the BITs that Ethiopia signed, does not employ the term 'indirect expropriation'. One may argue, however, that the term 'expropriation' under the Investment Proclamation

---

[67] Yihdego (2012), pp. 329–344.

[68] The term can also be described as de facto, equivalent, creeping, disguised, consequential, constructive expropriation. See Newcombe and Paradell (2009), p. 325.

[69] Reisman and Sloane (2003), p. 121.

[70] Newcombe and Paradell (2009), pp. 327–328.

[71] Expropriation of Landholdings for Public Purposes and Payment of Compensation Proclamation No 455/2005, Federal Negarit Gazette, 11th Year No 43, 15th July 2005.

[72] Payment of Compensation for Property Situated on Landholding Expropriated for Public Purposes Council of Ministers Regulation No 135/2007, Federal Negarit Gazette, 13th Year No 36, 18th May 2007.

[73] Re-enactment of Urban Land Lease Holding Proclamation No 272/2002, Federal Negarit Gazette, 8th Year No 19, 14th May 2002.

[74] Civil Code of the Empire of Ethiopia Proclamation No 165 of 1960, Negarit Gazette, Gazette Extraordinary, 19th year No 2, 5th May 1960.

[75] Currently, land is common property of nations, nationalities and peoples of Ethiopia. Hence, the word owner under the civil code is to be interpreted to refer to the 'landholder who owns the property situated upon the land'. See Abdo (2012), p. 359.

could be read to include both direct and indirect expropriation given that Ethiopia has endorsed such an approach in the many BITs it has signed with foreign countries. This interpretation of the investment law can be reinforced by the fact that the phrase 'indirect expropriation' appears in the Civil Code, though the meaning attributed to it is not similar to the meaning of the phrase under international investment jurisprudence. Article 1485 of the Code, under the title 'indirect expropriation', allows the competent authorities to take the property of individuals for setting up installations or construction works without undergoing through expropriation proceeding. The subsequent provisions deal with its application and limitation. While the authorities may undertake construction works on the property, in effect expropriating the property, without going through the expropriation proceedings such as the requirement of notification, they are required to effect payment of compensation. The purpose of the provision seems to be to allow the state to expropriate private property without complying with normal expropriation procedures.[76]

From this it can be observed that the concept of indirect expropriation as incorporated in the BITs that Ethiopia has signed is unknown to the Ethiopian domestic law of expropriation. However, the investment laws must be interpreted to accommodate such a notion if/when Ethiopian international legal commitments are taken into account, as further considered in a while.

The second point relates to the requirement of compensation. One condition that the state is required to fulfil during expropriation, as indicated in its BITs and article 25 of the Investment Proclamation, is the payment of compensation. All the BITs that Ethiopia has signed guarantee payment of 'adequate, prompt and effective' compensation, otherwise known as the 'Hull formula', for all expropriations, including nationalisation. Under article 25 of the Investment Proclamation, nationalisation of foreign investment will result in the payment of 'adequate or appropriate' compensation. While 'adequate compensation' is understood to mean a figure reflecting the market value of the property expropriated, that is not the case for 'appropriate compensation', which is a 'reference to a flexible standard which could range from the payment of full compensation, the amount of future profits lost, to the payment of no compensation at all in circumstances where the foreign investor had visibly earned inordinate profits from the investment while the host state had no benefits at all from it'.[77]

In addition, other pieces of domestic legislation dealing with expropriation and compensation reveal that compensation will be paid on the basis of the replacement cost of the property expropriated.[78] The Civil Code under article 1474/1 states that the amount to be paid as compensation will be equal to the amount of present and certain damage caused by the expropriation.[79] The implication of qualifying the

---

[76] Abdo (2012), p. 362.

[77] Sornarajah (2010), p. 446.

[78] Abdo (2012), p. 385.

[79] While the English version of the code says that the compensation shall be equal to the amount of actual damage, the Amharic version qualifies it to 'present and certain' damage. The Amharic version of the law is the one that has prevalence in case of conflict or ambiguity between the two versions.

amount to 'present and certain' damage is that future loss is not compensable even when it may be certain to occur.[80] Hence, consequential damage like loss of profit and transportation costs might be disregarded from the calculation.[81]

It is notable that while the 'Hull formula' is broadly favoured by developed countries, the 'appropriate compensation' standard is often invoked by developing countries such as China.[82] The Ethiopian FDI compensation regime appears to have adopted a mixture of the two. This might create practical problems when issues of compensation arise, although with respect to relevant BITs in which the Hull formula is incorporated, Ethiopia would not be able to opt for its standard of compensation enshrined in its domestic law.

While one may argue that foreign investors are better protected through the BITs, it should not be forgotten that there is interplay between the IIAs that a host state has ratified and its municipal law. While the IIAs extend protection for the investments or property of foreign investors, the question of whether a foreign investor has a right *in rem* over a particular piece of property, as well as the scope of such right, will be determined by the municipal law of the host state.[83] The treaties that extend protection for investment that concerns property do not contain substantive rules of property law, thereby necessitating a *renvoi* to the municipal law of the host state.[84] In the event of a dispute, the municipal law also helps in determining the conditions imposed or assurances granted for the operation of the investment, as well as the nature and scope of a government measure in breach of the agreement.[85] This highlights the importance of coherence between the national laws and the international investment agreements that a country participates in. BITs, once ratified by the Ethiopian parliament, however, constitute part of the laws of the land and are therefore self-executing before a court of law.[86] If a conflict arises between a domestic law such as the 1960 Civil Code and a specific BIT commitment, it is proposed that the legislator and the courts should resolve and harmonise them without violating Ethiopian international legal commitments but without disregarding domestic law.[87] This is, of course, notwithstanding the well-established principle that a state cannot invoke domestic law to justify non-compliance with international law.

To conclude, this section signals that Ethiopian FDI law and regulation is robust, yet formulating a full picture of the nature of such a law and regulation necessitates looking into relevant reforms and policy interventions.

---

[80] Krzeczunowick (1977), p. 173.
[81] Abdo (2012), p. 380.
[82] Shan (2012), p. 52.
[83] Douglas (2003), p. 198.
[84] Douglas (2003), p. 198. See also Sasson (2010), p. xxx.
[85] Newcombe and Paradell (2009), p. 94.
[86] Woldemariam (2016), p. 77.
[87] Ibid., p. 85.

## 4 Legal and Institutional Reforms and Assertive Interventions

### *4.1 Context: Ambitious Policy*

The Government of Ethiopia has set the year 2025 for the country to achieve lower middle income status.[88] The country has made significant progress towards this goal by registering an average growth rate of 10% over the last several years. The national strategies that the country adopted over the years are cited as primary reasons for the recorded growth. The first 5-year Growth and Transformation Plan (GTP I, 2010–2015), while described as ambitious, laid the foundation for industrialisation through significant investment in infrastructure and technical skills. Though the country has recorded impressive growth under the GTP I period, the structural transformation achieved was not as originally envisioned. By the end of 2015, the industry sector[89] contributed only 15.1% of the total GDP from which only 4.8% goes to the manufacturing sector.[90] This shortfall in the manufacturing sector was attributed to the poor growth performance of micro and small-scale manufacturing industries and delay in the implementation of large manufacturing projects.[91] Cognizant of this shortfall in the manufacturing sector performance, the second GTP (GTP II, 2016–2020) recognises the need for accelerated growth in the manufacturing industry to help achieve fundamental structural transformation. This accelerated growth of the manufacturing sector is to be promoted through expanding new investments mainly in export-oriented manufacturing, as well as by improving the productivity and competitiveness of domestic investment firms.[92] By employing a developmental state model, the government seeks to transform its economy through major investments in economic infrastructure and engagements in those sectors identified as priority sectors. The objective is to make the country a leading manufacturing hub in Africa.[93]

---

[88] The World Bank classifies countries in to four groups based on Gross National Income (GNI) per capita. For the 2018 fiscal year, lower middle-income economies are those with a GNI per capita between $1006 and $3955. Ethiopia's per capita income was reported as $590 in 2017. See http://www.worldbank.org/en/country/ethiopia/overview.

[89] The industry sector includes manufacturing, construction and mining among others.

[90] National Planning Commission (2016), p. 28.

[91] Ibid.

[92] Ibid., p. 135.

[93] National Planning Commission (2016), p. 136.

## 4.2 Legal and Institutional Reforms

Investment, both domestic and foreign, is a fundamental tool to achieve accelerated growth of the manufacturing sector. This requires prudent and continuous institutional reforms as observed in the Ethiopian investment regime over the last decade. The Ethiopian Investment Agency (EIA), which was previously under the Ministry of Industry, was restructured as the Ethiopian Investment Commission (EIC), an autonomous federal government office with its own legal personality and directly accountable to the Prime Minister.[94] The Ethiopian Investment Board, chaired by the Prime Minister and composed of different government officials designated by the Prime Minister and the Investment Commission, is the highest body in formulating and executing the investment policy of the country. For example, the Board is empowered to authorise the granting of new or additional incentives other than what is outlined under the existing regulations. It may also authorise foreign nationals to participate in investment areas that are otherwise exclusively reserved for domestic investors. Under the previous law, power was given to the Council of Ministers to determine such areas by issuing regulation. Giving such power to the Board will reduce the time needed to make a decision.

Another institutional development that occurred in 2014 is the establishment of the Industrial Park Development Corporation (IPDC), which is accountable to the Prime Minister. The Ethiopian Investment Commission serves as the regulatory body of the IPDC. GTP II emphasised the need to develop industrial parks, also known as special economic zones, as vital tools for the industrial transformation of the country through economic diversification, increased investment and export. The Industrial Park Proclamation[95] calls for the establishment of industrial parks with very broad objectives, including achieving planned and systematic development of industries, and urbanisation, as well as mitigation of the impact of pollution on the environment and human beings. Embedded in these objectives and common to all special economic zones, one can find FDI attraction, alleviating large-scale unemployment and supporting wider economic reform strategies as some of the reasons for setting up industrial parks.[96] Industrial parks can also be used as experimental tools for the application of new polices. Such policies have been widely introduced.[97]

---

[94] Ethiopian Investment Board and Ethiopian Investment Commission Establishment Council of Ministers Regulation No 313/2014, 20th year, No 63, August 2014.

[95] Industrial Park Proclamation No 886/2015, Federal Negarit Gazette, 21st year No 39, 9th April 2015.

[96] Farole and Akinci (2011), pp. 3–4.

[97] Ibid.

## 4.3 Assertive Intervention: The Case of Building Industrial Parks

With these objectives in mind, the Government of Ethiopia, through the IPDC, has embarked on the development of industrial parks in different parts of the country. Two of the IPs built by the IPDC, in Addis Ababa and Hawassa, have already become operational.[98] The Bole Lemi industrial park phase I has created about 11,000 job opportunities in the apparel sector and has been operational since 2014. The Hawassa Industrial Park (HIP), the IPDC's flagship project, was inaugurated in June 2017.[99] HIP is a specialised park in textile and garment production with 37 completed manufacturing sheds and aims to host 60,000 workers.[100] There are around eight industrial parks that are currently being built by the IPDC. The first phases of two of these, the Kombolcha and Mekelle Industrial parks, were inaugurated in early July 2017.

Parallel to the projects undertaken by the IPDC, the regional governments have also laid down their plans to set up industrial parks, the major aim of which is to create links between local suppliers and enterprise investors. The country plans to construct 17 integrated agro-industrial parks in all regions, four of which have commenced construction.[101] While the country has great potential in the agriculture sector, further integration of farmers into the commercial value chain will be a turning point in transforming the country's economy. Ethiopia's advantage in the agriculture sector is challenged on account of poor links with agro-industry and the presence of numerous middlemen between farmers and consumers,[102] which the integrated agro-industrial parks are expected to address. These industrial parks are state sponsored. There are also privately developed and administered industrial parks in Dukem town on the south-western outskirts of Addis Ababa, which strengthen the aims of the Ethiopian developmental state ambitions.

The industrial parks are also meant to address some of the challenges faced in investment promotion and facilitation. Many reports have indicated that one of the major challenges in promoting investment in the country is lack of capacity to provide serviced land for investment. Servicing land is mainly done by investors themselves and requires investing significant resources. The industrial parks will address this concern as serviced land in the form of factory sheds is made available. Water, electricity and other utilities are made available in the industrial parks, thus addressing another concern of investors.

---

[98] Addis Industrial Village which was built and became operational in the 1980s, is also administered by the IPDC, bringing the number of operational industrial parks in the country currently to 3.
[99] http://www.ipdc.gov.et/index.php/en/industrial-parks/hawasa.
[100] 'In Full Swing' Addis Fortune News Paper (June 25, 2017).
[101] Shiferaw (February 18, 2017).
[102] UNIDO (2016) Integrated Agro-Industrial Parks in Ethiopia, p. 4 https://isid.unido.org/files/Ethiopia/Integrated-Agro-Industrial-Parks-in-Ethiopia-booklet.pdf.

The construction of these industrial parks is one step towards achieving GTP II, i.e. to increase investment and create a million jobs in the manufacturing sector. In this regard, reports indicate that FDI inflows have constantly been increasing in the past years. The recorded FDI flow for the year 2016 was $3.2 billion, a 46% increase compared to the 2015 figure of $2.2 billion,[103] putting the country as the second largest LDC host economy in Africa.[104] While it is too early to attribute this success to the industrial parks, improvements in infrastructure and advances in industrialisation are considered as some of the contributing factors.

The Industrial Park Proclamation[105] requires industrial park enterprises to observe the laws of the country, especially environmental and labour laws. But at times the implementation of such a requirement is not properly observed. For example, a report based on working conditions in one of the privately run industrial parks indicated that wages paid to employees are not sufficient to cover their living expenses.[106] Employees are also required to work beyond the legally mandated work hours in order to meet the stringent delivery time requirements that park enterprises agree with their clients.[107] The report also indicated that workers are not allowed to form associations and those who attempt at organising the workers see their contract terminated on shaky grounds.[108] While the law requires inspectors to inspect the workplace at any time, it was reported that those inspectors were not allowed to go through the gates of the parks unless they set up an appointment before the visit.[109] As indicated above, the report is based on one of the industrial parks that are operated privately and may not necessarily represent the practices in all industrial parks.

In summary, the ambitious plans, laws and institutions that have been introduced since 2010 are significant, as further analysed later. However, as this and the proceeding sections show, there are also challenges.

## 5  Some Challenges and State Responses

Among the challenges that foreign (and domestic) investment faces in Ethiopia relate to land management and other interpretative, technical and procedural matters, which are considered in turn.

---

[103] UNCTAD (World Investment Report 2017b), p. 46.
[104] Ibid.
[105] Industrial Park Proclamation No 886/2015, Federal Negarit Gazette 21st year No 39, 9th April 2015, Addis Ababa.
[106] Redae (May 2016), p. 6.
[107] Ibid, p. 5.
[108] Ibid.
[109] Ibid.

## 5.1 Land Management Practices, Issues and Responses

One of the challenges related to investment in Ethiopia is large-scale land deals. Land in Ethiopia is the common property of nations, nationalities and peoples with the responsibility of administering it falling on the government.[110] Private individuals, including investors, can lease land from the government. This system of leasing land to private individuals began long before the global land rush started in the aftermath of the 2008–2009 global food crisis.[111] Dessalegn Rahmato classifies the land investment programmes of the country under the Ethiopian Peoples' Revolutionary Democratic Front (EPRDF)-led government into three phases. The first phase, which runs from the mid-1990s to 2000, witnessed land transfers with relatively small sizes (less than 500 hectares) to almost exclusively domestic investors.[112] The second phase, with transfer of small to medium-sized land to domestic as well as foreign investors, runs from 2001 to 2007.[113] During this period, a new investment law, which introduced different incentives for investments in identified priority areas, was issued. This period also witnessed an increase in agricultural investment, especially in the floriculture business where many foreign investors were given land close to urban centres with easy access to transport facilities.[114]

Intensification in large-scale investment in farmland was observed globally following the 2008 global food crisis. Rising energy demands leading to global hike in oil price coupled with the financial crisis in 2007–2008 and subsequent food crisis were some of the factors behind the global land rush.[115] It was during this period that the third phase of large-scale land investment in Ethiopia occurred. The adoption of GTP I in 2010 shifted the focus from smallholder-based agriculture, which was the main pillar of the 'Agricultural Development Led Industrialization' (ADLI)[116] strategy, to large-scale agriculture, aimed at intensifying 'production of marketable farm products for domestic and export markets'.[117] GTP I specifically noted:

> This strategy will support strongly the intensified production of marketable farm products for domestic and export markets, by smallholders and private agricultural investors. Fundamentals of the strategy include a shift to production of high value crops, a special

---

[110] Article 40 of the Constitution. Article 52/2/d of the constitution gives the regional states the power to administer land and natural resources within their respective boundaries, in accordance with federal laws. While regions were originally the ones allocating land for large-scale agriculture investment purposes, later on the mandate to allocate land above 5000 hectares was passed, through delegation, to the Ministry of Agriculture and Rural Development, a Federal entity. See Imeru Tamrat (April 2010).

[111] Rahmato (2014), p. 28.

[112] Ibid.

[113] Ibid.

[114] Melese and Helmsing (2010), as cited by Rahmato (2014), p. 28.

[115] Deninger and Byerlee (2011).

[116] It should also be noted that 'the first PRSP left a space for large scale agriculture' as well. Lavers (2012), p. 112.

[117] MOFED (2010), pp. 22–23.

focus on potential high-productivity areas, intensified commercialisation, and support for development of large-scale commercial agriculture where it is feasible. The commercialisation of smallholder farming will continue to be the major source of agricultural growth. Concerted support will be given to increase private investment in large commercial farms.[118]

In the pursuit of its GTP objectives, the government rolled out a large-scale land lease programme[119] targeting foreign investors who were given farm land at an average price of below USD 10 per hectare.[120] One of the premises on which such large-scale land deals were conducted is the idea that there is extensive underutilised or 'empty land' in the lowland areas of the country.[121]

However, several concerns were raised, including lack of consultation with affected communities, lack of adequate environmental impact assessment and lack of clarity about the communal land tenure system relating to such land deals. One of the criticisms challenges the very premise on which land was transferred in the low lands—there is no such thing as 'empty land'. These were mainly left idle because they were either being fallowed or used for grazing purposes.[122] Accordingly, characterising such land as empty seems to emanate either from a misunderstanding of the traditional communal land holding system or the belief that there is a need to impose change on the lifestyle of the people living in such areas.[123]

Another criticism regarding large-scale land transfer in Ethiopia is the lack of proper consultation with the affected people, which might be attributed to the developmental state approach to decision-making concerning foreign investment or other economic activities.[124] In many of the areas in which land was transferred to investors, either none or very limited consultation was undertaken with the local people. One report indicated that consultation on land investments has taken place in the Afar region, where the deals were made with the clans.[125] In all the other regions

---

[118] MOFED (2010), pp. 22–23.

[119] Rahmato (2014), p. 29. According to a World Bank report, around 1.2 million hectares of land was transferred to 406 investors during 2004–2009. Deninger and Byerlee (2011), p. xxxiii. The Oakland Institute estimates around 3.6 million hectares of land given out to 1349 investors by the end of 2011. Oakland Institute (2011), p. 20. The report of the Ethiopian Government, on the other hand, indicates that a total of 3.31 million hectare of land was identified and transferred to the federal land bank, of which 473 thousand hectares was transferred to investors by 2012/13. MOFED (2014), p. 38. Worthy of note is the government is also another big investor in the agriculture sector. One of the key components of the GTP is the development of the sugar sector. The Government has identified the sugar sector as one of the high potential sectors and made heavy investments through the Ethiopian Sugar Corporation.

[120] Rahmato (2014), p. 29.

[121] Makki (2012), p. 92.

[122] Abdo (2014), p. 235. Investors who were given land in those areas attested that the land is very rich and fertile. This richness is attributed to the manner of cultivation of the land which includes fallowing the land in rotation. See Pearce (2012), p.

[123] Abdo (2014) cited above for detailed analysis of the communal land holding system in rural Ethiopia and the implication of the large-scale land transfers.

[124] Rahmatto (2014), p. 41.

[125] Keeley et al. (2014), p. 45.

where large-scale land transfer took place, there was no public consultation.[126] There is also no public engagement in the computation of compensation to be paid for the expropriated land. As noted by Tagliarino, the government is the sole decision-maker in compensation and benefit package computation.[127]

In addition, many asserted that the transfers were made without conducting proper assessments on the environmental impact of the transfers and planned investments, for example, on wildlife. A tendency on the part of the investors to consider the animals as a 'problem' was reported.[128] And at times, the land transferred is covered by natural forests. A case in point is the transfer of 3012 hectares of land in the Gambella region, Mezhenger zone, covered by natural forests.[129] Despite protests by the local community and other vocal advocates in the country, including the former president of the country, President Girma Woldegiorgis, the contract was upheld.[130]

These concerns coupled with the poor employment opportunities in the affected regions led to varying degrees of public disaffection and resentment around the country and appear to have contributed to the recent political instabilities in the country.[131] People expressed their anger in the form of groups of young men plotting to 'fight for [their] land'.[132] This went, in one incident, to the extent of attacking farm workers, including expatriates.[133]

The government, although slow, responded to these concerns in different ways, including by promising to review the compensation regime and to take measures to support those who have already lost their lands without adequate compensation.[134]

There was also failure on the part of the investors; most of them who took those large tracts of land either failed to develop them completely[135] or wanted to use them

---

[126] Pearce (2012), reported that there was no public consultation regarding the matter in the Gambella region while Keeley et al. (2014) reported absence of consultation in SNNP region and other parts. Similar accounts are reported by Imeru Tamrat (2010) and Deninger and Byerlee (2011).

[127] Tagliarino (2017), p. 17.

[128] Pearce (2012). In an interview with Karaturi regarding the antelopes that migrate between South Sudan and Ethiopia, the investor referred to the wildlife as 'problems' which will disappear through time. p. 15. Later on, the amount of land given to Karaturi was reduced. One of the reasons claimed by the government for such reduction was 'to create an 8000 hectare corridor through Karaturi's land for a one million strong migration of white-eared kob, a type of antelope'. Stebek (2011), p. 199.

[129] The land was transferred to an Indian Company Verdant Harvests PLC, See Elias Stebek (2011), p. 200.

[130] See Elias Stebek (2011), pp. 200–201.

[131] Pearce (2012), p. 14.

[132] Pearce (2012), p. 14.

[133] 'Five Saudi Star Workers Killed in Gambella' The Ethiopian Reporter, (2 May 2012) as cited by Abdo (2014), p. 241.

[134] An office has been setup under the Addis Ababa Bureau of Labor and Social Affairs to rehabilitate farmers displaced from their land on grounds of development, see http://bolsa.gov.et/en_US/web/guest/rehabilitation-project-office-for-displaced-peasants-dueto-development.

[135] MOFED (2014), p. 38. In the government's own account made in 2014, of the 473 thousand hectares of land transferred to investors, only 11% was developed by the investors.

for purposes other than agriculture as had been agreed with government.[136] It was as a result of these and other factors that, in 2016, the government suspended such large-scale land lease programme.[137] This was followed by revocation of some foreign investor and trade licences by the state to enforce the contracts, which led some to threaten, or indeed commence, arbitration.[138]

This may well be the reason why GTP II avoids large-scale farming by foreign investors, as one of the key economic plans, and emphasises as follows:

> A significant shift in productivity and production of the horticulture sector and ensuring quality will be effectively undertaken through combined efforts of smallholder farmers among themselves, joint efforts between small scale investors and emerging educated youth, as well as joint efforts between domestic and foreign investors. Such a joint undertaking enables these operators efficiently utilize markets, infrastructure and logistics supply and let smallholder farmers participate in areas of specialization that facilitate structural transformation.[139]

However, GTP II also encourages 'large scale commercial farming'[140] and aims to improve effective participation of large-scale investors in agriculture development by bridging the infrastructure deficit and addressing governance issues, including what the government calls rent seeking.[141] It is not clear whether the target investors here are domestic or foreign or both.

Ethiopia's developmental efforts, including through inward FDI, cannot be free from ups and downs. Mistakes and poor decisions over policy or implementation are inevitable. The decision of the authorities to suspend the practice of rushed large-scale land deals should be seen as a sensible measure. However, the literature and reports considered earlier suggest that the problem is systemic—lack of transparency, participatory and prudent leadership and decision-making, which might be associated with the statist model of development and governance,[142] have contributed to the failure. The governance deficit in the country is openly acknowledged by the authorities as their top priority to be addressed swiftly.[143]

The problems associated with the statist approach to development and foreign investment, such as susceptibility to corruption, non-democratic decision-making, incompetence in effectively managing FDI issues, including the inability to timely respond to complaints, can be tackled or mitigated by 'devising sound and effective

---

[136] Deninger and Byerlee (2011), p. 118.

[137] Maasho (March 25, 2016).

[138] Nizar Manek (21 September 2017). the Indian farm conglomerate-Karuturi Global, which was given a large swash of land in the Gambela region in the form of lease, has been subjected to revocation of its foreign investor and trade licences by the state in 2016.

[139] National Planning Commission (2016), p. 122.

[140] Ibid, p. 100.

[141] Ibid, p. 128.

[142] Mbate (2016), p. 7.

[143] 'Ethiopian PM urges high-level cadres to address concerns of good governance'. Xinhua (23 May, 2017). GTP II also refers to good governance in all aspects of economic development, the realisation of which remains to be seen.

institutions',[144] led by far-sighted political leadership. For example, 'industrial development in South Korea and Taiwan' was attributed 'to state interventions in coordinating public and private investment, visionary political leadership …'.[145] In this respect, the institutional developments and achievements considered in the preceding section need to be commended, although managing FDI in a transparent and accountable manner requires robust and effective institutions that are able to promote and protect the interests of communities and investors. This should include matters of poor land management and other technical and procedural hurdles to attracting and supporting the flow of responsible and quality FDI to the country.

### 5.2 Some Interpretative, Technical and Procedural Issues

While the legal and institutional reforms that have been made have addressed some pertinent shortcomings in previous laws, one can still find some grey areas that are sources of confusion. With regard to the investment law that is currently in force, *one* challenge relates to the manner in which the law is to be understood and interpreted. This pertains particularly to entry conditions, especially with regard to areas open for foreign participation. Unlike the repealed 2002 investment law,[146] which contains a schedule that specifically indicates areas of investment that are excluded from foreign participation, the schedule in the current (2012) law[147] provides for investment areas that are open for foreigners. One practical problem in such approach is that unless the proposed area of investment squarely fits in one of the areas included in the schedule, the foreign investor will not be allowed to participate in the area. Sometimes it is difficult to categorise a business activity either as falling under the schedule or not. One example can be investment in the engineering sector. Investment in engineering works is one of the areas open for foreigners. Will maintenance of electronic equipment like automated teller machines (ATMs) be considered as engineering works and hence foreigners will be allowed to engage in such business or will it be considered as any other maintenance in which case it will be presumed that it can be done only by Ethiopians and hence not open for foreigners?[148]

---

[144] Mbate (2016), p. 7.

[145] Ibid., p. 3.

[146] Investment Proclamation No 280/2002, Federal Negarit Gazette, 8th year No 27, July 2002 as amended by proclamation No 375/2003 and Council of Ministers Regulation on Investment Incentives and Investment Areas reserved for Domestic Investors No 84/2003, Federal Negarit Gazette, 9th Year No 34, February 2003 [all of which are replaced by the 2012 investment legislations].

[147] Investment Proclamation 769/2012 as amended and Investment Regulation 270/2012 as amended.

[148] This happens to be a real case in which a firm jointly owned between national and foreign investors that won a bid to maintain ATM machines was latter informed that it cannot engage in ATM maintenance service as the area is not open for foreigners. The argument of the firm was that ATM maintenance was part of an engineering work and hence, the reason for initially issuing the investment permit.

From within the areas of investment illustrated in the schedule as 'open' for foreigners, there are certain exclusions. When one considers such exclusions, it seems that some are excluded for no reason. For example, in the education sector, it seems that what is excluded from foreign participation is provision of kindergarten, elementary and junior secondary education through construction of an investor's own building. But can a foreign investor engage in educational activities by renting a building? A similar issue arises with regard to the health sector in the provision of diagnostic and clinical services. It is not clear what purpose such exclusion serves. One may argue that the fact the schedule was originally meant to govern (and provide for) investment areas eligible for incentives contributed to the confusion.

Another grey area that needs attention is the definition given to domestic investors in the investment law vis-à-vis treaty protection given to foreign investors of Ethiopian origin. 'Domestic investor' under article 2/5 of the Investment Proclamation includes a foreign national treated as a domestic investor in other relevant law. A proclamation issued in 2002[149] gives foreign nationals of Ethiopian origin the right to be treated as domestic investors.[150] Hence, Ethiopian-born individuals who have changed their nationality can still be considered as domestic investors and participate in areas that are otherwise not open to foreign nationals. Assuming the nationality of the investor in question is of a country that has signed a BIT with Ethiopia, in case of dispute, would such investor be allowed to rely on the BIT and submit his or her claim against the host state in international tribunals?[151] Or can we assume that such investors should be treated like other domestic investors regarding dispute settlement? The issue can also extend to repatriation of profit and compensation money in convertible currency, among others. The mere fact that this investor chose to be treated as domestic investor does not mean that he/she revoked his/her foreign nationality. Hence, he/she gets all the privileges from being considered as domestic investor while his/her right under the BIT is still intact. This will tighten the state's regulatory space. One way to address this will be to include 'denial of benefit'[152] clauses in the BITs. This, unfortunately, will either be limited to future BITs or entail renegotiation of existing BITs, both of which require the full cooperation of the other contracting countries, which may not be easy to obtain.

---

[149] Proclamation Providing Foreign Nationals of Ethiopian Origin with Certain Rights to be Exercised in their Country of Origin No 270/2002, Federal Negarit Gazette, 8th Year No 17, February 2002.

[150] See Article 5/5 Proclamation 270/2002. Such person must hold Identification Card to be issued either by the Ministry of Foreign Affairs or the Authority for Security, Immigration and Refugee Affairs indicating his/her status as foreign national of Ethiopian origin. See article 7 of proclamation 270/2002.

[151] For jurisprudence in relation to this question see Schreuer (2009), pp. 521–527.

[152] 'Denial of benefit' clauses are those clauses under which 'states reserve the right to deny the benefits of a treaty to an company that does not have economic connection to the state on whose nationality it relies', Dolzer and Schreuer (2012), p. 55. For the case at hand, what is suggested is a modified version of such clause where the investor will be denied benefit of the BIT where he/she wishes to be treated as domestic investor.

The *second* challenge concerns the trade name requirement for the investment. One of the particulars to be specified at the time of registering a business is the trade name of the business.[153] Article 105 of the Commercial Code includes trade name as one of the particulars to be specified while applying for registration of a business. Hence, registration of trade name precedes commercial registration of the business. For this purpose, a trade name register that is administered by the Ministry of Trade has been established. The registration of, and search for, a trade name is conducted at the Ministry, where the entrepreneur proposes five different company names, and as the service at the Ministry is partially computerised, the search is quick.[154] The proposed trade name will be registered once the officer in charge is satisfied that none of the causes for preventing the registration of a trade name enumerated under article 16 of the business registration proclamation[155] are present.[156]

As part of the legal reform targeted towards addressing the concerns of business persons, the current commercial registration and licensing proclamation was issued in 2016. Apart from addressing the concerns, the law also introduces forms of business that were not covered under the previous laws, though were well known internationally. One improvement made in the current law relates to the conditions that need to be fulfilled while registering a trade name. One requirement under the previous commercial registration law[157] to register a trade name was that it should not be generic or common. The question then is: what factors are considered to determine if a trade name is generic or common? Considering the confusion that such term created in the registration process, it is omitted from the new law. The other problematic condition was the requirement that the trade name should not be like the names of public bodies, such as 'bureau', 'ministry', etc. If an internationally renowned entity has a trade name that contains any of those words, for example bureau, the likelihood of having its trade name registered in Ethiopia is slim even though it may have operations bearing similar trade names in other countries.

---

[153] Article 105 of the Commercial Code. Following this stipulation of the Commercial Code, article 5 of the Commercial registration and licensing proclamation requires the trade name to be included in the commercial registration. See Commercial Registration and Licensing Proclamation No 980/2016, Federal Negarit Gazette, 22nd Year No 101, Addis Ababa, August 2016.

[154] World Bank (2016), p. 20.

[155] Commercial Registration and Licensing Proclamation No 980/2016, Federal Negarit Gazette, 22nd Year No 101, Addis Ababa, August 2016.

[156] Article 16 of the Registration and Licensing Proclamation lists the causes for refusing registration. These are: the suggested trade name is identical to a previously registered trade name or business organisation, it includes name of a celebrity but no written consent of such celebrity is provided, where the name does not include the sector of business, where the name is renowned in Ethiopia or around the world even if not registered in Ethiopia, where the name is contrary to commendable conduct or ethical values, is identical or misleadingly similar to name of government institution, religious institution, political party, tribes and clans, any other business organisation or association, organisations of nations or states, charities and societies.

[157] Commercial Registration and Business Licensing Proclamation No 686/2010, Federal Negarit Gazette, 16th Year No 42, 2010 as amended by Proclamation No 731/2012, Federal Negarit Gazette, 18th Year No 19, 2012.

At times, the ground for rejecting the internationally renowned trade name could be the fact that 'some small local enterprise has already taken the name'.[158] Both the previous and current commercial registration proclamations require that the trade name whose registration is sought should not be renowned in Ethiopia or around the world even if not registered in Ethiopia.[159] Any person that wished to use such internationally renowned trade name needs to get authorisation from its owner. It may be difficult to trace globally known trade names when such trade names are not registered in Ethiopia. Consequently, local businesses may have such internationally known trade names registered without permission. The question then is: what will be the fate of the foreign investor, the rightful owner of the well-known trade name, when it wants to start business in Ethiopia? While the logical thing to do in such scenarios is to cancel the trade name given to the local business, such a remedy was not clearly available under the previous law. One possible ground for cancellation in such circumstances, under the previous law, was invoking fraud. But one can see how difficult it would be to prove fraud. One improvement made in this regard is broadening the grounds for cancellation of trade names to include erroneous registrations.

The *third* challenge is lack of operational coordination from different government agencies with respect to certification of a business. Getting a commercial registration certificate is contingent on a positive decision by the designated competence-certifying agency (agencies). As noted, 'there are 35 different competence-certifying agencies, which clearly could benefit from rationalization'.[160] The competency certificate, just like the business licence and the commercial registration certificates, had to be renewed annually, a requirement that has been waived by the new commercial registration law; today, only the business licence is required to be renewed annually. This is a commendable step in addressing concerns of business persons and improves coordination among the different government agencies.

*Finally*, Ethiopian commercial law was not broad enough to embrace some forms of business known internationally. To remedy that, the new commercial registration law has introduced such concepts and practices as franchise agreements and holding companies,[161] which were not recognised as such under the previous law, which subjected them to general contract law. The new law gives definition of franchise agreement[162] and requires the franchisee to function on the same standard as the

---

[158] Yibeltal and Tsegaye (2015).

[159] Article 24/3/I Commercial Registration Proclamation No 686/2010 as amended and article 16/1/e Commercial Registration Proclamation 980/2016.

[160] World Bank Group (July 2015), p. 44. The agencies that certify competence are Ministry of Agriculture, Ministry of Education, Ministry of Health, Food, Medicine and Healthcare Administration and Control Authority (FMHACA), Ministry of Mining, Ministry of Industry etc. See Ethiopian Standard Industrial Classification (ESIC), Rev.1 for more. The problem with competence certification is at times, multiple of institutions may be required to certify a single business.

[161] See article 37 and 34 of Commercial Registration Proclamation 980/2016 for franchise agreement and holding companies, respectively.

[162] See article 2/33 of Commercial Registration Proclamation 980/2016 for definition of franchise agreement.

franchiser while leaving the details for the registration of the franchise for future regulation. As far as holding companies are concerned, while the commercial code mentions them in a few instances, the details were not sufficient to implement and regulate the relationship between companies.[163] The new law lays down the liability of the holder company to its members and gives the Ministry of Trade the mandate to undertake registration of such companies.

In sum, there remain challenges in the Ethiopian FDI regime, namely (1) ambiguities over areas of investment, (2) what privileges should be granted to foreign nationals of Ethiopian origin, (3) the acquiring of trade names and business certificates and (4) the non-recognition of some common business practices. However, there is cause to hope, as a result of the positive continuous measures taken by the Ethiopian government in response to lessons learnt, that progress is being made.

## 6 Conclusions

The article provides insights into major aspects of Ethiopian FDI law and practice in light of the various standards of IIL and the liberal and statist approaches to foreign investment regulation. This article set out to answer a number of specific questions. Firstly, on the question of the relationship between Ethiopian law and IIL, it finds that Ethiopian FDI law mirrors what most national laws do; the rules, principles and standards of investment promotion and protection are broadly aligned with the overall direction of IIL. Like many other developing countries, Ethiopian FDI law (in certain areas) provides extra incentives and protections to foreign investors. The government also demonstrated its commitment to the protection of investment when it launched a compensation scheme available to foreign companies affected by the 2016 riots in the country.[164] At the same time, Ethiopian law also attempts to strike the right balance between attraction and protection of FDI, and protecting and promoting the national interest, including in the form of knowledge and skill transfer obligations, local employment and local content requirements, and protection of communities and the environment.[165] Indeed, this is a positive step to promoting investor confidence.

Secondly, on the question of whether Ethiopia has a *laissez-faire* or a statist approach to foreign investment regulation, the article finds that the selected laws, policies and practices considered above do not seem to prove the classical divide between investor (often developed) and host (often developing) countries' approaches to governing FDI; nor do they clearly suggest that Ethiopian FDI law and practice are dictated by a liberal or statist approach to FDI. The regulatory

---

[163] Bekele (June 2016).

[164] Getnet (November 15, 2016). It should further be noted here that the 1999 Ethiopia-UK BIT, under Article 4, provides that foreign investors should be compensated if they sustain damages as a result of armed conflict, state of emergency and the likes.

[165] See e.g. EIC (2017), employment data obtained on file which cover the years 1992–2016.

framework appears to combine both liberal and statist elements in its treatment of FDI. The underlying principles of FDI law, including the signed BITs, are based upon globally endorsed principles such as national treatment, MFN clause and the commitment to comply with other international standards. There is no doubt that Ethiopia has opened its doors for foreign investors to come and compete in an environment of free market. While this is in line with the general trend in IIL and practice,[166] this liberal approach is subject to satisfying national and local expectations.

The reforms on substantive laws, policies and institutional changes and recent developments considered in the fourth section, however, show the aggressively statist nature of the Ethiopian FDI regime, which is openly led and inspired by a developmental state philosophy. The statist nature of Ethiopian FDI law and practice goes beyond strictly regulating inward FDI and facility provision by the state. It must be noted that, despite persistent pressure from outside, especially from global financial institutions 'to shift its [Ethiopia's] public sector-led growth strategy to a private investment-led model',[167] the state sees itself as the main investor and driver of economic growth, as unequivocally stated in its two growth and transformation plans. This may explain why the FDI regime remains selective and restrictive. These ongoing robust measures of a legal, policy and operational nature provide strong evidence of a statist approach to development and investment; this does not necessarily exclude the key elements of the *laissez-faire* philosophy as considered. And the approaches and measures taken by Ethiopia are not only played within the rules of IIL but also reinforce the latter through state intervention and the several BITs to which Ethiopia is a party.

Thirdly, on the question about the evolution of the FDI regime and its negative/positive implications for promoting foreign investment in Ethiopia, the article, based upon Sects. 3 and 4, further finds that the authorities do not only regularly update the laws and institutions to meet new situations but also actively engage in facilitating a conducive environment through investment in infrastructure such as those of building industrial parks. They do not stop there; they also aggressively work to find foreign investors that are willing to make use of the industrial parks before and after building them using public funds.[168] The taking of actions when things go wrong, as shown in the large-scale land deals, should also be mentioned here.

Fourthly, on the question of challenges and lessons to be learnt from the laws, policies, practices and institutional frameworks considered in Sect. 5 and also other relevant parts of the article, it appears to be apparent that the statist approach adopted and the achievements registered so far are not without challenges—these are summarised as follows: (1) local employment attributable to FDI appears to be low, as mentioned earlier, compared to the huge demand for employment from the (educated and trained) youth in the country; (2) dispossession of land from locals, in the name

---

[166] Shan (2012), p. 75.
[167] Solomon (2015). Porter (1999), p. 380.
[168] Girma (2016).

of investment, lack transparent, participatory and accountable legal frameworks and protections—which highlights the need for a responsible investment regime capable of dealing with land management issues in an equitable and participatory manner; (3) there are still grey areas with respect to the economic sectors permitted/excluded for foreign investors. The laws intend to resolve this issue by empowering the Ethiopian Investment Board to perhaps decide on a case-by-case basis. This might provide some flexibility in managing FDI as an absolute and rigid listing of items may be detrimental to the goal of attracting investment. Such a flexible approach, without appropriate and transparent guidelines and processes, may also be a cause for concern for investors in terms of combating government malpractice; (4) the favourable treatment that foreign nationals of Ethiopian origin are afforded under the Ethiopian investment regime is defendable for socio-economic reasons, such as bringing skills and capital to the country, thereby combating brain drain, although some of the confusion around their legal implications requires appropriate clarification; and (5) the ambiguity over selecting and endorsing trade names is also a vital question, which begs for capacity building to make sure that international and domestic business names are not repeatedly used or abused by new investments. While investors have a legal responsibility to not deliberately make use of an already existing trade name, the primary, though not exclusive, responsibility to make sure this does not happen rests on state authorities. Much coordinated effort by all concerned institutions and authorities is required to address this, and the problem of involving several institutions in granting a business certificate is discussed in Sect. 5.2.

Of course, the reforms and improvements carried out in these areas, including the inclusion of the new concepts such as franchise agreements and holding companies, as well as other changes made in the new commercial registration law, are indicative of the government's efforts towards improving the business environment for investors and the evolving nature of FDI law and practice in the country. Though it is not possible for now to quantify the effects of such improvements in terms of the amount of foreign investment flow to the country, one can still draw the link between improving business environment and FDI attraction. One key message that might be deduced from the challenge of lack of coordination among the several state agencies that deal with FDI issues, a one-stop shop in which an inter-agency unit would be established composed of all regulatory agencies in the country and with the authority to issue all required certification under one roof, may provide a consistent, equitable and speedy service to foreign investors, communities and other stakeholders.

In conclusion, Ethiopia, as a sovereign state, with an ambition to transform its economy, has adopted a statist (or developmental state) approach to (foreign) investment. This has been the case without ignoring general rules and norms of IIL and good practices in the field. Without endorsing or rejecting the statist approach in its entirety and without denying the accomplishments thus far, democratic governance requires an open, accountable, participatory and inclusive approach to foreign and domestic investment. This must be upheld to achieve multiple objectives at once—attracting and protecting FDI on the one hand and promoting sovereign, community and individual interests on the other, in a balanced and equitable manner. This is what IIL is all about, as rightly stated by Professor Desta at the outset. Democratic values, including the rule of law, are better defended in liberal political and economic systems than other forms of governance. There is no reason why the developmental state model to investment and to governance more generally should not learn positive lessons from liberal values, as others, such as Taiwan and South Korea have done, without compromising on host states' socio-economic and sovereign interests.

**Acknowledgement** The authors are grateful to the external reviewers, editors of the yearbook for their critical and constructive comments. In particular, the authors would like to thank Professor Melaku Desta for the invaluable ideas and suggestions he has offered on various versions of the article. Any error belongs to the authors.

# References

Abdo M (2012) Ethiopian property law: a text book. Addis Ababa
Abdo M (2014) State policy and law in relation to land alienation in Ethiopia. PhD Thesis, University of Warwick. http://go.warwick.ac.uk/wrap/74132. Accessed 10 Jan 2017
Addis AK, Zuping Z (2016) Foreign direct investment in Ethiopia and its contribution to the socio-economic status. Int J Bus Manag 4(8):226–236
Aseffa A (2014) The Ethiopian developmental state and its challenges. https://www.academia.edu/18138282/The_Ethiopian_Developmental_State_and_its_Challenges. Accessed 5 Jan 2017
Bekele A (June 2016) The New Commercial Registration and Business Licensing Proclamation No 980/2016. Legal Update II(VI). https://www.mtalawoffice.com/legal-update
Brown C (2015) International agreements-history, approaches, schools. In: Bungenberg M, Griebel J, Hobe S, Reinisch A (eds) International investment law. C.H. Beck/Hart/Nomos
Brungenberg M, Griebel J, Hobe S, Reinisch A (2015) General introduction to international investment law. In: Bungenberg M, Griebel J, Hobe S, Reinisch A (eds) International investment law. C.H. Beck/Hart/Nomos
Caldentey EP (2008) The concept and evolution of the developmental state. Int J Polit Econ 37(2):27–53
Civil Code of the Empire of Ethiopia Proclamation No 165 of 1960, Negarit Gazette, Gazette Extraordinary, 19th year No 2, 5th May 1960
Commercial Code of the Empire of Ethiopia Proclamation No 166 of 1960 Negarit Gazette, Gazette Extraordinary, 19th Year No 3, 5th May 1960
Commercial Registration and Licensing Proclamation No 980/2016, Federal Negarit Gazette, 22nd Year No 101, Addis Ababa, 5th August 2016
Convention on the Settlement of Investment Disputes between States and Nationals of other States 1965, 18 March 1965, 575 UNTS 159 (entered into force 14 Oct 1966)
Deninger K, Byerlee D (2011) Rising global interest in farmland: can it yield sustainable and equitable benefits? World Bank
Derso B (2017) Ethiopia: Nation's Foreign Direct Investment Rising During State of Emergency. The Ethiopian Herald, (21 February 2017). http://allafrica.com/stories/201702210199.html. Accessed 6 July 2017)
Desta MG (2016) Competition for natural resources and international investment law: analysis from the perspective of Africa. In: Yihdego Z, Desta M, Merso F (eds) Ethiopian yearbook of international law, vol 2016. Springer, Cham, pp 117–149

Dolzer R, Schreuer C (2008) Principles of international investment law, 1st edn. Oxford University Press, Oxford
Dolzer R, Schreuer C (2012) Principles of international investment law, 2nd edn. Oxford University Press, Oxford
Douglas Z (2003) The hybrid foundations of investment treaty arbitration. Br Yearb Int Law 74:151–289
Ethiopian Investment Board and Ethiopian Investment Commission Establishment Council of Ministers Regulation No 313/2014, 20th year, No 63, August 2014
Ethiopian Investment Commission Investment Guide (2014) http://www.ethiopianembassy.org/PDF/Ethiopia_Investment_Guide_2014.pdf. Accessed 15 Aug 2016
'Ethiopian PM urges high-level cadres to address concerns of good governance' (2017) Xinhua (23 May 2017). http://news.xinhuanet.com/english/2017-05/23/c_136308293.htm
Expropriation of Landholdings for Public Purposes and Payment of Compensation Proclamation No 455/2005, Federal Negarit Gazette, 11th Year No 43, 15th July 2005
Farole T, Akinci G (2011) Special economic zones: progress, emerging challenges and future directions. The World Bank, Washington DC
Five Saudi Star Workers Killed in Gambella (2012) The Ethiopian Reporter (2 May 2012). http://www.ethiopianreporter.com/news/293-news/6168-2012-05-02-06-50-57.html. Accessed 13 June 2016
Footer ME (2009) Bits and pieces: social and environmental protection in the regulation of foreign investment. Mich State J Int Law 18(1):33–64
Freyer D, Herlihy D (2005) Most favored Nation treatment and dispute settlement in investment arbitration: just how "Favored" is "Most Favored"? Foreign Invest Law J 20(1)
Getnet T (2016) Investment Commission calls on insurers to compensate damaged businesses. Capital (15 November 2016). http://capitalethiopia.com/2016/11/15/investment-commission-calls-insurers-compensate-damaged-businesses/. Accessed 20 Jan 2017
Girma S, Gong Y, Görg H (2009) What determines innovation activity in Chinese state-owned enterprises? The role of foreign direct investment. World Dev 37(4):866–873
Girma Z (2016) Ethiopia: industrial parks way forward for economic transformation. The Ethiopian Herald. http://allafrica.com/stories/201608161195.html. Accessed 12 May 2017
Gómez-Palacio I, Muchlinski P (2008) Admission and establishment. In: Muchlinski P et al (eds) Oxford handbook of international investment law. Oxford University Press
Hahn M (2015) EU and obligations related to investment. In: Bungenberg M, Griebel J, Hobe S, Reinisch A (eds) International investment law. C.H. Beck/Hart/Nomos
Hobe S (2015) The development of the law of Aliens and the emergence of general principles of protection under public international law. In: Bungenberg M, Griebel J, Hobe S, Reinisch A (eds) International investment law. C.H.Beck/Hart/Nomos
In Full Swing (2017) Addis Fortune News Paper (25 June 2017). https://addisfortune.net/articles/in-full-swing/. Accessed 28 June 2017
Industrial Park Proclamation No 886/2015, Federal Negarit Gazette 21st year No 39, 9th April 2015
Investment Amendment Proclamation 849/2014, Federal Negarit Gazette, 20th year, no.52, 22 July, 2014
Investment Incentives and Investment Areas Reserved for Domestic Investors Council of Ministers Regulation, Federal Negarit Gazette, 19th year, No. 4, 29 November, 2012
Investment Incentives and Investment Areas Reserves for Domestic Investors Council of Ministers (Amendment) Regulation 312/2014, Federal Negarit Gazette, 20th Year, No.62., 13 August, 2014
Investment Proclamation No 769/2012, Federal Negarit Gazette, 18th Year, No. 63, 17 September, 2012
Keeley J, Seide WM, Eid A, Kidewa AL (2014) Large-scale land deals in Ethiopia: scale, trends, features and outcomes to date. IDRC and IIED, London

Knutsen CH, Rygh A, Hveem H (2011) Does state ownership matter? Institutions' effect on foreign direct investment revisited. Bus Polit 13(1). https://doi.org/10.2202/1469-3569.1314

Krzeczunowick G (1977) The Ethiopian law of compensation for damages. Addis Ababa University Faculty of Law

Kumar N (2002) Globalization and the quality of foreign direct investment. Oxford University Press, Oxford

Lavers T (2012) 'Land Grab' as development strategy? The political economy of agricultural investment in Ethiopia. J Peasant Stud 39(1):105–132

Maasho A (March 25, 2016) Ethiopian Body Suspends Farm Lease Program after Poor Results. http://af.reuters.com/article/topNews/idAFKCN0WR10P?sp=true. Accessed 25 Jan 2017

Makki F (2012) Power and property: commercialization, enclosure and the transformation of Agrarian relations in Ethiopia. J Peasant Stud 39(1):81–104

Manek N (2017) 'Karuturi Demands Compensation From' Ethiopia for Failed Land Deal'. Bloomberg (21 September 2017)

Mbate M (2016) Structural change and industrial policy: a case study of Ethiopia's leather sector. J Afr Trade 3(1):85–100. http://www.sciencedirect.com/science/article/pii/S2214851517300026

McLachlan C, Shore L, Weiniger M (2007) International investment arbitration: substantive principles. Oxford University Press, Oxford

Melese A, Helmsing AHJ (2010) Endogenisation or enclave formation? The development of the Ethiopian cut flower industry. J Mod Afr Stud 48:35–66

Memorandum on the Foreign Trade Regime: Ethiopia Ministry of Trade and Industry December 2006 Addis Ababa, Ethiopia http://www.ethdiaspora.org.et/phocadownloadpap/Publications/moti-memorandumonthe-ftr.pdf

Miller AS (April 1959) Protection of private foreign investment by multilateral convention. Am J Int Law 53(2):371–378

MOFED (2010) Growth and Transformation Plan 2010/11-2014/15

MOFED (2014) Growth and Transformation Plan Annual Progress Report for F.Y 2012/2013

National Planning Commission (May 2016) Growth and Transformation Plan II (GTP II) (2015/16-2019/20)

Newcombe A, Paradell L (2009) Law and practice of investment treaties: standards of treatment. Wolters Kluwer

Oakland Institute (2011) Understanding land investment deals in Africa: Country Report-Ethiopia. USA

Payment of Compensation for Property Situated on Landholding Expropriated for Public Purposes Council of Ministers Regulation No 135/2007, Federal Negarit Gazette, 13th Year No 36, 18th May 2007

Pearce F (2012) The land grabbers: the new fight over who owns the earth. Peacon Press

Porter M (1999) The Ethiopian investment law. Icsid Rev Foreign Invest Law J, pp 362–380. https://academic.oup.com/icsidreview/article-pdf/14/2/362/2611931/14-2-362.pdf. Accessed 12 Aug 2017

Proclamation Providing Foreign Nationals of Ethiopian Origin with Certain Rights to be Exercised in their Country of Origin No 270/2002, Federal Negarit Gazette, 8th Year No 17, February 2002

Rahmato D (June 2014) The perils of development from above: land deals in Ethiopia. Afr Ident 12(1): 26-44

Redae M (May 2016) Investment and labor rights in Ethiopia: some challenges and opportunities. Proceedings of seminar series of the school of law, Addis Ababa University

Re-enactment of Urban Land Lease Holding Proclamation No 272/2002, Federal Negarit Gazette, 8th Year No 19, 14th May 2002

Reisman WM, Sloane RD (2003) Indirect expropriation and its valuation in the BIT generation. Br Yearb Int Law 74:115

Rodriguez AF (2008) The most favoured nation treatment clause in international investment agreements: a tool for treaty shopping? J Int Arbitr 25(1)

Sasson M (2010) Substantive law in investment treaty arbitration: the unsettled relationship between international law and municipal law. Kluwer Law International

Sauvant KP, Nolan MD (2015) China's outward foreign direct investment and international investment law. J Int Econ Law 18:893–934. https://doi.org/10.1093/jiel/jgv045

Schreuer C (2009) Nationality of investors: legitimate restrictions vs. business interests. ICSID Rev 24(2):521–527. https://doi.org/10.1093/icsidreview/24.2.521

Shan W (2012) The legal framework governing foreign investment. In: Shan W (ed) The legal protection of foreign investment: a comparative study. Hart, Oxford

Shiferaw A (2017) Ethiopia: integrated agro-industrial parks for economic transformation. The Ethiopian Herald (18 February 2017). http://allafrica.com/stories/201702180279.html. Accessed 28 June 2017

Solomon T (2015) Ethiopia: IMF urges private sector involvement in economy. African Reporter, 19 June 2015. http://www.theafricareport.com/East-Horn-Africa/ethiopia-imf-urges-private-sector-involvement-in-economy.html. Accessed 20 Aug 2016

Sornarajah M (2010) The international law on foreign investment. 3rd edn. Cambridge University Press

'State of the Union 2017 - Trade Package: European Commission proposes framework for screening of foreign direct investments', Brussels 14 September 2017. http://europa.eu/rapid/press-release_IP-17-3183_en.htm. Accessed 23 Jan 2018

Stebek EN (2011) Between 'Land Grabs' and agricultural investment: land rent contracts with foreign investors and Ethiopia's normative setting in focus. Mizan Law Rev 5(2):175–214

Tagliarino NK (2017) The status of National Legal frameworks for valuing compensation for expropriated land: an analysis of whether national laws in 50 countries/regions across Asia, Africa, and Latin America comply with international standards on compensation valuation. Land 6:37. https://doi.org/10.3390/land6020037

Tamrat I (April 2010) Governance of Large Scale Agricultural Investments in Africa: The Case of Ethiopia. Paper presented at the World Bank Conference on Land Policy and Administration Washington. http://siteresources.worldbank.org/EXTARD/Resources/336681-1236436879081/5893311-1271205116054/tamrat.pdf. Accessed 15 June 2016

The Economist (13 October 2016) 'Ethiopia: State of emergency declared'

UNCTAD (2017a) Investment Policy Hub. http://investmentpolicyhub.unctad.org/IIA/CountryBits/67. Accessed 15 June 2017

UNCTAD (2017b) World Investment Report 2017: Investment and the Digital Economy. United Nation Publications (UNCTAD/WIR/2017)

UNIDO (2016) Integrated Agro-Industrial Parks in Ethiopia. https://isid.unido.org/files/Ethiopia/Integrated-Agro-Industrial-Parks-in-Ethiopia-booklet.pdf. Accessed 16 May 2017

Wang S, Tong TW, Chen G, Kim H (2009) Expatriate utilization and foreign direct investment performance: the mediating role of knowledge transfer. J Manag 35(5):1181–1206

Ward H (2008) Overview. In: Dufey A, Grieg-Gran M, Ward H (eds) Responsible enterprise, foreign direct investment and investment promotion: key issues in attracting investment for sustainable development. International Institute for Environment and Development, London

Woldemariam GA (2016) The place of international law in the Ethiopian legal system. In: Yihdego Z, Desta M, Merso F (eds) Ethiopian yearbook of international law 2016. Springer, Cham, pp 61–94

World Bank (2016) Priorities For Ending Extreme Poverty and Promoting Shared Prosperity Systematic Country Diagnostic. Report No: 100592-ET (March 30, 2016). http://documents.worldbank.org/curated/en/913611468185379056/pdf/100592-REVISED-P154064-PUBLIC-Ethiopia-SCD-March-30-2016-web.pdf. Accessed 12 Sept 2017

World Bank (2017) World Economic Prospects: a Fragile Recovery. https://openknowledge.worldbank.org/bitstream/handle/10986/26800/9781464810244.pdf?sequence=14&isAllowed=y. Accessed 29 Sept 2017

World Bank Group (July 2015) 4th Ethiopia Economic Update: Overcoming Constraints in the Manufacturing Sector

Yibeltal K, Tsegaye K (2015) Is Ethiopia becoming a 'No Go Zone' for Investors? Addis Standard. http://addisstandard.com/is-ethiopia-becoming-no-go-zone-for-investors. Accessed 23 June 2016

Yihdego Z (2012) Ethiopia, Chapter 19. In: Shan W (ed) The legal protection of foreign investment: a comparative study. Hart, Oxford

Zarsky L (2008) FDI and sustainable development: challenges and opportunities in the ICT sector. In: Dufey A, Grieg-Gran M, Ward H (eds) Responsible enterprise, foreign direct investment and investment promotion: key issues in attracting investment for sustainable development. International Institute for Environment and Development, London

**Martha Hailu** is an assistant professor of law at Addis Ababa University, Ethiopia.

**Zeray Yihdego** is a Reader in public international law at the University of Aberdeen, UK.

# Comparative Perspective on Exhaustible Resource Development in Ethiopia: Lessons from the Norwegian Legal Framework and Experience

Tina Hunter

**Abstract** This paper analyses the Ethiopian Petroleum Operations Proclamation (the Proclamation) and other relevant laws and regulations to determine whether the current structure and function of the law support Ethiopia's goals of sustainably developing the petroleum resources for the benefit of the Ethiopian people, which is set out in the preamble to the principal Proclamation. This analysis is undertaken by looking at the form and substance of the Proclamation, as well as its interaction with other Ethiopian proclamations, to determine if they support the goal of the law. Further analysis is also undertaken by considering the Proclamation against the Norwegian (and other) legal framework, which has successfully encouraged the optimal extraction of petroleum for sustainable development for over 40 years. Upon analysis of the Proclamation, this paper finds that although some elements of the Proclamation do support sustainable development, there are several functions, such as field development planning and depletion policy, that should be addressed in order to sustainably develop Ethiopia's petroleum resources for the benefit of the Ethiopian people.

## 1 Introduction

The presence of petroleum (especially gas at this stage) in Ethiopia is little known outside of corporate circles, and certainly not a focus for many commercial actors. The extraction[1] of petroleum resources has economic consequences for Ethiopia. By extracting the petroleum, the 'asset' is liquidated, revenue from the asset is

---

[1] In this chapter, the term 'extraction' is used to encompass all upstream activities required for the production of petroleum. This includes petroleum exploration, the development of a potential petroleum deposit and the actual production of petroleum from the field.

T. Hunter (✉)
University of Aberdeen, Aberdeen, UK
e-mail: thunter@abdn.ac.uk

© Springer International Publishing AG, part of Springer Nature 2018
Z. Yihdego et al. (eds.), *Ethiopian Yearbook of International Law 2017*,
Ethiopian Yearbook of International Law 2017,
https://doi.org/10.1007/978-3-319-90887-8_3

gained and the state can no longer realise revenue from this asset[2]—once the petroleum is extracted and sold. Like any other non-renewable asset, it is permanently lost. This creates an imperative for Ethiopia to extract the petroleum in a manner that provides enduring social and economic benefits for the state and its community.

The discovery of petroleum in any state, but particularly an African state, brings opportunities and pitfalls in equal measures. For the state, there is the opportunity for economic development, particularly, in terms of international investment in petroleum and associated infrastructure such as roads and ports. In addition, the development of petroleum resources brings newfound wealth to the state, providing opportunities for economic and social development. However, oil has not been called 'the devil's excrement' for nothing. In 1975, Venezuelan Pablo Perez Alfonzo, in referring to the development of oil in his country, lamented that oil brings trouble: waste, corruption, consumption and debt.[3] At the heart of such trouble is the 'Dutch disease', where the non-resource tradable sector of an economy contracts as resources take over and dominate the economy.[4] Persistent Dutch disease can provoke a rapid, distorted growth of the services, transportation and other non-tradable sectors whilst simultaneously discouraging industrialisation and agriculture.[5] When combined with other barriers to long-term productive activity characterised by exhaustible[6] resource exploitation, such as those described by several academics, including Hotelling[7] and Robinson et al.,[8] the impacts of Dutch disease can be dramatic, particularly, in developing countries, leading to a phenomenon known as 'resource curse'[9] or the 'paradox of plenty'.[10]

Whilst the development of Dutch disease and the resource curse is not a foregone conclusion for a developing country that seeks to exploit its petroleum resources, there have nonetheless been many examples of such an outcome: Venezuela in the 1970s (thus leading Alfonzo to refer to oil as 'the Devil's excrement'), Nigeria,[11]

---

[2] For a discussion of the economic value of petroleum, see Lee (2006).

[3] Perez Alfonzo in Strønen (2017), p. 317.

[4] The Netherlands experienced a severe decline in its manufacturing sector in the 1960s after the giant Groningen Gas Field was discovered and came into production in the 1950s, because of the high appreciation of the Dutch Guilder. For a further explanation of this concept, see Corden and Neary (1982), pp. 825–848.

[5] Kari (1997), p. 5.

[6] In this chapter the concept 'exhaustible' is used to mean those resources that are non-renewable. Therefore, the terms 'exhaustible' and 'non-renewable' are interchangeable. The term exhaustible has been chosen as it is the same term utilized by Robert M Solow in his groundbreaking work, *Intergenerational Equity and Exhaustible Resources* (1973).

[7] Hotelling (1931), pp. 137–175.

[8] Robinson et al. (2002).

[9] The concept of Resource Curse has been considered in detail in Sachs and Warner (2001), pp. 827–838.

[10] The paradox of plenty in relation to oil is considered in Kari (1997).

[11] Sala-i-Martin and Subramanian (2003).

Mexico and the Gulf states.[12] An impact of resource curse and the 'paradox of plenty' is that as a state's petroleum resources are developed, economic growth and social development are hampered. A study by Sachs and Warner demonstrates that almost without exception, resource-abundant countries have economically stagnated since the early 1970s, with little or no economic growth (export led or otherwise).[13] A meta-analysis of oil-rich nations and the paradox of plenty by Dauvin and Guerreiro support this view and identify three factors that influence the impact of non-renewable natural resources on economic growth[14]: the type of resources considered, the institutional framework of the resource-rich county and the way the resources are measured.

For Ethiopia, on the cusp of developing its petroleum resources, the prospect of such resource curse could prove to be a decisive strain on a country already suffering from domestic inflationary pressure and a devalued currency, combined with an external environment that has created volatility in the Ethiopian economy at a time when the country seeks to implement its *Growth and Transformation Plan*.[15] This chapter focuses on one of the factors defined by Dauvin and Guerreiro that influence natural resource extraction and the development of resource curse: the institutional framework. It examines the legal framework that regulates the extraction of petroleum in Ethiopia, considering both the policy and the laws enacted. It seeks to assess whether the current Ethiopian regulatory framework will provide socio-economic benefits for Ethiopia and Ethiopians in accordance with the aims of the government policy on developing petroleum resources[16] or whether, like many other developing nations that have developed their exhaustible petroleum resources, it will result in negative impacts such as resource curse.

For Ethiopia to avoid such consequences, it is vital that petroleum resource extraction is optimised in a manner that provides enduring social and economic benefits for the state and its community. By undertaking the sustainable development[17] of its resources from the outset, and, in particular, by optimising the extraction of its petroleum resources, such benefits can be realised. The sustainable development of the petroleum resources in any state occurs by virtue of the legal framework that governs the extraction of petroleum. By analysing a state's petroleum legal framework,[18] it is possible to analyse whether sustainable development of petroleum currently occurs. An analysis of Ethiopia's legal framework in determining sustainable development is necessary since it is acknowledged that sound legal frameworks assist developing countries in promoting economic growth and

---

[12] Sachs and Warner (2001), p. 828.
[13] Sachs and Warner (2001), p. 837.
[14] Dauvin and Guerreiro (2017), p. 225.
[15] National Planning Commission Ethiopia (2016), p. 1.
[16] Ethiopian Ministry of Mines (2017).
[17] Sustainable development and the narrower concept of sustainable extraction are considered in detail in section 4 below.
[18] This framework is defined as both the laws and policies pertaining to the extraction of petroleum.

national development.[19] Rossouw notes that a legal framework is essential for the sustainability of the petroleum sector. Furthermore, Li and Flier argue that the governance environment (rule based or otherwise) will have an impact on investment and, therefore, petroleum development,[20] thereby impacting on the petroleum because of reliance on foreign investment for the development of petroleum resources in developing countries. This chapter, therefore, poses the question: does the current petroleum regulatory framework of Ethiopia encourage the sustainable development of petroleum resources through the optimisation of petroleum extraction?

In answering this question, the chapter will analyse the concept of sustainable development (which is synonymously used with terms such as 'optimisation' and 'prudent production' for this chapter purposes) of resources, focusing on the legal framework associated with optimising recovery, and then provide an overview of the legal framework for the extraction of petroleum in Ethiopia. It will then focus on the capacity of the Ethiopian law to sustainably extract petroleum. In doing so, there will be a focus on two main aspects of the legal framework: the structure of the legal framework and the content of the law. By undertaking this analysis, the chapter will then determine whether the current Ethiopian petroleum legal framework optimises petroleum extraction, thereby encouraging the sustainable development of its petroleum resources.

In addition to using doctrinal research methodology,[21] the socio-legal issues are considered in the study, thereby placing Ethiopia's petroleum laws within the socio-legal context in which the laws have developed. Furthermore, to understand the capacity of Ethiopian laws to encourage sustainable development of petroleum, a comparative legal methodology is utilised.[22] The limit of comparative method is that 'only similar legal systems can be compared'[23] and that incomparable rules arising from different legal systems cannot be compared.[24] However, functional analysis methodologies overcome such limitations since legal concepts, principles and rules that fulfil similar functions are compared.[25] This chapter comparatively analyses petroleum extraction law of Ethiopia, and the petroleum extraction legal framework of Norway, widely regarded in the literature as a system of regulation that exhibits best practice in extracting petroleum extraction for socio-legal benefit.[26] It also draws upon experiences in Queensland where the regulation of the extraction of

---

[19] Armstrong (2003), p. 12.

[20] Li and Filer (2007), pp. 83–84.

[21] Doctrinal methodology is defined as 'a synthesis of rules, principles, norms, interpretive guidelines and values. It explains, makes coherent or justified a segment of the law as part of a larger system of law. A doctrine can be abstract, binding, or non-binding'. See Mann and Blunden (2010).

[22] The first International Congress of Comparative Law was held in Paris in 1900, and brought together experts from Europe to consider this area of legal methodology. See Smits (1998), p. 442.

[23] Orucu (1998), p. 442.

[24] Zweigert and Kotz (1998), p. 34.

[25] Zweigert and Kotz (1998), p. 34.

[26] See for example Larsen (2004), Hunter (2014), Ryggvik (2010), and Al-Kasim (2006).

coal seam gas is not seen as best practice in encouraging sustainable socio-economic development. In addition, the mineral extraction law of Ethiopia will be considered as a good example of sustainable development of non-renewable resources.

To assist with assessing the content of the law and the capacity of the law to support the optimisation of petroleum extraction, this paper will apply the elements of the World Bank Policy Research Working Paper *Legislative Frameworks Used to Foster Petroleum Development.*[27]

In short, the contribution of this chapter is that it looks at the law on extraction of petroleum resources for the benefit of all Ethiopians *before* actual extraction occurs. Too often, such assessment is carried out when it becomes evident that petroleum extraction has not provided economic and social benefits and perhaps may have caused harm, such as in the case of Nigeria,[28] requiring remedial legislative reform that may be difficult to enact.[29] To date, much analysis of the concept of optimising the benefits of petroleum extraction for sustainable development has been confined to the assessment of well-developed legislative frameworks, such as Australian and Norwegian laws, whilst this chapter provides an assessment of the structure and content of the legal framework regulating the extraction of the petroleum resources of a developing state.

## 2 Overview of Ethiopian Petroleum Resources and Law

### 2.1 Petroleum Resources and Their Place in the Ethiopian Economy

Ethiopia has one of the largest endowments of natural gas in Africa. It was discovered in 1972 by the US company Tenneco, which was subsequently expelled from Ethiopia by the Derg in 1977. Initial attempts to exploit the field by the USSR company Soviet Petroleum Exploration Expedition (SPEE) abruptly concluded in 1994 when SPEE was also expelled after the ruling military regime fell. Further attempts to develop the resources of the Calub field have failed, despite the World Bank extending a loan of US$74.31 million to the Government of Ethiopia (GoE).[30] Such failure is particularly disappointing for Ethiopia given that approximately one quar-

---

[27] Onorato (1995).

[28] Sala-i-Martin and Subramanian (2003).

[29] In order to reform its laws relating to the extraction of petroleum, Nigeria introduced the *Petroleum Industry Bill* into the Parliament in 2009. A watered-down form of the Bill (which became known as the *Petroleum Industry Governance Bill, or PIGB*) was passed in May 2017, and will implement sweeping changes in the legal framework and institutions that govern the Nigerian petroleum industry. Such reform has occurred over 70 years after petroleum extraction first occurred in Nigeria, and more than 25 years after protests regarding the law and institutions governing petroleum extraction.

[30] World Bank (2016), p. 5.

ter of the population live below the poverty line.[31] Despite this lack of ability to develop the gas resources to date, Ethiopia has experienced strong, broad-based economic growth since 2003/2004, averaging 10.4% growth/annum, compared with the regional average growth of 5.4%.[32] This growth has partly been reinforced by the first *Growth and Transformation Plan* (GTP I) from 2011 to 2016, which successfully increased agricultural productivity and assisted in reducing the import dependency ratio.[33] The development of exhaustible resources during the period was significant, generating approximately US$2.62 billion from mineral exports,[34] which contributed to economic growth. However, no export earnings were realised from the extraction of petroleum resources. Altogether, the transformation of the domestic private sector under GTP I was low and remains a priority for GTP II.[35] The development of Ethiopia's large gas reserves has the potential to significantly contribute to economic growth under GTP II, and therefore the development of these resources is critical for long-term economic development.

In order to increase its foreign currency earnings, the GoE has set a strategic goal of increasing the exploitation of its gas resources, particularly, in the Ogaden Basin in eastern Ethiopia, where the Calub and Hilala gas fields are estimated to hold 1.33 Tcm (trillion cubic metres) of gas.[36] Most importantly, the GoE established the Ethiopian Petroleum and Natural Gas Development Enterprise (EPNGDE),[37] where the GoE participating interests under the Petroleum Production Sharing Agreement (PPSA) are to be transferred to the EPNGDE.[38] The objectives of the EPNGDE are to engage in petroleum and natural gas development, to invest in companies engaged in petroleum development, to represent the government in its equity participation in private companies and to engage in other activities necessary to attain the objectives.[39]

The establishment of the EPNGDE supports the petroleum policy of the GoE, which seeks to promote and strengthen the development of existing fields and the exploration for further oil reserves.[40] The policy position of the GoE with respect to oil and gas is laid down in section 4 (general policy) of the National Energy Policy of Ethiopia, which states a commitment to 'promote and strengthen the development and exploration for natural gas and oil'.[41] The GoE's Ministry of Mines, Petroleum and Natural Gas (MoM) reiterates and expands this policy, noting that the Petroleum

---

[31] National Planning Commission Ethiopia (2016), p. 6.
[32] World Bank (2017).
[33] National Planning Commission Ethiopia, *GTP II*, pp. 20–21.
[34] National Planning Commission Ethiopia, *GTP II*, pp. 33–34.
[35] National Planning Commission Ethiopia, *GTP II*, pp. 22–23.
[36] 'Ethiopia eyes gas production and exports from potential reserves' Oil Review Africa (2015).
[37] Established by Council of Ministers Regulation No. 264/2012 (26 June 2012).
[38] Council of Ministers Regulation to Provide for the Establishment of the Ethiopian Petroleum and Natural Gas Enterprise Council of Ministers Regulation No. 264/2012 (26 June 2012), r10.
[39] Council of Ministers Regulation to Provide for the Establishment of the Ethiopian Petroleum and Natural Gas Enterprise Council of Ministers Regulation No. 264/201 (26 June 2012), r6.
[40] World Bank (2016), p. 8.
[41] Government of Ethiopia, p. 4.

Licencing and Administration section of the MoM should work to implement the main objectives of the MoM, which include the advancement of petroleum exploration and development activities to enhance the overall development of the country, the establishment of petroleum operations as one of the major contributors to the national economy and the undertaking of exploration activities to unearth natural resources and make use of them for the benefit of the country and the people at large.[42] By establishing the goal to exploit natural resources for the benefit of Ethiopia and Ethiopians, the GoE has expressed a desire to develop its petroleum resources to ensure that both the people (this generation) and the future prosperity of the country (impliedly including future generations) benefit from the exploration and development of petroleum. Of course, such development necessarily includes the attraction of foreign investment; however, there is also a strong sense of ensuring that the development benefits the Ethiopian people and contributes to economic growth.[43] Such goals are in line with the definition of sustainable development.

## 2.2 Petroleum Resource Extraction Framework

The Ethiopian policy position with regard to oil and gas has its basis in the Ethiopian Constitution. There are two sections of the Ethiopian Constitution that are relevant for the development of Ethiopia's petroleum resources for the benefit of all Ethiopians:

- Article 43 (1): The Peoples of Ethiopia as a whole, and each Nation, Nationality and People in Ethiopia in particular have the right to improved living standards and to *sustainable development*; and
- Article 89 (1): The government shall have the duty to formulate policies which ensure that all Ethiopians can benefit from the country's legacy of intellectual and *material resources*.[44]

The policy position regarding the development of Ethiopian petroleum resources is currently implemented through a regulatory framework that consists of the Petroleum Operations Proclamation (POP),[45] the Tax Proclamation[46] and the Environmental Assessment Proclamation.[47] In addition, a Model Petroleum Production Sharing Agreement (PPSA), established in 1986 and revised in 2011, sets out the terms of each Production Sharing Agreement (PSA), with some allowances for negotiation between the GoE and a contracting party.[48] An overview of the legal

---

[42] Ethiopian Ministry of Mines (2017).
[43] The policy position regarding petroleum development is outlined in the *Petroleum Operations Proclamation 1986* Proclamation No. 295/1986, and discussed in detail in section 5.2 below.
[44] Italics added by author.
[45] Petroleum Operations Proclamation 1986 Proclamation No. 295/1986.
[46] Tax Proclamation, Proclamation No. 296/1986.
[47] Environmental Assessment Proclamation, Proclamation No. 299/2002.
[48] Model Petroleum Production Sharing Agreement (2011).

**Fig. 1** Legal framework for petroleum resource exploration and development in Ethiopia (Source: Compiled by Author)

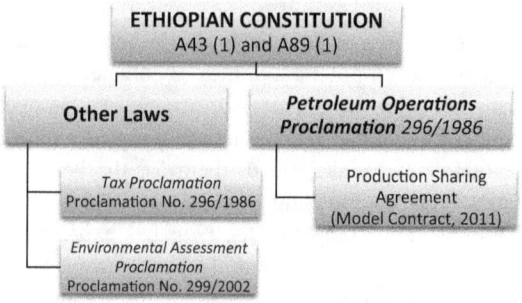

framework for the development of Ethiopian petroleum resources is represented in Fig. 1.

The Environmental Assessment Proclamation will be considered in relation to environmental protection requirements of the core petroleum legislation and an extraction licence. The Tax Proclamation will, however, be excluded from the scope of this study in the interest of economy of space.

Established in 1986 (along with the implementation of the associated PPSA), the POP is somewhat sparse in detail. It comprises 28 sections in all and contains an interesting accumulation of provisions. After a preamble setting out the goals of petroleum development, Article 2 of the POP provides definitions of terms, Article 3 outlines the scope of the POP, Article 4 stipulates that ownership of petroleum belongs to the state. Article 5 outlines the role of the government in undertaking petroleum activities, whilst Articles 6 and 7 relate to the Minister's representation and powers. Article 8 of the Proclamation sets out the capacity of the Minister to make directives in relation to the method for inviting and evaluating petroleum bids, the content of petroleum applications and the requirements of applicants when applying to undertake petroleum operations. This section amounts to a discretionary capacity of the Minister to stipulate the terms for the grant of a licence, and is similar to what is obtainable in other jurisdictions, as considered later. Articles 9–28 set out the requirements for a contractor under a PPSA and includes matters such as insurance, records, disposal of assets, operating standards, transfer and assignment, duration of the agreement and obligations under the PPSA. Thus, the POP is a mix of an enabling Act and a checklist/outline for the content of the PPSA. This combination is unusual, particularly, given that sections of the Model PPSA also cover these requirements: asset disposal (section 3.3) insurance (section 3), records (section 3.4), operating standards (sections 3.7.2 and 8.1.1), transfer and assignment (section 3.1.3) and duration of the agreement (section 5.3.2). Thus, there is repetition and overlap between the two Ethiopian instruments.

Of great importance in relation to prudent production and extraction is the preamble to the POP, which broadly outlines the need for optimal extraction of petroleum for the benefit of all Ethiopians. A detailed analysis of the content of the preamble is analysed in section 5.2.2 below. The structure and content of the POP is the subject of this analysis, to determine whether it provides a suitable framework for the optimal extraction of petroleum resources in Ethiopia.

## 3 The Concepts of Sustainable Development and Optimising Extraction

### 3.1 Sustainable Development

The concept 'sustainable development' was first defined by the World Commission on Environment and Development (the 'Brundtland Commission') in its report to the United Nations General Assembly[49] as 'development which meets the needs of the present without compromising the ability of the future generations to meet their own needs'.[50] The Commission emphasised that sustainable development provides 'successive generations [with] not only man-made wealth but also natural wealth … in adequate amounts to ensure continuing improvements in the quality of life'.[51] The World Commission recommended sustainable development as a guiding principle to governments and private enterprises.[52]

Whilst respecting a state's sovereignty over its natural resources,[53] the United Nations specifies that protecting and managing the natural resource base for economic and social development are overarching objectives of, and essential requirements for, sustainable development.[54] Although the World Commission first applied the concept of sustainable development only to the environment, the principle has been expanded to encompass three interdependent but mutually reinforcing pillars—economic development, social development and environmental protection.[55] This expanded definition was affirmed by the United Nations Development Programme (UNDP) and the World Energy Council in its energy assessment, where they defined sustainable development as 'energy produced and used in ways that support human development over the long term, in all its social, economic and environmental dimensions'.[56] It is this definition that has been adopted for use in this chapter, focusing on the social and economic aspects[57] of the sustainable development of petroleum resources. As such, in this chapter, the term 'sustainable development' focuses on maximising the economic and social benefits from the development of the petroleum resources, although it does briefly refer also to the first pillar of environmental sustainability.

---

[49] World Commission on Environment and Development, (1987), (known as the Brundtland Commission).

[50] Report of the World Commission on Environment and Development (1987), p. 1.

[51] Report of the World Commission on Environment and Development (1987), p. 1.

[52] Report of the World Commission on Environment and Development (1987), p. 1.

[53] As laid down in UN Resolution 1803 (1962).

[54] UN Resolution 1803 (1962).

[55] World Summit Outcomes, [48] UN GAOR 60th session UN Doc A/60/L.1 (2005).

[56] United Nations Development Programme (2000), p. 3. This is UNDP citation, whilst the quote refers to the World Energy Council?

[57] Economic benefits include, but are not confined to, economic diversification of industry, and the capturing of production cost spending. Social development includes increases in knowledge, development of skills and competence, and increased social welfare.

## 3.2 Optimising Petroleum Extraction for Sustainable Development

The extraction of petroleum resources can be defined as the production of petroleum from the ground, thereby liquidating the petroleum asset for sale.[58] It is the extraction of petroleum resources that create many challenges. Economic challenges arise since by extracting the petroleum, a state depletes a valued resource that cannot be replaced and is permanently lost.[59] Since these resources are precious and will influence both current and future generations' prosperity, a major focus of resource extraction in sustainable development needs to be the optimisation of petroleum extraction to ensure that as much of the resource is recovered. This creates regulatory challenges for the state in how it regulates the extraction of petroleum. The optimisation of the extraction of petroleum seeks to balance the commercial imperatives of the companies that extract the petroleum with the aim of the state to sustainably develop the resources for current and future generations. It is through the regulatory framework, which encompasses the laws governing a company's petroleum extraction activities and the policy setting in which those laws have been constructed, that the notions of optimised extraction can be implemented.

Nobel Prize winning scholar Joseph Stiglitz, who states that the extraction of non-renewable resources such as petroleum lowers the wealth of a country, has expressed the view that resources extracted mean that the country has less wealth unless the funds generated are invested in other forms of wealth.[60] Therefore, it is essential for a country's economic well-being that as much of the exhaustible resources are extracted to *convert* the wealth generated from the exhaustible resources' resource rent to other forms of wealth for future generations.[61] Converting this wealth requires social,[62] political and economic strategies.[63] This conversion can be accomplished through the development of appropriate taxation strategies that adequately capture the value of the resource rent,[64] the establishment of sovereign wealth funds[65] and the investment of the petroleum wealth in human capital and infrastructure.[66] A country can only retain the wealth that extracting petroleum brings if it reinvests that income

---

[58] This can be delineated as upstream petroleum activities. Upstream Petroleum is defined as all the petroleum activities that occur up to the point of transfer of the petroleum for the transport, sale and refining of the product. It includes exploration and production activities.

[59] Hartwick (1977), p. 972.

[60] Stiglitz (2005), p. 14.

[61] Sachs (2007), p. 180.

[62] Sachs (2007), p. 175.

[63] Sachs (2007), pp. 178–180.

[64] Sachs (2007), pp. 178–180.

[65] For a discussion on the utility of Sovereign Wealth Funds, particularly in developing countries, see Curto (2010). For a discussion of the Norwegian Pension Fund—Global, see Clark and Monk (2010).

[66] For a discussion on the conversion of natural capital to human capital, see Stiglitz (2005), p. 16; Humphreys et al. (2007).

earned into capital, be it human, physical or natural capital, to offset the loss of the wealth from natural resources.[67] Whilst acknowledging the importance of converting the petroleum extracted into other forms of capital, this chapter focuses solely on optimising the extraction of petroleum.

The optimisation of petroleum extraction seeks to maximise the recovery of petroleum from individual licence areas, whole fields and reservoirs to prevent or reduce resource sterilisation.[68] This means that the extraction of petroleum is done in a manner consistent with the three pillars of sustainable development (i.e., social, economic and environmental). The optimisation of recovery relies on the structure and function of the legislative and policy frameworks and the role of the law in regulating field development, and it is influenced by the allocation of petroleum licences.[69]

## 4 Law and the Optimisation of Petroleum Extraction

In undertaking an assessment of the capacity of the Ethiopian petroleum framework to enable the optimal extraction of petroleum resources, this section compares both within the Ethiopian jurisdiction where necessary (between the mineral extraction proclamations and the petroleum proclamation) and a specific comparison to Norway.

Norway is widely recognised as an example of a successful system where 'best practices' have been utilised to develop petroleum resources for the benefit of all Norwegians, including future generations.[70] In developing its petroleum regulatory framework in the early 1970s, Norway relied on previous experience of state-controlled natural resource development, especially state control of foreign companies that developed those resources. The petroleum licencing system utilised the principles of the Norwegian natural resource management system, which had its roots in the management of hydropower resources[71] in the early twentieth century, where the state exerted control through regulation of companies developing the water resources.[72]

It was this experience that Norway relied upon when developing a framework for the regulation of petroleum resource development. In particular, it utilised its experience in managing foreign investment and companies that are used to develop the resource. The resulting system of petroleum resource management had been

---

[67] Sachs (2007), pp. 178–180.

[68] Resource sterilisation (also known as a stranded field) occurs where some petroleum is unable to be developed because of reservoir geology, access to the field, or access to facilities for development, or when individual companies develop fields on an individual basis with the combined effect of stranding some petroleum in the reservoir: see Schulte and Asshert (2012).

[69] Hunter (2012), pp. 4–6.

[70] Discussion of the success of Norway is found in a number of academic works, including the following: Ryggvik (2010), Larsen (2004), Hunter (2014), and Al-Kasim (2006).

[71] The Ethiopian government is also managing its hydropower in a similar manner. See National Planning Commission Ethiopia, *GTP II*.

[72] Lieberman (1970).

recognised by several institutions as best practice,[73] representing a 'potent example of the successful development of the petroleum sector and surrounding industry'.[74]

However, this does not mean that the Norwegian system offers a one-size-fits-all 'model' for petroleum regulation,[75] nor does any other petroleum regulatory framework. Rather, it is suggested that the Norwegian petroleum regulation is an example of a successful system that encourages sustainable development from extraction through to wealth conversion whilst having avoided the worst manifestations of the natural resource curse because of many factors.[76] As stated in the introduction, however, the Ethiopian legal framework of petroleum extraction can benefit from the Norwegian experience, as considered next.

This chapter builds on previous analyses of sustainable production of petroleum resources[77] through an analysis of the structure and the content of the Ethiopian petroleum framework to determine whether it promotes sustainable development through the extraction of petroleum resources.

## 5 Ethiopian Law and Optimal Extraction of Petroleum: A Comparative Analysis

### 5.1 An Introduction to the Structures of the Legal Framework

Generally, there is commonality of petroleum law content across the globe. This 'globality' of petroleum law is not a construct of international law or treaties. Rather it is a 'transnational petroleum law' that arises from the internationalisation of business practice, customs and usage of the members of the international petroleum industry,[78] leading to the coining of the concept *Lex Petrolea*.[79] It is this global nature of the activities associated with petroleum extraction and the laws that regulate them that give rise to an 'international' petroleum law and the ability to undertake a functional analysis of the petroleum laws between jurisdictions. Generally, a petroleum extraction regulatory framework will contain provisions for the regulation of the following: administration; role and capacity of the state; access to petroleum (award of a licence or granting of a PPSA); environmental regulation; pollution

---

[73] Organisation for Economic Cooperation and Development (2005), p. 11.

[74] Gordon and Stenvoll (2007), p. 1.

[75] It is important to realise that Norway does not necessarily provide an example of the 'best' system of petroleum regulation. Rather, Norway provides an example of a successful system where petroleum resources have been developed for the benefit of all Norwegians, including future generations.

[76] Humphreys et al. (2007), p. 273.

[77] Hunter (2012); Hunter (2014), pp. 48–58.

[78] Wawryk (2015), p. 21.

[79] Wawryk (2015), pp. 21–22.

liability and damage; safety, including that of personnel, platforms, structures and wells; and field development planning and rates of production.[80]

The main purpose of a petroleum legal framework should be to provide the basic context for framework governing petroleum operations and to regulate them as they are carried out by domestic, foreign and international enterprises.[81] It should encompass legal instruments such as primary legislation, subordinate legislation, a contractual framework and administrative decisions made by public officials utilising policy guidelines. The structure of such a framework by a state is a fundamental tool in the administration of petroleum activities[82] and has a major influence on how the legal framework implements the petroleum policy and how the law is applied and interpreted.[83] Essentially, there are two main forms of structuring regulation—principle-based regulation and rule-based regulation. Between these two types of structures, there may be varying combinations of rules and principles, established to suit the individual needs of a state.

Rule-based regulatory frameworks rely on legislatively entrenched rules to regulate petroleum activities, directing what they need to do and how they should do it.[84] This type of regulation is also known as prescriptive regulation, because the rule specifies in relatively precise terms what is required to be done.[85] These systems often require a large number of detailed laws and require new rules every time a new regulatory situation arises.[86] Such a large number of changes can be difficult for legislators, can lead to regulatory inconsistencies, and rigidity, and are prone to creative compliance in order to adjust to new situations.[87] Traditionally, the petroleum industry has relied on the use of prescriptive regulation to ensure regulatory enforceability, which is appropriate where there is a single commonly agreed means of controlling a hazard or risk.[88]

However, prescriptive/rule-based regulation is seen as an inappropriate regulatory structure for an activity such as petroleum extraction since it has changing technology and circumstances, which requires constant regulatory updates to ensure that the law keeps up to date with activities. If updates do not occur, then the rigidity of such laws can be detrimental for the activity being undertaken.[89] The use of such

---

[80] This list has been determined by examining the contents of the primary petroleum Act in Norway, Australia, Canada and the UK.

[81] Onorato (1995), p. 3.

[82] Such structure is rule-based (prescriptive) or principle-based (sometimes known as objective-based). For a discussion on these see Black (2007), p. 3; Frieburg (2017), pp. 239–247.

[83] The role of petroleum policy in considered in section 6 below.

[84] Frieberg (2017), p. 234.

[85] Frieburg (2010), p. 89.

[86] Black (2007), p. 7.

[87] Black (2007), p. 7. An excellent example of this is the regulation of coal Seam Gas extraction in Queensland, Australia, where thousands of amendments have been made since 2000.

[88] Frieburg (2010), p. 89.

[89] Frieburg (2010), p. 89. It is important to note that the prescriptive based regulatory framework that existed at the time of the Deepwater Horizon blowout and oil spill was seen as a contributor to

prescriptive legislation is also seen as outdated, discouraging innovation and technological development, and carrying high administrative and compliance costs for companies.[90] As such, for many petroleum jurisdictions, even those in the common law, there is a move away from such type of regulation.

In contrast to rule-based regulation, principle-based regulation relies on broadly stated principles or objectives to set the requirements for the conduct of petroleum operations.[91] It is often known as objective-based regulation since it seeks to implement the policy objectives using broad principles rather than specific rules. Generally, principle-based regulation is drafted at a high level of generality, intending to be overarching requirements rather than rigid rules.[92] This type of legislation makes reference to general rules that express fundamental obligations that participants are required to observe when conducting petroleum operations observe.[93] By utilising general rules, this type of regulation provides flexibility for both the regulator and the regulatee, and as a result of the more discretionary nature of the regulatory regime, it is able to respond to new issues as they arise. This ensures that the legislation has a broad application to a wide range of circumstances, for example the development and implementation of new technologies, consistent with the general principles imbued in the regulatory framework.[94]

## 5.2 The Structure of the Ethiopian Legal Framework and Sustainable Development: A Norwegian Perspective

The Norwegian petroleum regulatory framework provides an example of such principle-based regulation.[95] After independence in 1905, a series of laws were passed culminating in the *Concession Act 1917* (Norway) (CA),[96] requiring any

---

the event, and the report from the National Academy of Engineering and National Research Council recommended that the prescriptive regulatory framework be reformed to a hybrid system based on principle-based regulation that incorporates some prescriptive elements. See National Academy of Engineering and National Research Council (2012), pp. 112–121.

[90] Government of Victoria (2016), pp. 3–8.
[91] Black (2007), p. 7.
[92] Black (2007), p. 7.
[93] Black (2007), p. 7.
[94] Black (2007), p. 7.
[95] Act 12 of 21 June 1963 relating to exploration for and exploration of submarine natural resources. This Act contained three basic principles:

1. The right to submarine natural resources was vested in the State.
2. The King may grant Norwegian or foreign persons, including legal persons the right to explore for or exploit natural resources.
3. The King may issue regulations concerning such activities. See Arnesen et al. (2007), p. 896.

[96] Liberman (1970), Chapter 1.

foreign company wishing to invest in hydropower plants to gain approval from the Norwegian parliament and comply with certain corporate structure and governance rules,[97] including the use of capital, the use of Norwegian goods and services and the relinquishment of property to the state after the expiration of the licence.[98] It was this experience that Norway relied upon when developing a framework for the regulation of petroleum resource development, with the resultant system of petroleum resource management and concomitant legal framework recognised as best practice[99] in the sustainable development of resources by the International Energy Authority[100] and scholars,[101] representing a 'potent example of the successful development of the petroleum sector and surrounding industry'.[102] The exploitation of petroleum in Norway occurs under the *Petroleum Activities Act 1996* (Norway) (PAA) and the associated *Petroleum Regulations 1997* (Norway) (PR), which are subsidiary instruments amended by Royal Decree, pursuant to the PAA.[103] The PAA is a brief, principle-based Act (only 30 pages) conferring rights and duties on participants exploring for and producing petroleum in Norway. It sets out the principles relating to all aspects of exploration production of petroleum, as well as general provisions relating to state interests and other industries.[104]

The World Bank recognises that objective-based regulation for petroleum resource development is superior to the rule-based form in order to provide optimal resource management. Onorato, in his World Bank Working Paper *Legislative Frameworks That Foster Petroleum Development*, sees short, thorough, broad and generic petroleum legislation as 'the cornerstone of effective petroleum legislative framework'.[105] The World Bank view is that principal legislation should not be

---

[97] Liberman (1970), Chapter 1.

[98] Nelsen (1991), pp. 22–23.

[99] Organisation for Economic Cooperation and Development (2005), p. 11.

[100] See International Energy Agency (IEA) (2005a, b). The IEA notes that 'Norway's skill in the development of its large oil and gas resources has made Norway Europe's largest exporter of oil and gas, and is contributing significantly to Europe's security of supply'. It also noted that 'The government's transparent and forward-looking way in which it intends to manage the expected decline is commendable as well as its plans to extend production for as long as possible. It has taken strong action to increase exploration for new fields and to open the industry further to smaller companies. It has also made important progress since the last review in reducing state involvement with the partial privatisation of Statoil. Altogether, Norwegian management of its petroleum resources is an example of best practice for the management of valuable natural resources in a small economy'.

[101] Norway's petroleum policy and framework are recognised as 'a potent example of the successful development of the petroleum sector and surrounding industry', since it successfully combined the development of State-owned Oil Company and international oil companies as it sought to develop petroleum resources whilst transforming the economy and creating an industry. See Gordon and Stenvoll (2007), p. 1. In addition, see Bunter (2003).

[102] Gordon and Stenvoll (2007), p. 1.

[103] See section 1-1 of the *Petroleum Activities Act 1996* (Norway).

[104] Such fluctuations may include the price of oil, changes in technology, the availability of capital, and the prospectivity and attractiveness of the jurisdiction.

[105] Onorato (1995), p. 3.

overly detailed and should be accompanied by enabling regulations that can be altered without parliamentary process in order to respond to the flexible needs of the petroleum industry, thereby providing clarity and detail to the principal legislation.[106] Completing the legislative framework should be an appropriate contractual arrangement, ensuring that both parties have clear legal framework to develop petroleum resources.[107] In recognising the flexibility provided by objective-based regulation, the World Bank acknowledges that such a framework is likely to encourage participant behaviour that fulfils states' regulatory objectives.[108]

In contrast to Norway, the rigid, rule-based nature of regulation is demonstrated by the petroleum legislation in Queensland, Australia (Qld). The primary legislative instrument is the *Petroleum and Gas (Production and Safety) Act 2004* (Qld) (PGPSA). At over 1400 pages, the PGPSA outlines, in minutiae, the 'rules' for the new industry of coal seam gas extraction, relying on legislatively entrenched rules to regulate petroleum activities. Therefore, every time legal alterations are required because of changes in petroleum operations, which are constant given that the Qld government utilises 'adaptive management'[109] as a regulatory tool, legislative reform is necessary.[110] Since 2004, the PGPSA has been subject to multiple and major amendments: an examination of the endnotes of the PGPSA identifies over 1000 amendments to the PGPSA, with more than forty consolidated versions of the Act released since 2005. The PGPSA will be further altered under the *Modernising Queensland Resources Acts Program* (MQRA), which is integrating five separate resource Acts into a single Act by 2019.[111] Therefore, it is likely that much of the legal framework already created will substantially be altered again. Together, these existing and impending changes have created a legal framework that is ever shifting, thereby affecting both investment and stakeholders.

Contrary to the rigidity of the PGPSA, the Norwegian petroleum framework has been assessed to meet the criteria of an effective petroleum regulatory framework, as defined by the World Bank.[112] The short PAA and the PR clearly outline the requirements for petroleum activities to take place. This is combined with a contractual framework (the Model Joint Operating Agreement—MJOA) that all participants are required to sign in order for petroleum activities to commence.

---

[106] Onorato (1995), p. 3.

[107] Onorato (1995), pp. 3–4.

[108] Black (2007), pp. 7–8.

[109] Department of State Development (Qld) (2012). This method of 'learning by doing' is implemented in Queensland primarily through the imposition of layered monitoring and reporting duties on the CSG operator alongside obligations to compensate and 'make good' any harm caused. For a discussion on adaptive management see Swayne (2012).

[110] Such as changes in the regulatory framework for the disposal of water from petroleum extraction activities.

[111] The MQRA is an ambitious legislative reform programme that commenced in 2013 and is expected to be finalised in 2017 and integrates the Mineral Resources Act 1989, the Petroleum and Gas (Production and Safety) Act 2004, the Petroleum Act 1923, the Greenhouse Gas Storage Act 2009 and the Geothermal Energy Act 2010.

[112] Refer to Hunter (2012, 2014).

The Ethiopian POP demonstrates elements of both rule-based and principle-based regulation. Section 7 of the POP establishes the discretionary powers of the Minister, which include the issuing of any regulations necessary for the effective implementation of the provisions of the POP. As such, under the current petroleum law, it would be possible for the GoE to establish regulation for petroleum activities. Similarly, section 10 (areas precluded from petroleum operations) confers discretion on the relevant Minister to liaise with the appropriate state organs to determine the areas where operations may not be conducted, rather than binding the state to areas listed in the POP.

Section 9 of the POP outlines the particulars required in a petroleum agreement[113]; although the section is structured in a manner that appears to be highly prescriptive by listing the content required in an MPPSA, it provides sufficient flexibility by outlining the need for the condition to be in the petroleum agreement, but not the detailed requirements. This is an excellent example of establishing and outlining the law (i.e., what is required) but not the minutiae of details required in order to meet the requirements of what the law *is*. For example, Article 9(3) of the POP stipulates that the minimum work obligations, minimum expenditure and periodic surrender of areas must be contained in the petroleum agreement but does not stipulate the period of obligation or the amount to be spent. It leaves such detail to the individual petroleum agreement, thus creating a relationship between the POP and the PPSA. Such obligations are set out in section 5 of the MPPSA. However, unlike the Norwegian legal framework (under the PAA, PPR and MJOA), the obligations, expenditure and budgetary terms are defined in the MPPSA.[114] Rather, these are left to be negotiated between the government and the participants. However, once these terms have been agreed, neither party is able to unilaterally alter the conditions of the PSA. Onorato sees such a relationship between the POP and the MPPSA as indicative of a framework that fosters petroleum development.

Whereas much of the Ethiopian POP is flexible as a result of the relationship between the POP and the MPPSA, it also contains elements of prescriptive regulation, even though it is a brief principal legislation (28 sections). Such stipulations, although making the requirements clear, render the POP inflexible and unable to respond with changing requirements as petroleum activities progress. For example, section 18 stipulates that the contractor is required to keep a complete set of books of accounting in Ethiopia[115] and submit to the Minister on an annual basis the financial statements, including balance sheets and profit and loss accounts.[116] Rather than prescribing the financial statements that are to be submitted to the Minister, principle-based regulation is crafted in a manner that still requires the reporting to occur but gives the state the scope to determine what it requires. For example, section 18(1)(b) could have been drafted into a higher level of generality: 'contractors must submit to the Minister annually financial records of petroleum operations as

---

[113] See sections 9 (1)–9 (17) of the POP.

[114] These are found under section V of the MPPSA.

[115] Section 18(1)(a) of the POP.

[116] Section 18(1)(b) of the POP.

stipulated by the Minister'. Such generality ensures that the Minister is not confined only to financial statements, balance sheets and profit and loss accounts, thereby widening the scope and authority of the Minister and ensuring that the state has greater control over petroleum operations.

Other articles of the POP outline in detail the requirements of the PPSA.[117] Whilst it is important that these requirements are stipulated, the primary legislation is not the place for such details as the state may wish to alter the terms of the PPSA for future participants and activities (such as changes required in Queensland and Nigeria, both of which are briefly mentioned below). Such alternations will only have effect on future contracts as the government cannot alter existing contracts unilaterally and retrospectively. Generally, what the law requires is set out in the principal legislative instrument, and the necessary actions to achieve it are placed in subordinate legislation, policy or tools. According to Onorato, such details should be contained in regulations and supported in the contractual agreement.[118]

The difficulties faced when failing to do so is demonstrated in Queensland. As new petroleum activities progress, there is often a need for legislative change, which has resulted in thousands of legislative changes occurring to maintain a coherent, stable law. By enshrining all of the details in the primary legislation, legislative response to the requisite changes can be considerable, and may also be slow. The passage of the Nigerian Petroleum Industry Bill is such an example of slowness: the Bill took almost nine years to be approved by the parliament.

Given that the use and development of technology in the development of Ethiopian petroleum resources is a cornerstone of Ethiopian petroleum policy,[119] the rigid and prescriptive nature of rule-based regulation is unlikely to establish a satisfactory regulatory environment that encourages the use of technology. Furthermore, given that Ethiopia is an emerging petroleum jurisdiction, it is likely that there will be a greater use of technology as petroleum activities progress and intensify, especially if there are geological features that present challenges in the extraction of petroleum.

As outlined in section 3 above, the Ethiopian POP comprises 28 sections, which can be divided into four main areas:

---

[117] These include the duration of the PPSA, training and preferences for local content provisions, transfer and assignment of interests, operating standards, disposal of assets, record-keeping, insurance and indemnity, supply of petroleum to the domestic market, duties and levies, exemptions, royalties, taxes, payment of contractors, and arbitration/choice of law forum.

[118] Onorato (1995), pp. 7–8.

[119] As outlined in the preamble of the *Petroleum Operations Proclamation,* Proclamation No. 295/1986.

- administration,[120]
- role and capacity of the state,[121]
- access to petroleum,[122] and
- conditions of access (through petroleum agreements).[123]

As stated earlier, the POP has no sub-regulations. Therefore, all the laws relating to the regulation of petroleum operations are contained in the POP. Upon close examination, it can be seen that some aspects of petroleum extraction regulation have been either omitted from the POP or addressed in passing, giving little regulatory scope to the area.[124] The areas that have been omitted or poorly considered under the POP and its implication for optimising extraction of Ethiopian petroleum extraction are wide, and shall be considered in turn.

The regulation of environmental impacts arising from petroleum operations is critical for the sustainable development of petroleum. If a state fails to regulate the environmental impacts of petroleum activities and to attribute liability and require compensation where damage occurs, there is likely to be a substantial impact on local populations, particularly on their health, as well as the socio-economic strata of communities. For example, in August 2008, a fault in the Trans-Niger pipeline resulted in a prolonged (approximately 4 weeks) oil spill in Bodo Creek, Ogoniland (Nigeria), affecting swamps and creeks and killing marine life.[125] As a consequence, drinking water was polluted and food sources for the local population destroyed. Such environmental damage can cause social dislocation and economic decline as indigenous people have to leave traditional lands in order to earn money to purchase food and water or search further afield for food and water. The POP provides little regulation of environmental damage, save for section 9(11), where the particulars in a petroleum agreement will include *requirements relating to environmental protection*.

---

[120] Sections 3 and 4 are administrative in nature, outlining the scope of the Proclamation (s 3) and the ownership of the resources (s 4), domestic supply reservation (s 20), arbitration provisions (s 25), applicable laws (s 26), and conflict of laws (s 27).

[121] The role of the government (s 5) and Ministers (s 6 and s 7) relating to the Minister's representation and powers and Ministerial discretion to make directives relating to petroleum activities (s 8); set out the capacity of the Minister to make directives in relation to the method for inviting and evaluating petroleum bids, the content of petroleum applications and the requirements of applicants when applying to undertake petroleum operations.

[122] S 9 of the POP.

[123] Sections 9–28 set out the requirements for a contractor under a PPSA, and includes matters such as particulars to be contained in the petroleum agreement (s 9), Areas precluded from petroleum operations (s 10) duration of agreements (s 11), local content provisions (s 12) transfer and assignment (s 13), operating standards (s 14), disposal of assets (s 15), access to property (s 16), protection of historical sites and other minerals (s 17), Books and records (s 18), insurance and indemnity (s 19), and financial requirements (royalties, tax, etc.—s 21–s 24).

[124] These include environmental regulation.

[125] Vinent-Akpu et al. (2015), p. 135.

To ensure that the exploitation of petroleum resources in Ethiopia *contributes to the economic growth and welfare of the Ethiopian broadmasses*,[126] it is critical that the legal framework addresses the issue of environmental harm. In undertaking the exploitation of mineral resources in Ethiopia, the licensee is required to conduct mining operations in such a manner as to minimise the damage or pollution to the environment.[127] Furthermore, under the Mining Sustainable Development Proclamation (MSDP),[128] the licence holder is required to undertake[129] and have an approved environmental impact assessment.[130] Where the community is in danger, the licensing authority has the capacity to suspend mining activities where this is the only remedy available.[131] Furthermore, the licensing authority has the power and duty to ensure that mining operations carried out by licensees take into account the environment and are beneficial to the mining communities.[132]

Under part 7 of the MSDP (environment), there is a requirement for a mine rehabilitation fund and a community development plan to assist the peoples within the licence area. Such provisions for environmental protection and community development during the extraction of petroleum are not iterated under the POP. However, it is important to note that under section 3.7 of the MPPSA, the contractor has a general obligation to undertake environmental and safety measures, as well as a requirement to contribute financially to ecological and environmental protection under section 4.14. However, as stressed by Onorato, an effective framework is one that states a legal requirement in the enabling law and actioned through subordinate legal tools. Therefore, to address the gaps in the petroleum legal framework relating to the environment and its impact on sustainable extraction, the GoE should consider expanding the environment provisions of the MSDP to encompass the extraction of petroleum or to draft a similar Sustainable Development Proclamation that applies to the extraction of petroleum.

Similar to the environment, the regulation of the safety of people, installations and wells in petroleum operations is critical for the sustainable extraction of petroleum activities. If the safety of workers is not protected under the POP, then sustainable development of petroleum is compromised since there will be a substantial social and health impact on local populations. Accidents leading to the disability or death of workers create social and economic impacts for families and communities.

---

[126] As outlined in the preamble to the POP.

[127] Proclamation to Promote the Development of Mineral Resources, Proclamation No. 52/1993.

[128] Proclamation to Promote Sustainable Development of Mineral Resources, Proclamation No. 678/2010.

[129] S18(1) (c) of the Proclamation to Promote Sustainable Development of Mineral Resources, Proclamation No. 678/2010.

[130] S 26(1) (c) of the Proclamation to Promote Sustainable Development of Mineral Resources, Proclamation No. 678/2010.

[131] S 44(1) of the Proclamation to Promote Sustainable Development of Mineral Resources, Proclamation No. 678/2010.

[132] S 52(4)(j) of the Proclamation to Promote Sustainable Development of Mineral Resources, Proclamation No. 678/2010.

The POP has three general provisions relating to safety. Firstly, the contractor is required to obtain and maintain workers compensation insurance in reasonable amounts and coverage.[133] Secondly, the petroleum agreement is required to set out the safety requirements and programmes and other matters related to the working conditions of employees engaged in petroleum operations.[134] Thirdly, contractors are required to conduct petroleum operations in accordance with generally accepted international petroleum industry standards and practices in a manner that is compatible with the consideration of petroleum and other resources and the protection of human life, property and the environment.[135] This general requirement for worker safety is also contained in the Mining Proclamations, and neither Proclamation makes further elaborations relating to worker safety. However, the right of the worker for a healthy and safe work environment is imbued in Article 42 (2) of the Ethiopian Constitution (1994), set out in the *Labour Proclamation*,[136] and the role of the Ministry of Labour and Social Affairs in regulating safety is enunciated under Proclamation No. 4/1995.[137]

One of the critical aspects of sustainable extraction of petroleum is the rate of production and the full development of petroleum fields (known as field development planning). The regulatory requirement for a field development plan (FDP) that optimises the amount of petroleum extracted and ensures that smaller fields are not left stranded is critical since once a field is abandoned, it is exceptionally difficult to recommence operations and the remaining petroleum is unable to be recovered. This means that less petroleum is extracted, and therefore less benefits flow to the people. Although the POP has a general preamble to develop Ethiopia's petroleum for the good of the people, it lacks a specific requirement for field development planning to optimise the extraction of petroleum. As such, under the POP, there is no requirement for optimal extraction of petroleum.

Under the MPPSA, there is some control exerted over production. Section 5.3 of the MPPSA requires the notification of a discovery of petroleum to the GoE and the requirement to submit a work programme for the development of the discovery. The section also enables the GoE to request changes to the work programme. However, the work programme stipulates a programme only for that contract area and has no impact or bearing on the extraction of petroleum under other PSAs. As such, whilst the GoE exerts control over individual work programmes, there appears to be no coordinated approach to the development of reservoirs as a whole in order to optimise extraction. Section 5.4 requires a plan for development and production in accordance with sound engineering and economic principles to ensure that there is no excessive decrease in the rate of production. In addition, the GoE can impose changes to the development plan for the development of infrastructure and to assist

---

[133] POP, s 19.

[134] POP, s 9(2).

[135] POP, s 14.

[136] Labour Proclamation No. 377/2003, see section 3.

[137] Proclamation to Provide for the Definition of Powers and Duties of the Executive Organs of the Federal Democratic Republic of Ethiopia, Proclamation No. 4/1995.

national needs. However, this applies to a single area that is subject to the PSA, and once the plan is approved and accepted, changes cannot be made without the agreement of both parties. As such, the GoE negotiates development of petroleum resources on a contract-by-contract basis. Such an arrangement has two major repercussions. Firstly, by being negotiated on an individual contract basis, the GoE cannot regulate a wider reservoir extraction plan to ensure that extraction is optimised. Secondly, given the contractual nature of the agreement, and the lack of field development planning law in the POP, the GoE has no capacity to alter the terms of the agreement and therefore impose conditions relating to optimising extraction and therefore encouraging sustainable development. The GoE requires notification of the rate of production under section 8.1. However, such notification is for the purposes of production sharing and sale rather than for field development control.

The Norwegian framework requires a field development plan (known as a plan for development and operations or PDO) for all petroleum activities under the principal Act, the PAA. By imbuing the requirement for field planning in the legislation, the state has the right to continually evaluate the method of extraction and to maximise extraction. When a new field has been discovered and the licence holder wishes to extract the petroleum, the licensee is required to submit a PDO for approval,[138] in accordance with the *prudent production* requirements set out in section 4-1 of the PAA, utilising appropriate technologies and sound economic principles to ensure that as much of the petroleum resources are recovered.[139] To satisfy the requirements of prudent production, the PDO must contain an account of the economic, resource, technical, commercial and environmental aspects of the production from not just the field being developed but also its relationship with the rest of the reservoir.[140] The Ministry must also approve the expected production schedule, which can be altered if warranted by the need to manage the resource or other significant social considerations.[141] The regulation of the rate of production and depletion is not for the purpose of controlling overall production output but rather to ensure the effective and efficient production from the field and to protect the reservoir, thereby ensuring the optimal extraction of petroleum.

The regulatory requirement for a PDO in Norway is to not only optimise extraction of petroleum resources in the stipulated field but also ensure that petroleum extraction is for the benefit of Norwegian society as a whole.[142] The information that the state receives in the PDO is used to enable the Norwegian state to obtain and maintain an overall view of petroleum resource production, enabling strategic planning of field depletion, production and use of facilities.[143] It is this strategic planning and overview of resource depletion, made possible by the combination of the requirement for a detailed field development plan and the legislated capacity of the

---

[138] Norwegian Petroleum Directorate (2000).

[139] Petroleum Activities Act 1996 (Norway), s 4-1.

[140] Petroleum Activities Act 1996 (Norway), s 4-2.

[141] Petroleum Activities Act 1996 (Norway), s 4-4.

[142] Bygdevoll (2006), p. 5.

[143] Bygdevoll (2006), p. 5.

Norwegian state to coordinate petroleum extraction under section 1-2 of the PAA, that enable sustainable petroleum extraction to occur in Norway. Presently, the Ethiopian POP has no such field development requirements, and this lack of field development requirements severely hampers the capacity of the legal framework to encourage sustainable development through the optimisation of petroleum extraction.

If an international oil company is not required to maximise the recovery of petroleum from the field, it is highly unlikely that it will undertake to maximise recovery on its own volition.[144] Such reticence on the part of an international oil company to maximise extraction is illustrated in the example of *Ekofisk* on the Norwegian continental shelf, where the legal requirement to maximise production from the field under section 4-1 of the PAA enabled the recovery of billions more of barrels of oil than if recovery from the field was decided wholly by the commercial imperatives of the operator, ConocoPhillips. When oil was initially discovered in the *Ekofisk* area in 1969, the field's lifetime was estimated to be 25 years. The original (1971) PDO for *Ekofisk* estimated the total recovery of petroleum from the field to be 17% as a result of the complex chalk formations in the field.[145] Predictions for recovery from the field in 1988 were that only 20–30% of the field would be recovered.[146]

In the early 1990s, there were concerns regarding the safety of *Ekofisk* on account of subsidence and poor maintenance, with the operator Phillips (now ConocoPhillips) seeking to decommission parts of the *Ekofisk* field because of falling production and subsistence in the production facilities.[147] However, the Norwegian Petroleum Directorate (NPD) insisted that ConocoPhillips submit a revised PDO in 1994, resulting in the redevelopment of *Ekofisk* production facilities and the use of increased recovery techniques.[148] Today, the use of improved oil recovery technology and the revised PDO submitted under the *prudent production*[149] requirements of the Norwegian petroleum legislative frameworks means that the revised recovery of petroleum for *Ekofisk* at the end of its production life will be around 50%, a great improvement on the original estimation of 17%.[150] Given that the *Ekofisk* field contains around four billion barrels of oil.[151] This increased recovery means that instead of around 680 million barrels of oil being recovered, around 2 billion barrels of oil will be recovered in the future, yielding an extra 1.32 billion barrels of oil. The benefit of optimising extraction of petroleum can be seen when it is considered in terms of wealth generation. Even if each extra barrel of oil recovered provided $1.00 in revenue, the state would have received an extra $1.32 billion in revenue.

---

[144] As demonstrated in Hunter (2012).

[145] Norwegian Petroleum Directorate (2008).

[146] Kvendseth (1991), p. 194.

[147] Ekofisk Redevelopment Plan Chronology (1994).

[148] Ekofisk Redevelopment Plan Chronology (1994).

[149] For a discussion of prudent production requirements, see section 5.3.

[150] Norwegian Petroleum Directorate (2008).

[151] Norwegian Petroleum Directorate (2017).

The experience of Norway in optimising petroleum extraction from Ekofisk highlights the role and experience of the Norwegian state in the development of its petroleum resources: however inexperienced the Norwegian government was in exploiting petroleum resources, the state still exerted control over the exploitation over the resources it owned. The revised rate of recovery from *Ekofisk* as a result of the field development requirements of the Norwegian PAA demonstrates how optimal petroleum extraction can occur as a result of the content of the legal framework. At present, the Ethiopian POP does not contain the legislative capacity to compel companies to submit a field development plan that optimises field extraction, thereby failing to sustainably develop its petroleum resources. Unless the POP and the MPS contains a requirement for oil companies to maximise their extraction as part of the requirement of the field development plan, it is difficult to see that the Ethiopian petroleum regulatory framework will contribute to sustainable development in the country.

## 5.3 Imbuing Policy in the Law

Whatever the structure and content of the legal framework a state chooses to exploit its petroleum, it must be able to regulate petroleum activities and encourage development of petroleum from a field in a manner that is consistent with the overarching development objectives of that state. Therefore, the legal and administrative framework must be constructed as a function of a state's petroleum policy framework. As such, it is critical that the legal framework is constructed in a manner that articulates the policy of the jurisdiction. The policy of Ethiopia is to 'promote and strengthen the development and exploration for natural gas and oil'. In Ethiopia, this policy position of the government is reiterated in the preamble to the POP, which states, inter alia, the following:

1. The exploitation of petroleum resources of the country will greatly contribute to the economic growth and welfare of the Ethiopian broadmasses.
2. Petroleum operations should be carried out in accordance with modern technology and sound principles of resource conservation and should provide a better knowledge of the petroleum potential of the nation.
3. It is necessary to develop domestic expertise and petroleum infrastructure by fostering the acquisition of petroleum technology; to achieve these ends, it is essential to promulgate a special law on taxation operations.[152]

The capacity to give effect to this policy requires a legal framework that supports these aims, thereby encouraging sustainable development of petroleum. However, although these statements are noble and articulate what the GoE wishes to be the result of the extraction of petroleum, the current content of the POP does not support these aims. This is attributable to the lack of field development planning

---

[152] Petroleum Proclamation, Proclamation 286/1986, preamble.

requirements in the POP, which is also much more fundamental. Whilst the preamble contains these statements, there is no specific provision within the POP that implements these statements.

An excellent example of the transformation of policy into the regulatory framework can be found in the Norwegian petroleum legal framework. In 1971, the principles of Norwegian petroleum policy were laid out in the 'Ten Oil Commandments',[153] a set of goals and strategies to guide national involvement in the development of petroleum resources and that still stand today.[154] They were formally declared in 1972 by the *Royal Decree of 8 December 1972 Relating to Exploration of and Exploitation of Petroleum in the Seabed and Substrata of the Norwegian Continental Shelf* and implemented through conditions attached to the granting of licences from the third petroleum licensing round.[155]

Norwegian petroleum policy laid down in the Ten Oil Commandments over forty years ago continues to be imbued within the Norwegian legislative framework. In particular, two sections of the PAA reflect Norwegian petroleum policy. Firstly, section 1-2 of the PAA states:

> Resource management of petroleum resources shall be carried out in a long-term perspective for the benefit of Norwegian society as a whole. In this regard the resource management shall provide revenues to the country and shall contribute to ensuring welfare, employment and an improved environment as well as to the strengthening of Norwegian Trade and Industrial development...[156]

This section is in many aspects similar to the preamble in the Ethiopian POP. However, the difference between the Norwegian and Ethiopian legal frameworks is that the Norwegian policy in enunciated in specific legislative provisions

---

[153] The Norwegian ten oil commandments were approved by the Norwegian Storting (Parliament) on 14 June 1971, and comprised the following: 1. that national supervision and control must be ensured for all operations in the Norwegian continental shelf; 2. that petroleum discoveries are exploited in a way that makes Norway as independent as possible of others for its supplies of crude oil; 3. that new industry is developed on the basis of petroleum; 4. that the development of an oil industry must take necessary account of existing industrial activities and the protection of nature and the environment; 5. that flaring of exploitable gas on the Norwegian Continental Shelf must not be accepted, except during brief periods of testing; 6. that petroleum from the Norwegian Continental Shelf must as a main rule be landed in Norway, except in those cases where sociopolitical considerations dictate a different solution; 7. that the State becomes involved at all appropriate levels, and contributes to a coordination of Norwegian interests in Norway's petroleum industry as well as the creation of an integrated Norwegian oil community which sets its sights both nationally and internationally; 8. that a State oil company be established which can look after the government's commercial interests and pursue appropriate collaboration with domestic and foreign oil interests; 9. that a pattern of activities is selected north of the 62nd parallel which reflects the special socio-political conditions prevailing in that part of the country; and 10. that large Norwegian petroleum discoveries could present new tasks for Norway's foreign policy. See Lerøen (2002), p. 46.

[154] Olsen (2002), p. 2.

[155] Nelsen (1991), pp. 71–75. This round occurred in 1974, therefore it was the first official implementation of the procurement policy from the 1972 Decree. However, there had been some development of local industry prior to this official decree.

[156] Section 1-2 of the Petroleum Activities Act 1996 (Norway).

and supported by other legal requirements, such as field development planning requirements set out in chapter 4 of the PAA, which gives effect to the policy. Further legislative support to the policy that seeks to optimise extraction is section 4-1 of the PAA, the so-called *Prudent Production* requirements:

> Production of petroleum shall take place in such a manner that as much as possible of the petroleum in place in each individual petroleum deposit, or in several deposits in combination, will be produced. The production shall take place in accordance with prudent technical and sound economic principles and in such a manner that waste of petroleum or reservoir energy is avoided. The licensee shall carry out continuous evaluation of production strategy and technical solutions and shall take the necessary measures in order to achieve this.[157]

These prudent production requirements of the Norwegian PAA ensure that both technology and economic principles are utilised to optimally extract petroleum within a flexible, objective-based regulatory framework containing specific legislative provisions that require the oil companies to continuously evaluate the field to ensure that extraction of petroleum is optimised. The present Ethiopian POP does not contain any provisions that implement the petroleum policy objectives, and there is no requirement for PPSA holders to maximise recovery of petroleum. Without such provisions, there is little capacity for the legal framework to optimise extraction and sustainably develop the resources for the Ethiopian broadmasses. However, the Norwegian legislation can provide some guidance for Ethiopian legislative drafters. The principle-based provisions of sections 1-2 and 4-1 of the PAA may provide an example of the type of sections that could be drafted in the POP that would compel the PPSA holder to optimally extract petroleum from Ethiopian fields, thereby providing a greater 'contribution to the economic growth and welfare of the Ethiopian broad masses'.

## 6 Conclusion

This chapter has assessed the POP for its capacity to sustainably and optimally produce petroleum from Ethiopian oil and gas fields in order to provide benefits for present and future generations. The assessment has found that whilst some aspects of the structure of the POP encourage the optimisation of extraction, the content of the POP is generally underwhelming in encouraging optimisation of production, which is necessary to achieve the goal of sustainable development. In particular, the lack of imbuing of the fundamental principles of the petroleum policy in the POP undermines the capacity of the POP to optimise extraction. Furthermore, without the inclusion of field development planning and optimisation of extraction requirements, such as those required in section 4-1 of the PAA, there is little possibility of the POP enforcing the optimisation of the recovery of Ethiopian petroleum resources for the benefit of the people. There is a need for broad reform of the POP in order to

---

[157] Section 4-1 PAA Norway.

provide the GoE with the necessary tools to optimise the extraction of its petroleum resources.

**Acknowledgements** The author thanks Lillnna Kifle for her excellent research help on Ethiopian law. The author also wishes to thank the peer reviewers for their excellent and insightful feedback, which contributed to the improvement of this paper. All errors are, of course, the author's.

# References

## Books, Articles and Web Sites

Al-Kasim F (2006) Managing petroleum resources: the Norwegian model in a broad perspective. Oxford Institute for Energy Studies, Oxford

Armstrong P (2003) Status report on corporate governance reform in Africa. Paper presented at the 2003 Pan Africa Consultative forum on Corporate Governance

Arnesen F, Hammer U, Høisveen HP, Kaasen K, Nygard D (2007) Energy law in Europe. In: Martha MR, Catherine R, Inigo DG, Anita R (eds) Energy law in Europe: national, EU and international regulation, 2nd edn. Oxford University Press, Oxford

Black J (2007) Principles based regulation: risks challenges and opportunities. London School of Economics

Bunter M (2003) A new approach to petroleum licencing. Oil Gas Energy Law Intell 1. https://www.ogel.org/article.asp?key=1023. Accessed 19 July 2017

Bygdevoll J (2006) Field development plan. Norwegian Petroleum Directorate. http://www.ccop.or.th/ppm/document/PHEXV5/PHEXV5DOC03_bygdevoll.pdf. Accessed 12 July 2017

Clark GL, Monk AHB (2010) The legitimacy and governance of Norway's sovereign wealth fund: the ethics of global investment. Environ Plan 42:1723–1738

Corden WM, Neary JP (1982) Booming sector and deindustrialisation in a small open economy. Econ J 92:825–848

Curto S (2010) Sovereign wealth funds in the next decade. In: Canuto O, Guigale M (eds) The day after tomorrow: a handbook for future economic policy in the developing world. The World Bank, Washington DC

Dauvin M, Guerreiro D (2017) The paradox of plenty: a meta-analysis. World Dev 94:212–231

Department of State Development (Qld) (2012) Chapter 9 adaptive management. https://www.statedevelopment.qld.gov.au/resources/report/gbr/chapter-9-adaptive-management.pdf. Accessed 24 July 2017

Ekofisk Redevelopment Plan Chronology (1994) Oil Gas J 92. http://www.ogj.com/articles/print/volume-92/issue-47/in-this-issue/drilling/ekofisk-redevelopment-plan-chronology.html. Accessed 31 July 2017

'Ethiopia eyes gas production and exports from potential reserves' (2015) Oil Review Africa, 31 March 2015. http://www.oilreviewafrica.com/gas/gas/ethiopia-eyes-gas-production-and-exports-from-potential-reserves. Accessed 12 July 2017

Ethiopian Ministry of Mines (2017) Petroleum and licensing administration. http://www.mom.gov.et/Petroleum.aspx. Accessed 16 July 2017

Frieberg A (2017) Regulation in Australia. Federation Press, Sydney

Frieburg A (2010) The tools of regulation. Federation Press, Sydney

Gordon R, Stenvoll T (2007) Statoil: a study in political entrepreneurship James. The James A. Baker III Institute for Public Policy, Rice University. https://www.bakerinstitute.org/media/files/page/9ffcb110/noc_statoil_gordon_stenvoll.pdf. Accessed 12 July 2017

Government of Ethiopia (n.d.) Energy policy of Ethiopia. http://www.abyssinialaw.com/policies-and-strategies?download=1197:national-energy-policy-english

Government of Victoria (2016) Guide to regulation. Commissioner for Better Regulation. http://www.betterregulation.vic.gov.au/files/98181269-905c-4893-bff3-a6bb009df93c/Victorian-Guide-to-Regulation-PDF-final.pdf

Hartwick JM (1977) Intergenerational equity and the investing of rents from exhaustible resources. Am Econ Rev 67:972

Hotelling H (1931) The economics of exhaustible resources. J Polit Econ 39:137–175

Humphreys M, Sachs J, Stiglitz JE (eds) (2007) Escaping the resource curse. Columbia University Press, New York

Hunter T (2012) The role of regulatory frameworks in encouraging the sustainable extraction of petroleum resources in Australia and Norway. Oil Gas Energy Law Intell 10 (online)

Hunter T (2014) Law and policy frameworks for local content in the development of petroleum resources: Norwegian and Australian perspectives on cross-sectoral linkages and economic diversification. Miner Econ 27:115–126

International Energy Agency (IEA) (2005a) Energy policies of IEA countries – Norway. 2005 Review. http://www.oecd-ilibrary.org/energy/energy-policies-of-iea-countries-norway-2005_9789264109360-en

International Energy Agency (IEA) (2005b) IEA commends Norwegian energy policy for exemplary management of resources and wealth, but outlines challenges on climate change and energy security. https://www.iea.org/newsroom/news/2005/november/2005-11-28-.html. Accessed 21 July 2017

Kari TL (1997) The paradox of plenty: oil booms and petro-states. University of California Press, Berkeley

Kvendseth SS (1991) A history of Ekofisk through the first 20 years. Phillips Petroleum Company, Norway. https://www.nb.no/ekofisk/funn_eng.pdf

Larsen ER (2004) Escaping the resources curse and Dutch disease? When and why Norway caught up with and forged ahead of its neighbors. Discussion Papers No. 377, May 2004, Statistics Norway, Research Department

Lee M (2006) Measure of the in situ value of exhaustible resources: an input distance function. Ecol Econ 62:490

Lerøen BV (2002) Drops of black gold: Statoil 1972–2002. Statoil Publishers, Stavanger

Li S, Filer L (2007) The effects of governance environment on the choice of investment mode and the strategic implications. J World Bus 42:80–98

Liberman S (1970) The industrialization of Norway 1800–1920. Universitetsforlaget, Oslo

Mann T, Blunden A (eds) (2010) Australian law dictionary, 1st edn. Oxford University Press, Oxford

National Academy of Engineering and National Research Council (2012) Macondo well deepwater horizon blowout: lessons for improving safety. https://docs.lib.noaa.gov/noaa_documents/NOAA_related_docs/oil_spills/mocando-well_lessons_2011.pdf. Accessed 12 July 2017

National Planning Commission Ethiopia (2016) Growth and Transformation Plan (GTP II) (2015/16 – 2019/20), Volume I, main text. https://www.africaintelligence.com/c/dc/LOI/1415/GTP-II.pdf

Nelsen BF (1991) The state offshore: petroleum, politics and state intervention on the British and Norwegian continental shelves. Praeger Publishers, New York

Norwegian Petroleum (2017) *Ekofisk*. http://www.norskpetroleum.no/en/facts/field/ekofisk/. Accessed 1 Aug 2017

Norwegian Petroleum Directorate (2000) Guidelines to plan for development and operation of a petroleum deposit (PDO) and plan for installation and operation of facilities for transport and utilisation of petroleum (PIO) 2000. http://www.npd.no/Global/Engelsk/5-Rules-and-regulations/Guidelines/PDO-PIO-guidelines_2010.pdf. Accessed 22 July 2017

Norwegian Petroleum Directorate (2008) Invitation to apply for petroleum production license. Ministry of Petroleum and Energy, Oslo

Olsen WH (2002) Petroleum revenue management – an industry perspective. Paper presented at the Oil, Gas, Mining and Chemicals Department of the WBG and ESMAPO, Workshop on Petroleum Revenue Management, Washington DC, 23–24 October, 2004, p 2

Onorato WT (1995) Legislative frameworks used to foster petroleum development. World Bank Policy Research Paper WPS 1420

Organisation for Economic Cooperation and Development (2005) Economic Survey: Norway

Orucu E (1998) A 'methodology of comparative law'. In: Smits JM (ed) Elgar encyclopedia of comparative law. Edward Elgar Publishing Ltd, Cheltenham

Robinson JA, Torvik R, Verdier T (2002) Political foundations of the resource curse. CEPR Discussion Paper No. 3422

Ryggvik H (2010) The Norwegian oil experience: a toolbox for managing resources. Centre for Technology, Innovation and Culture, University of Oslo

Sachs JD (2007) How to handle the macroeconomics of oil wealth. In: Humphreys M, Sachs JD, Stiglitz JE (eds) Escaping the resource curse. Columbia University Press, New York

Sachs JD, Warner AM (2001) The curse of natural resources. Eur Econ Rev 45:827–838

Sala-i-Martin X, Subramanian A (2003) Addressing the natural resources curse: an illustration from Nigeria. IMF Working Paper WP/03/139

Schulte RJ, Asshert A (2012) Stranded gas in the Netherlands: what is the potential. SPE Conference Paper SPE-152357-MS

Smits JM (ed) (1998) Elgar encyclopedia of comparative law. Edward Elgar Publishing Ltd, Cheltenham

Solow RM (1973) Intergenerational equity and exhaustible resources. Working paper 103, Department of Economics, MIT

Stiglitz J (2005) Making natural resources into a blessing rather a curse. In: Tsalik S, Schiffrin A (eds) Covering oil: a reporter's guide to energy and development. Open Society Institute, New York

Strønen IÅ (2017) Grassroot politics and oil culture in Venezuela: the revolutionary petro-state. Palgrave-Macmillan, Geneva

Swayne N (2012) Regulating coal seam gas in Queensland: lessons in adaptive environmental management approach? Environ Plan J 29:163–187

United Nations Development Programme (2000) The world energy assessment: energy and the challenge of sustainability. UNDP, New York

Vinent-Akpu IF, Tyler AN, Wilson C, Mackinnon G (2015) Assessment of physio-chemical properties and metal contents of water and sediments of Bodo Creek, Niger Delta Nigeria. Toxicol Environ Chem 97:135–147

Wawryk A (2015) Petroleum regulation in an international context. In: Hunter T (ed) Regulation of the upstream petroleum sector: a comparative study of licensing and concession systems. Edward Elgar Publishing Ltd, Cheltenham

World Bank (2016) Ethiopia oil and gas sector development: support for review and update of policy and regulatory framework final report. WB Reference No. 1170668. http://documents.worldbank.org/curated/en/516451468196767562/pdf/106190-WP-P151025-PUBLIC-Oil-and-Gas.pdf. Accessed 22 July 2017

World Bank (2017) World Bank in Ethiopia: overview. http://www.worldbank.org/en/country/ethiopia/overview. Accessed 22 July 2017

Zweigert K, Kotz H (1998) An introduction to comparative law, 3rd edn. Oxford University Press, Oxford

# Legal Instruments

## Australia

Petroleum and Gas (Production and Safety) Act 2004 (Qld)

## Ethiopia

Council of Ministers Regulation to Provide for the Establishment of the Ethiopian Petroleum and Natural Gas Enterprise Council of Ministers Regulation No. 264/2012 (26 June 2012).
Environmental Assessment Proclamation, Proclamation No. 299/2002.
Model Petroleum Production Sharing Agreement 2011. http://www.mom.gov.et/upload/Model%20Petroleum%20Production%20Sharing%20Agrement(MPPSA).pdf. Accessed 21 July 2017.
Petroleum Operations Proclamation, Proclamation No. 295/1996.
Proclamation to Promote the Development of Mineral Resources, Proclamation No. 52/1993.
Proclamation to Promote Sustainable Development of Mineral Resources, Proclamation No. 678/2010
Proclamation to Provide for the Definition of Powers and Duties of the Executive Organs of the Federal Democratic Republic of Ethiopia, Proclamation No. 4/1995
Tax Proclamation, Proclamation No. 296/1986

## Norway

Act 12 of 21 June 1963 Relating to Exploration for and Exploration of Submarine Natural Resources.
Petroleum Activities Act 1996 (Norway)
Petroleum Regulations 1997 (Norway)

## United Nations

UN Resolution 1803 (1962)
Report of the World Commission on Environment and Development. UN GAOR 96th Plenary Meeting, UN Doc A/Res/42/187(1987). www.un.org/documents/ga/res/42/ares42-187.htm. Accessed on 12 July 2017
World Commission on Environment and Development (1987) Our Common Future: Report of the World Commission on Environment and Development. http://www.un-documents.net/our-common-future.pdf. Accessed 12 July 2017

**Tina Hunter** is the Director of the *Aberdeen University Centre for Energy Law* (AUCEL) and the Professor in Energy Law at the University of Aberdeen. She has undertaken teaching, research and consultancy in numerous countries including the UK, Australia, Norway, Canada, Iceland, Greece, Finland, Russia, the USA and the Philippines.

# The GERD and the Revival of the Egyptian–Sudanese Dispute over the Nile Waters

Salman M. A. Salman

**Abstract** The Tripartite National Committee (TNC), established by Egypt, Ethiopia, and Sudan on the Grand Ethiopian Renaissance Dam (GERD), abruptly ended its seventeenth meeting in Cairo on November 12, 2017. The meeting was intended to discuss the inception report prepared by two French firms, BRLi and Artelia, on two studies on the GERD. These studies have been under discussion and planning since 2013, and hitherto major differences over them arose among the three countries. The TNC meeting failed to agree on the inception report, with Sudan and Ethiopia on one side and Egypt on the other. Neither a joint statement, nor an agreement on a date for the next TNC meeting, was issued. More importantly, the meeting revealed the growing rift between Egypt and Sudan on the GERD and the studies, revived their century-old dispute on the entire Nile water relations, and confirmed the widening crack in their long-time alliance against the other Nile riparian countries. This article aims to explore the historical and current (The developments considered in this article are up-to-date as of 23 January, 2018.) legal contradictory claims by Egypt and Sudan over the Nile waters in light of the GERD negotiations and the two studies and offers some thoughts for the future relations of the Nile Basin countries.

## 1 Introduction

The Grand Ethiopian Renaissance Dam (GERD), which Ethiopia started building on the Blue Nile in April 2011, some 20 km from its borders with Sudan, is not the first project that has given rise to a dispute among the Nile Basin countries. Indeed, serious disputes over the sharing and uses of the Nile waters date back to the beginning of the last century when Sudan started planning the Gezira Scheme, to be

---

S. M. A. Salman (✉)
IWRA, Khartoum, Sudan

irrigated from the Blue Nile waters. Egypt opposed the Scheme vehemently as it regarded that any uses by Sudan of the Nile waters would be at its expense.

After a series of committees were established and their reports issued, an agreement was reached between the two countries that the size of the Scheme would not exceed 300,000 feddans,[1] and a specified, limited amount of Nile waters was allocated for the Scheme. However, as Sudan started planning the expansion of the Scheme, the dispute with Egypt over Sudan's needs of the Nile waters continued to simmer. After a series of lengthy committee reports, and difficult negotiations, the Egyptian–Sudanese dispute on the sharing of the Nile waters was resolved through the bilateral 1959 Nile Waters Agreement. However, the close alliance between Egypt and Sudan, which the Agreement established, recently started to crack, following Sudan's endorsement, after some initial hesitation, of the GERD, which Egypt vehemently opposed.

Shortly prior to the endorsement of the GERD by Sudan, and following a series of meetings and protests from Egypt and Sudan, Ethiopia agreed to the establishment of an International Panel of Experts. The Panel consisted of two members from each of the three countries, plus four members from outside the Nile Basin countries. Its terms of reference centered on studying the GERD and its impacts on Sudan and Egypt.

The Panel report did not identify any serious flaws with, or significant harm resulting from, the GERD but recommended two more in-depth studies, one on modeling and the other on downstream impacts of the GERD. Egypt demanded a halt to the construction of the GERD until the studies are completed, but Ethiopia refused that request, claiming that no such recommendation was made by the Panel. Egypt further demanded that the two studies be undertaken by international experts, which Ethiopia also rejected, stating that the studies would be carried out by Ethiopian experts. Meanwhile, Sudan reconfirmed its full support of the GERD in December 2013, listing the extensive benefits it would reap from the project.

Although Sudan's move prompted a major outcry in Egypt, the three countries continued to meet to discuss the differences on the GERD. On March 23, 2015, the three countries concluded the Agreement on Declaration of Principles on the GERD, recognizing the right of Ethiopia to use the Nile water resources for development and endorsing the GERD. The Agreement pointed out that the two studies would be carried out by two international firms, under the guidance and supervision of a Tripartite National Committee (TNC), which would consist of two members from each of the three countries. More details on the two studies were included in the Khartoum Document, which was signed on December 28, 2015, by the Minister of Water Resources, as well as the Minister of Foreign Affairs, of each of the three countries.

After a series of delays, two firms were selected, and they presented their inception report on the two studies to the TNC on 11th and 12th of November 2017. The report raised some issues regarding the baseline data for measuring the effects that may result from the GERD. The report was rejected by both Sudan and Ethiopia,

---

[1] One feddan equals 4200 $m^2$; or 0.42 ha; or 1.038 acres.

which claimed that the firms have expanded the terms of reference beyond those agreed upon by the three parties, while Egypt welcomed the inception report and the expanded terms of reference.

The hydrological data to be used by the firms to determine the effects that may result from the GERD have also become an acrimonious matter as each of Egypt and Sudan presented different notions of uses and rights over the Nile waters. Thus, the TNC meeting ended abruptly, and Egypt returned to square one in raising its major concerns about the GERD, and sometimes even opposing it, despite its signature of the Agreement on Declaration of Principles on the GERD in March 2015, as well as the Khartoum Document in December 2015.

The crack in the relations between Egypt and Sudan has turned now into an open dispute over the sharing of the Nile waters between the two countries and over what Egypt considers as its current/existing and acquired uses of the Nile waters and what Sudan regards as its existing lawful rights under the 1959 Nile Waters Agreement.

This article will trace Egypt and Sudan's initial dispute over the sharing of the Nile waters and discuss the agreements they concluded to resolve this dispute, particularly the 1959 Nile Waters Agreement. The article will then explain how and why this Agreement itself and its implementation have now become a source of a major and a bitter dispute between Egypt and Sudan, prompted by the GERD and the two studies thereon. The article will conclude with some thoughts on the GERD, as well as on the future relations of the Nile Basin countries.

## 2 Genesis of the Egyptian–Sudanese Dispute over the Nile Waters: The Gezira Scheme

Following the conquest of Sudan by the Anglo-Egyptian forces in 1898, Lord Cromer, the British Consul-General in Egypt at that time, sent Sir William Garstin, a British engineer with the Egyptian Public Works Department in Cairo, to Sudan. Mr. Garstin was to be assisted by Mr. Charles Dupuy, another British engineer stationed in Cairo. The purpose of their mission was to undertake a study on the best ways of harnessing the Nile waters for the growing uses in Egypt, as well as for new development projects in Sudan, but without causing harm to Egypt's water uses.

It is worth noting that the decision regarding Mr. Garstin's mission and its terms of reference came from Cairo and not from London, which administered the two countries at that time. The message that the Nile waters in Sudan would be managed from Cairo, and not from Khartoum or even London, was clear. To reconfirm that message, a new post called "Inspector General of Egyptian Irrigation in the Sudan" was established, and Mr. Dupuy was appointed as the first officer in that position.[2] That post continued and was strengthened during the colonial era and exits today under a modern title—Undersecretary of Egyptian Irrigation in the Sudan.

---

[2] See Collins (1996), p. 23.

Mr. Garstin made his first visit in 1900 and the second one in 1902, accompanied by Mr. Dupuy. The two engineers completed their extensive studies and issued their report in 1904.[3] Although written more than a century ago, the report remains one of the most comprehensive and authoritative studies of the Nile River. The report made several recommendations for increasing and regulating the Nile water flow for the benefit of Egypt. These recommendations included the building of storage reservoirs in Ethiopia and Uganda and the digging of the Jonglei canal for conserving some of the waters of the swamps of the then Southern Sudan and adding such waters to the White Nile, all for increasing the Nile waters' flow for uses in Egypt.

The third recommendation dealt with starting an irrigation scheme in the peninsula between the Blue Nile and White Nile, south of Khartoum, for the benefit of Sudan, called "the Gezira Scheme."[4] That was the first time in history for Sudan to use the Nile waters for irrigation through a government project. Given this critical historical fact and the expected size of the Scheme, the report made several suggestions for ensuring that this Scheme would not harm Egypt's existing uses of the Nile waters.

This recommendation, which was debated and refined within a few years, sowed the seeds of the Gezira Scheme as a development project, for growing cotton as a cash crop.[5] The Scheme would have two main purposes: improving the living conditions of some of the people of Sudan, and providing the colonial administration in Khartoum with income to defray the costs of administering Sudan, and starting the provision of some basic services for its people.

The immediate response to the Gezira Scheme proposal in Cairo was anger and dismay. The Egyptians—government and people—opposed the Scheme vehemently for some reasons: First, they all agreed that any Nile waters to be used by the Scheme in Sudan would be at the expense of Egypt and would reduce the flow of the Nile waters reaching the Egyptian farmers.

Second, the Scheme simply meant for them opening the door for Sudan to become a user of the Nile waters, not only in Gezira but also in other future schemes as well. That clearly meant a potential continuous reduction of the Nile waters reaching Egypt.

The third reason related to the idea of growing cotton in Sudan, which the Egyptians saw as resulting in major economic problems for Egypt. The problems would be caused by more supply of cotton from Sudan to the European markets, which would inevitably result in a sharp competition and subsequently in the

---

[3] Garstin (1904).

[4] Gezira is the Arabic word for "peninsular."

[5] A few years after inauguration of the Scheme, farmers were allowed to grow sorghum for use by the farmers and their families. That decision provided the basic and immediate needs of the farmers, and helped focus their attention and energies on cotton production as a cash crop. The profit from the sale of cotton, after deducting the cost of growing and marketing it, was initially divided as follows: 40% for the Sudanese government, 40% for the Sudan Plantation Syndicate—the company that managed the Scheme—and the remaining 20% for the farmers. *See* Gaitskill (1959).

lowering the international prices and consequently in less income to Egypt and its farmers.[6]

Negotiations between Khartoum and Cairo started and went on for a long time, with several committees established to study the Nile water uses in Egypt and Sudan and to make appropriate recommendations. Finally, an agreement consisting of two main components was reached. The first part was the establishment of the Gezira Scheme to be irrigated by a new dam to be built in Sennar on the Blue Nile River in Sudan, called the Sennar Dam. The second one consisted of another dam, the Jebel Aulia Dam, to be built on the White Nile, South of Khartoum, but whose waters would be reserved for the exclusive uses of Egypt.[7]

Thus, for Sudan to get a share of the Nile waters, it had to agree on compensating Egypt with another dam, built on Sudan's soil, with all its social and environmental costs borne by Sudan, for the exclusive benefit of Egypt. This is the first time in the history of international water resources that a dam was built totally in one country for the exclusive benefit of another country. As we will discuss later, Egypt regarded this formula of a dam for a dam as a precedent to which it would revert in its subsequent negotiations with Sudan over the Nile waters.

Moreover, and more importantly, it was agreed that the Gezira Scheme would not exceed 300,000 feddans, to be irrigated by a specified amount of water to be stored and released only during the monsoon season of the Blue Nile. Thus, the Gezira Scheme was officially born in July 1925, upon completion and inauguration of the Sennar Dam, but with major restrictions, and at a heavy price for Sudan.[8]

The Scheme would be irrigated through gravity irrigation, the cheapest and most effective and efficient mode of irrigation. In addition, the land of the Scheme is fertile, requiring little or no need for fertilizers, and the extremely high temperature of the summer would decrease the need for pesticides. Moreover, the people in the area have practiced rain-fed agriculture for ages and can easily be trained in irrigated agriculture. These factors helped in the immense success of the Scheme from its early years.

The success of the Scheme from the start prompted Khartoum to press for its expansion and, consequently, for increasing its uses and share of the Nile waters. However, this demand was fiercely resisted by Cairo. More committees were established to consider balancing the demands of Sudan for an equitable and reasonable share of the Nile waters, with the clinging of Egypt to the no-harm doctrine. Each of Egypt and Sudan continued to argue that international water law was on its side.

Negotiations and committee reports led, finally, to the conclusion of the 1929 Nile Agreement between the United Kingdom and Egypt.[9] The Agreement reserved the natural flow of the Nile for the benefit of Egypt from the 19th of January to the 15th of July (at Sennar), every year, subject to small amounts of pumping in Sudan,

---

[6] Tvedt (2004).

[7] Salman (2017a).

[8] *See* Gaitskill (1959).

[9] Exchange of Notes between Great Britain and Northern Ireland and Egypt in Regard to the Use of the Waters of the River Nile for Irrigation Purposes (1929).

defined in the agreement. Sudan would only commence using the Nile waters from the 16th of July, starting with certain quantities that would increase gradually and not to exceed certain limits. Those arrangements resulted eventually in Egypt's uses of the Nile waters, by virtue of the 1929 Agreement, reaching 48 billion cubic meters (BCM), while those of Sudan were only 4 BCM. The Agreement confirmed the construction of the Jebel Aulia Dam on the White Nile, South of Khartoum, for the exclusive use of Egypt.

However, the most noteworthy provision of the 1929 Agreement was paragraph 4 (b), which stated that "Save with the previous agreement of the Egyptian Government, no irrigation or power works or measures are to be constructed or taken on the River Nile and its branches, or the lakes from which it flows, so far as all these are in the Sudan or in countries under British administration, which would, in such a manner as to entail any prejudice to the interests of Egypt, either reduce the quantity of water arriving in Egypt, or modify the date of its arrival, or lower its level."

This paragraph, as the language suggests, granted Egypt veto power over the programs and projects of the other four upper riparians under the British control—Sudan, Kenya, Uganda, and Tanganyika (later Tanzania)—on the Nile River.[10] The paragraph sowed deep seeds of discontent and grievance in those countries. Indeed, the whole agreement, because of that paragraph, would soon come under heavy criticism and would be totally rejected by those countries as negating their right under international law to an equitable share of the Nile waters.[11] A similar paragraph exists in another treaty between Britain and Ethiopia, which Ethiopia also rejects.[12]

---

[10] See Krishna (1988), p. 23.

[11] Upon gaining independence in the early 1960s, the three states of Tanganyika, Kenya, and Uganda, adopted a strategy, later called the Nyerere Doctrine (after the first Prime Minister, and later President, of Tanzania, Julius Nyerere). The strategy gave the 1929 Agreement 2 years, during which it would either be replaced by another agreement, or it would simply lapse. Since no other agreement was concluded to replace the 1929 Agreement, the three countries announced that the Agreement lapsed in 1962. See Mekonnen (1984). As an example of the attitude of these countries toward the 1929 Agreement, Tanzania built a series of projects that convey water for drinking purposes from Lake Victoria to its North-western Region of Shinyanga, without notifying or consulting other riparians, claiming that Tanzania is not concerned with the 1929 Nile Waters Agreement. For more on these projects see: Nelson (2012).

[12] Treaty between Ethiopia and the United Kingdom relative to the frontiers between the Anglo-Egyptian Sudan, Ethiopia, and Eritrea (1902). The Treaty stated in Article III that Emperor Menelik II of Ethiopia "engages himself towards the Government of His Britannic Majesty not to construct, or allow to be constructed, any work across the Blue Nile, Lake Tsana, or the Sobat which would arrest the flow of their waters into the Nile, except in agreement with His Britannic Majesty's Government and the Government of the Sudan." Ethiopia claimed, a few years after the 1902 Treaty was concluded, that the Treaty was not ratified by any Ethiopian government organ, and that the English and Amharic versions of that particular paragraph were not congruent, and thus the treaty had no binding effect on Ethiopia. Ethiopia claimed further that, even assuming the 1902 Treaty was valid, it was concluded between Ethiopia and Britain, and Egypt was neither a party to the Treaty, nor could it possibly claim any rights through it. Egypt and Sudan on the other hand claim that the 1902 Treaty is valid and binding on Ethiopia. See Yihdego (2017).

Rather than try to resolve the bitter disputes over these two treaties, Egypt and Sudan concluded in 1959 another agreement confirming their full utilization and control of the Nile and the exclusion of other Nile riparians from sharing and uses of the Nile waters. The Agreement established an alliance between the two countries against the other Nile riparians. However, as will be discussed below, the Agreement is heavily tilted toward Egypt, and thus the alliance it established was not sustainable.

## 3 The 1959 Nile Waters Agreement: An Alliance Under Hydrohegemony?

The success of the Gezira Scheme exceeded the expectations of the colonial administration in Khartoum, as well as the Sudanese people. Hundreds of thousands of people started arriving in the Scheme from all over Sudan and from as far as West Africa, seeking to improve their living conditions.

However, with the water rights of Sudan reaching the limits of 4 BCM under the 1929 Nile Agreement, expansion of the Scheme had to stop at one million feddans by the early 1950s. Khartoum soon started carrying out more studies on the Scheme. Those studies led in 1953 to the proposal to build another dam on the Blue Nile River at Roseiris, upstream from Sennar Dam, to irrigate about 800,000 feddans of the Managil extension of the Gezira Scheme.[13] With Egypt holding firm to the 1929 Nile Agreement, and to what it saw as its acquired rights, Sudan was poised for another series of tough and difficult negotiations with Egypt. These negotiations started in 1954 and were concluded 5 years later with the signing in Cairo on November 8, 1959, of the Nile Waters Agreement between the two countries.[14]

The Agreement sanctioned the construction of the Aswan High Dam (AHD) by Egypt, in return for the Roseiris Dam for Sudan. Thus, the previous formula of a dam for a dam (Jebel Aulia and Sennar) was cited by Egypt as a precedent and was eventually replicated. However, Sudan gave larger concessions to Egypt this time than in the previous one.

Because the lake of the AHD would extend for more than 150 km inside the Sudanese territory, Sudan agreed to the relocation of more than 50,000 Sudanese Nubians as a result of the submergence of the main city in the area—Wadi Halfa—and 27 villages, with their entire infrastructure. More than 200,000 feddans of fertile land and more than one million palm and citrus trees were also submerged, together with large areas of rich archeological sites, as well as the second cataract

---

[13] Gibb (1953).

[14] Agreement (with Annexes) between the United Arab Republic and the Republic of the Sudan for the Full Utilization of the Nile Waters 1959 (hereinafter referred to as Nile Waters Agreement), and Protocol to the Agreement concerning the Establishment of the Permanent Joint Technical Committee; 453 United Nations Treaty Series 64 (1963).

that would have been a source of more than 650 MW of electricity.[15] Sudan demanded a compensation of 35 million Egyptian pounds, while Egypt insisted on paying only 10 million pounds. Sudan decreased its demand to 20 million, and the two parties eventually settled on 15 million Egyptian pounds.[16]

Sudan was also so generous when it came to the division of the Nile waters and granted Egypt similar extensive concessions. In December 1957, Sudan estimated its Nile water needs as 23 BCM[17] and presented this figure to the round of negotiations with Egypt, which took place that month. That figure was totally rejected by Egypt, which was willing to agree to no more than 14 BCM for Sudan.

The 1959 Nile Waters Agreement determined the total amount of the Nile waters reaching Aswan as 84 BCM; deducted 10 BCM, which represent the annual evaporation losses at the AHD lake; and divided the remaining balance of 74 BCM between the two parties—55.5 BCM for Egypt and 18.5 BCM for Sudan. Thus, by agreeing to share the evaporation losses in AHD Lake, Sudan had forgone five BCM, which could have been a part of its share.[18]

And as if this generosity was not enough, Sudan agreed to grant Egypt a water loan of 1.5 BCM from its share of the Nile waters until 1977.[19] Thus, the actual share of Sudan from the Nile waters was reduced to 17 BCM for the first 18 years following the conclusion of the 1959 Agreement. Strangely enough, the water loan was not referred to in the Agreement itself, only in an Annex to the Agreement.[20] Even more surprising is the fact that there is no mention anywhere in the 1959 Agreement (or the Annex) of when and how the water loan would be repaid by Egypt to Sudan. However, as will be discussed later, the issue of the repayment of the water loan has become an academic exercise because Sudan has failed since the conclusion of the 1959 Nile Waters Agreement to use more than 12 BCM of its share of 18.5 BCM specified in the Agreement. Nonetheless, this issue has now turned into a crucial and fundamental one for the entire Nile water relations between the two countries and for the two studies on the GERD, as the next parts of this chapter will show.

---

[15] See Dafalla (1975).

[16] *See* Nile Waters Agreement, Para Two (6), and Annex B to the Agreement. The figure of 15 million Egyptian pounds was determined by President Nasir of Egypt who was selected as arbitrator by the two delegations on this issue. He simply added the two figures (the 10 million pounds proposed by Egypt, and the 20 million proposed by Sudan), and divided them by two, as all arbitrators would usually do.

[17] *See* Mahgoub (2014).

[18] *See* Nile Waters Agreement, Para Two, (1 to 6), of the Agreement.

[19] *See* Nile Waters Agreement, Annex A.

[20] This situation should be compared to the 15 million Egyptian pounds to be paid under the Nile Waters Agreement by Egypt to the Sudan to compensate for the losses of the Sudanese Nubians who would be relocated as a result of the construction of the AHD. The figure of the compensation is specified in Para Two (6) of the Agreement, while the details regarding the amount of each of the four installments of the compensation, and the dates for their payment, are both specified in Annex B to the 1959 Nile Waters Agreement.

The share of Sudan from the Nile waters under the 1959 Agreement could get reduced even further if one of the other Nile riparians claims a share to the Nile waters and the two parties, after a study of the claim, decide to allot a share to such a riparian. The Agreement stipulates that "the value of this amount as at Aswan shall be deducted in equal shares from the share of each of the two parties."[21] It is strange that Sudan agreed that the deduction would be in equal shares and not in proportion to their shares under the 1959 Agreement of 55.5 and 18.5, as the global standards and practice dictate.

The Agreement stipulates that whatever Nile waters that may be allotted to another Nile riparian is the ultimate decision of the two parties (which may choose to allot none) and not a right to such a riparian under international water law. Indeed, under the Agreement, such allotted amount of the Nile waters to another riparian is more of a donation from Egypt and Sudan to such a riparian rather than a right. To confirm this, the Permanent Joint Technical Committee established under the 1959 Agreement "shall make arrangements with the concerned authorities in other territories in connection with the control and checking of the agreed amounts of Nile water consumption."[22] This stipulation is not consistent at all with the cardinal principle of international water law of the equality of all the riparians to a shared watercourse.[23] No wonder the other Nile riparians protested vigorously and loudly against and openly declared their rejection of the 1959 Nile Waters Agreement.

The Agreement established, as mentioned above, the Permanent Joint Technical Committee and sets forth its function, which is mainly joint action and facilitation of cooperation between the two parties. In case any question connected with the Nile waters needs negotiations with the governments of any riparian territories outside the Republic of the Sudan and the United Arab Republic, the two Republics would agree beforehand on a unified view in accordance with the investigations of the problem by the Committee. This unified view would henceforth form the basis of instructions to be followed by the Committee in the negotiations with the governments concerned.[24] Thus, Egypt was able to secure its close alliance with Sudan through the Committee.

The responsibilities of the Committee included ensuring continuation of the observation gauges and discharges of the Nile, and the Agreement stated that such tasks "shall be carried out under the supervision of the Committee within the

---

[21] *See* Nile Waters Agreement, Para Five (2).

[22] *See* Nile Waters Agreement, Para Five (2).

[23] The principle of equality of all the riparians in the shared watercourse was enunciated by the Permanent Court of International Justice (PCIJ) in *Case Relating to the Territorial Jurisdiction of the International Commission of the River Oder, (United Kingdom, Czechoslovakia, Denmark, France, Germany and Sweden v. Poland)*, (1929), Judgment No. 16. The PCIJ stated "[the] community of interest in a navigable river becomes the basis of a common legal right, the essential features of which are the perfect equality of all riparian Countries in the uses of the whole course of the river and the exclusion of any preferential privilege of any one riparian country in relation to the others." The principle was confirmed by the International Court of Justice (ICJ) in the *Gabcikovo-Nagymaros* case; *see* 1997 I.C.J Reports, p. 7.

[24] *See* Nile Waters Agreement. Para Five (I).

technical field by the engineers of the Republic of Sudan, and the staff of the United Arab Republic in the Sudan, and in Uganda." This clause of the Agreement confirms acceptance by Sudan of the presence and work of the Egyptian Irrigation Department staff in Sudan.[25] As discussed above, the presence of the Egyptian irrigation staff started at the beginning of the colonial era when the position of the "Inspector General of Egyptian Irrigation in the Sudan" was established.[26]

Similar functions and authority are given to Egypt with regard to the conservation of the waters of the swamps of South Sudan and to adding such waters to the Nile for use by Egypt and Sudan through the construction of canals. The Agreement stipulates that "the water benefit from such projects, as well as the total costs of construction, shall be shared equally by the two Republics."[27] However, the Agreement goes on to give Egypt a unilateral right to carry out such projects by itself if Sudan does not need such waters at that time. Egypt can carry out such a project by itself after notification of Sudan to this effect.[28] Accordingly, not only did the Agreement endorse and ratify the presence of the Egyptian irrigation staff in Sudan; it also allowed Egypt to carry out projects in Sudan after notification, and not approval, of Sudan. Thus, the provisions in the 1959 Agreement on the presence of the Egyptian irrigation staff in Sudan and the unilateral right of Egypt to build the canals in South Sudan have sealed the hydrohegemony of Egypt over Sudan and its Nile waters. Those provisions have raised serious concerns in Sudan as impinging on the sovereignty of Sudan.

All these substantial concessions have been granted by Sudan to Egypt so that Sudan would get 18.5 BCM of the Nile waters annually. It is ironic that despite all these concessions to get 18.5 BCM, Sudan has failed in using that amount of water from the very early days of the Agreement until now. Sudan's uses of the Nile waters throughout these years have remained below two thirds of this allotted amount, as discussed below.

---

[25] The Permanent Joint Technical Committee is headquartered in Khartoum. This has helped to serve as an umbrella to cover and hide all the Egyptian irrigation staff in the Sudan.

[26] *See* Collins (1996).

[27] *See* Nile Waters Agreement, Para Three (I).

[28] Para Three (2) of the 1959 Nile Waters Agreement reads "In case the United Arab Republic needs more water to cope with their progress in the agricultural expansion program, and therefore finds it necessary to take the necessary steps to carry out one of the above-mentioned schemes at a time when the need of the Republic of Sudan might not have arisen, the United Arab Republic will notify the Republic of Sudan of the date on which the former intends to start the execution, and in the course of two years from the date of such notification, each of the two Republics shall submit their program of expansion and the dates and quantities of their water requirements from the benefit of the scheme. Any such program shall be binding to both parties. At the expiration of the two years, the United Arab Republic shall start the execution of the project at its own expense ...."

## 4 Sudan's Embarrassment and Dilemma over Its Unused Share of the Nile Waters

As discussed earlier, the quantity of the Nile waters that Sudan needed for its irrigation projects remained a contentious issue from the start of negotiations with Egypt at the beginning of the last century. Although this matter was addressed by the 1929 Nile Waters Agreement, which allotted Sudan four BCM, Sudan soon called for renegotiations of that Agreement and demanded a higher figure. By 1957, Sudan estimated its water needs as 23 BCM, but Egypt was only willing to agree to no more than 14 BCM.

The incremental concessions that Sudan gave to Egypt during the 5 years of negotiations of the 1959 Agreement, particularly the submergence of Wadi Halfa town and its 27 villages, and the agreement to give Egypt a water loan helped eventually in increasing Sudan's share to 18.5 BCM. However, Egypt was clearly skeptical, and hopeful, that Sudan's actual uses of the Nile waters would be far less than that, and the water loan would end up as a permanent one.

Indeed, from the very early days following the conclusion of the 1959 Agreement, it became clear to both sides that Sudan was only able to use no more than two thirds, at best, of its Nile waters share of 18.5 BCM. Each side kept quiet about this fact for its own reasons. Sudan was hoping that this embarrassing and unfortunate situation would gradually change and Sudan would be able to put its Nile house in order by using its full share of water allotted under the 1959 Agreement. Egypt, on the other hand, did not want to embarrass its allies in the Ministry of Irrigation in Khartoum by divulging this critical fact and was hoping at the same time that this happy and unexpected situation would become permanent.

However, by the late seventies, after the AHD became fully operational, Nile water experts, as well as United Nations agencies and international financial institutions, started raising questions regarding the actual uses of the Nile waters of each of the two countries. The total flow of the Nile of 84 BCM measured at Aswan was also questioned in light of the fact that Egypt was able to fill the huge reservoir of the AHD of 162 BCM in less than 8 years.[29] The official answer from Khartoum remained unequivocal—Sudan was using its full and entire share of the Nile waters of 18.5 BCM allotted under the 1959 Agreement. Egypt did not respond to these issues.

And to confirm its position, Sudan indicated that it actually needed more Nile waters than its share of 18.5 BCM under the Nile Waters Agreement when it agreed

---

[29] Construction of the AHD started in early 1960, following conclusion of the Nile Waters Agreement in November 1959. Storage in its reservoir commenced in late 1962, and the AHD was completed in July 1970, and officially inaugurated in January 1971. Thus, it took about 8 years to fill the 162 BCM reservoir, which meant storage of about 20 BCM a year. Was Egypt really able to irrigate all its lands with 35.5 BCM only (55.5 minus 20 BCM)? Many experts believe that the Nile average annual flow since 1960 has been far higher than 84 BCM, and perhaps as high as 109 BCM annually, as suggested by the United Nations Development Programme (UNDP). For more discussion of this matter *see* United Nations Development Programme (2013).

with Egypt on the construction of the Jonglei canal in the late seventies.[30] The canal would add about five BCM of the waters from the swamps of South Sudan to the White Nile, for sharing equally by Egypt and Sudan. Work on the canal started in 1978 and was halted in 1983 because of the resumption of the civil way in South Sudan and the successful attack by the Sudan's People Liberation Army/Movement (SPLA/M) on the canal site.[31] Work on the canal never resumed.

However, by the late eighties and early nineties, the voices of the skeptics about Sudan's actual use of the Nile waters grew louder. The Nile expert Professor Robert Collins finally reconfirmed in writing what he had been saying privately, and in public lectures, about Sudan's failure to use its share of the Nile waters under the 1959 Agreement. Addressing that fact, the reasons therefor, and the consequences, Professor Collins wrote:

> The Sudan's depressed economy and the consequent deterioration of its agricultural infrastructure rendered it incapable of utilizing its share of the Nile waters. From the shaded windows overlooking the Blue Nile at the headquarters of the Permanent Joint Technical Commission and the Ministry of Irrigation in Khartoum, Sudanese officials watched in dismay as their gift to Egypt of 4 billion cubic meters passed silently below. The Sudan has been understandably reluctant to publicize its inability to consume its share of the Nile. The Egyptians characteristically remained as inscrutable as the Sphinx, delighted to receive the annual Sudanese contribution to Lake Nasser in the expectation that conditions in the Sudan would make permanent what the terms of the Nile Waters Agreement could not.[32]

Despite this clear and an unequivocal statement from a leading Nile expert, Khartoum continued denying that it had failed to use its share of the Nile waters and kept repeating that Sudan was indeed using its full share. Meanwhile, other reports started to surface indicating that Sudan's unused share may actually be higher than the figure of 4 BCM suggested by Robert Collins.

It was only in August 2011 that the then Sudanese Minister of Irrigation and Water Resources, Engineer Kamal Ali Mohamed, divulged the full story. Speaking during a television interview that was widely reported the next day, he said on this issue that Sudan had only been using 12 BCM of its annual share of the Nile waters of 18.5 BCM. However, he went on to add that Sudan had its plans to use its full share.[33]

The statement had a loud and wide echo, and the other Nile riparians and international and regional organizations concerned with shared water resources immediately took note of that earth-moving statement.[34] Egypt must have smiled and silently thanked their close ally for that statement since the concept of current uses and acquired rights has been the main principle of international water law that Egypt has been clinging to. Now, that principle can be extended to these waters that have

---

[30] *See* Howell et al. (1988).

[31] *See* Salman (2008), p. 299; *See* Salman (2014), p. 237.

[32] *See* Collins (2002), pp. 213–214.

[33] *See* Alsahafa newspaper (2011).

[34] For discussion of this matter; *see* Salman (2014). *See* also Braima (2014).

been crossing Sudan into Egypt for some time. The Minister's statement would, in Egypt's view, be a strong evidence of Egypt's actual current uses.

What prompted the then Minister of Irrigation and Water Resources of Sudan himself to make such a statement, after years of denial, may be difficult to know.[35] However, by 2009, Egypt and Sudan had decided to stand firm and break ranks with other Nile Basin countries on the negotiations over the Nile Basin Cooperative Framework Agreement (CFA) that became the principal component of the Nile Basin Initiative (NBI), as discussed below. Egypt has insisted on the full recognition of its existing/current water uses, and Sudan has demanded that its water rights under the 1959 Nile Waters Agreement be specifically acknowledged. The issues and terms "current water uses" and "current water rights" would keep the two allies together only for a short while because of the inherent contradiction in these two positions.

## 5 The Nile Basin Cooperative Framework Agreement, Water Security, and Current Uses and Rights

The Nile Basin Initiative (NBI), which was officially launched in Dar-es-Salam, Tanzania, on February 22, 1999, brought nine of the Nile Basin countries together, at the ministerial level, for the first time ever.[36] The NBI was established, through the minutes that were signed by the ministers, as a transitional arrangement to foster cooperation and sustainable development of the Nile River for the benefit of the inhabitants of those countries. The NBI is guided by a shared vision "to achieve sustainable socio-economic development through equitable utilization of, and benefit from, the common Nile Basin water resources."[37]

Work on an inclusive treaty called the Nile Basin Cooperative Framework Agreement (CFA) commenced soon after the official inauguration of the NBI, facilitated by the World Bank, the United Nations Development Programme (UNDP), and some other donors.[38] However, differences over the colonial treaties of 1902 and 1929 arose between Egypt and Sudan on the one hand and the Nile upper riparian countries on the other and soon derailed the entire work on the CFA. Egypt and Sudan invoked and demanded specific recognition of the other Nile treaties (1902, 1929, and 1959) in the CFA so they can protect what they saw as their "current uses"

---

[35] It should be added that Engineer Kamal Ali Mohamed was the longest serving Minister of Irrigation and Water Resources in the Sudan, having served as a minister from 1999 to 2011.

[36] Of the ten Nile riparian countries in 1999, nine countries, namely, Burundi, Democratic Republic of Congo, Egypt, Ethiopia, Kenya, Rwanda, Sudan, Tanzania and Uganda signed the minutes establishing the NBI. Eritrea decided to be an observer, and not a full member. South Sudan seceded from Sudan in 2011, and joined the NBI in 2012.

[37] See Nile Basin Initiative.

[38] See Brunnee and Toope (2002), p. 105.

(for Egypt) and "current rights" (for Sudan) on the Nile waters. This demand was totally rejected by other Nile riparians.

The facilitators and negotiators tried to break this impasse through the introduction of the concept of water security. They mistakenly thought that this concept would address the concerns of all the Nile riparian countries, and do away with colonial treaties, and decided to include it in the draft CFA.[39]

Article 2 of the CFA defines water security as "… the right of all Nile Basin Countries to a reliable access to and use of the Nile River system for health, agriculture, livelihoods, production, and environment." Furthermore, Article 14 of the CFA, titled "Water Security," stipulates that "Having due regard to the provisions of Articles 4 and 5, the Nile Basin Countries recognize the vital importance of water security to each of them. The Countries also recognize that the cooperation, management, and development of the waters of the Nile River System will facilitate achievement of water security and other benefits. Nile Basin Countries therefore agree, in a spirit of cooperation:

(a) to work together to ensure that all countries achieve and sustain water security;
(b) … the unresolved Article 14(b) is annexed to be resolved by the Nile River Basin Commission within six months of its establishment."[40]

It is worth adding that Articles 4 and 5 of the CFA deal, respectively, with the principle of equitable and reasonable utilization and the obligation against causing significant harm. Thus, the linkages between the two principles and the concept of water security were clearly in the minds of the negotiators and facilitators.[41]

All the Nile upper riparian countries participating in the negotiations (Burundi, Democratic Republic of the Congo, Ethiopia, Kenya, Rwanda, Tanzania, and Uganda) agreed to this proposal. However, the two lower riparian countries, Egypt and Sudan, rejected it. They demanded and insisted that Article 14 of the CFA should include a specific provision, to be added at the end of the article, which would oblige the basin countries "not to adversely affect the water security and current uses and rights of any other Nile Basin Country."[42]

Thus, the terms "current uses" and "current rights" were formally and officially unveiled by Egypt and Sudan in 2008, during the latter years of the negotiations of the CFA. Egypt insists on the word "uses" because the term includes all the water that Egypt is currently using. However, Sudan insists on the word "rights" to refer to what it considers as its water rights under the 1959 Nile Waters Agreement of 18.5 BCM.

---

[39] Mekonnen (2010), p. 430.

[40] The Nile Basin Cooperative Framework Agreement 2010 (CFA).

[41] It should, however, be clarified that the concept of water security is not a legal concept, and has no place in international water law. It is merely a socioeconomic and political concept. For an interesting discussion of the concept of water security, see generally, Wouters et al. (2009), pp. 97–135.

[42] For a detailed discussion of this matter see Salman (2013), p. 17; Salman (2017b), p. 18. See also Ibrahim (2012), p. 283.

As discussed earlier, Sudan has failed, since the 1959 Nile Waters Agreement was concluded, in using more than 12 BCM of its share of 18.5 BCM under the 1959 Agreement. Thus, Sudan could not possibly choose the word "uses," which would mean only 12 BCM and not 18.5 BCM. Accordingly, Sudan decided instead to use the term "rights" claiming it would capture the entire 18.5 BCM and would not be affected by its failure to use 6.5 BCM of that share.[43] Would Egypt's "current uses" include this 6.5 BCM that Sudan failed to use, and which have been pouring in the AHD lake, and used by Egypt? Egypt actually never used any figure to clarify what it means by "current uses," but this amount of water formed a good part of its current uses, as will be discussed later.

Egypt needed Sudan in the negotiations with the other Nile riparian countries on the CFA generally and in particular on this matter. For this reason, the two parties kept quiet on the possible differences, and indeed contradictions, over this issue, just as they kept quiet during the early years after the Agreement was signed on how much Sudan is actually using of its share of the Nile waters. However, a close look at the details of the concepts of current uses and current rights would reveal that Sudan and Egypt are actually at odds on the working and meanings of these concepts. This is because Sudan has defined its "current rights" to mean the 18.5 BCM allotted to it under the bilateral 1959 Nile Waters Agreement with Egypt. On the other hand, Egypt never publicly defined what it means by "current uses" and never attached a figure to that term. However, it is widely understood that Egypt's "current uses" would simply mean all the amounts of water that Egypt currently uses, including Sudan's 6.5 BCM unused portion of the 18.5 BCM allotted to Sudan under the 1959 Nile Agreement. Eventually, the GERD and its two studies will force open that Pandora's box and, as a result, will expose the inherent contradiction between the two concepts of rights and uses, as well as the fragility of the alliance between Sudan and Egypt, as will be discussed later.

## 6 The GERD, the Report of the Panel of Experts, and the Two Recommended Studies

As mentioned earlier, Ethiopia started construction of the GERD at the beginning of April 2011. The GERD is a large dam, with a height of 145 meters, storage capacity of 74 BCM,[44] and initial installed hydropower capacity of 6000 MW. However, Ethiopia indicated in February 25, 2017, that the installed hydropower capacity of the GERD has been revised upward from 6000 to 6450 MW "as a result of the

---

[43] *See* Salman (2014).
[44] The figure of 74 BCM capacity of the GERD should be compared with the figure of 162 BCM capacity of the AHD. It is interesting to note that the figure 74 BCM also represents the total annual flow of the Nile waters, measured as 84 BCM at Aswan, after deducting the evaporation losses in the AHD lake od 10 BCM, as per the 1959 Nile Waters Agreement. This is the figure that Egypt and Sudan divided among themselves under the 1959 Nile Waters Agreement; *see supra* note 14.

improvement made on generators to boost the capacity of the power plant."[45] This is more than three times the hydropower being generated by the AHD of 2100 MW.

The current estimates of the cost of the GERD are 4.8 billion dollars, which Ethiopia announced from the start that it intends to finance from its own resources. The GERD is being constructed by the Italian Company Salini Impregilo and will be, upon completion in 2018, the largest in Africa and the tenth largest in the world in terms of hydropower generation. Ethiopia stated repeatedly that the sole purpose of the dam is the generation of hydropower, and it is not intended for irrigation purposes since the terrain of the region does not allow the development of any irrigated agriculture.

Egypt and Sudan reacted immediately after the Ethiopian announcement was made, protesting and denouncing the Ethiopian decision and declaring their strong opposition to the GERD. Both countries contended that the GERD would decrease considerably the amount of the Nile waters reaching Sudan and flowing thereafter to Egypt. Egypt further claimed that the GERD would turn a large part of its irrigated lands into desert and will result in a considerable decrease of the hydropower generated by the AHD. Both countries demanded that the different studies for the GERD be provided to them so that they can assess the harm that the GERD will cause each of them. Sudan was also concerned about the safety of the GERD and the extensive harm that Sudan could suffer if the GERD were to crack, fail, or collapse.

However, the Sudanese position began to witness some gradual, but steady, changes, and many water experts and politicians started arguing that Sudan will actually benefit from the GERD. They explained that the benefits to Sudan include the entrapment of the huge sediments that the Blue Nile carries and brings annually to Sudan, which has caused the Sennar and Roseiris dams to lose more than half their storage and electricity-generating capacity. The benefits also include regulation of the flow of the waters of the river and putting an end to the recurrent flooding, and the destruction to property and crops, caused by the seasonal flow of the Blue Nile. Regulation of the flow, it is further argued, would help Sudan increase its crop rotations to two or even three a year, from the current single rotation dictated by the seasonality of the flow of the waters of the river. Indeed, the possibility of an increase in the number of Sudan's crop rotations and the resultant increase in the Nile water uses by Sudan have become the Egyptian unspoken focal point of concern on and opposition to the GERD, as will be discussed later.

Despite the Sudanese position favoring the dam, or perhaps because of that, the Egyptian opposition of the GERD continued to mount. Egypt continued to demand that Ethiopia formally notify both countries of the project, provide them with all available information, and allow time for their response before it moves on with the construction of the GERD. Ethiopia has always rejected the request for notification for any of its Nile projects, claiming that the hidden objective of Egypt's demand is for Egypt, after it is notified, to claim that the 1902 Agreement is valid and binding

---

[45] See 'GERD increases installed generation capacity to 6,450MW' Fana News (2017).

on Ethiopia. Furthermore, Ethiopia contends that Egypt and Sudan never notified Ethiopia of any of their projects on the Nile.

As the impasse persisted, Egypt and Sudan agreed with the Ethiopian proposal of September 2011 of establishing an International Panel of Experts, consisting of ten members, two from each of the three countries and four from outside the Nile Basin countries. The terms of reference of the Panel included identifying any negative impacts of the GERD on Sudan and Egypt and recommending ways of mitigating such impacts. The Panel was established in November 2011 and issued its report, which was signed by all ten members, 18 months later, on May 31, 2013.[46] The report was issued 3 days after Ethiopia announced on May 28, 2013, that it had diverted the Blue Nile on May 28, 2013, to start constructing the GERD. Egypt protested diversion of the river and the fact that such diversion was made only 3 days before the report of the Panel was due. The diversion was one clear signal of Ethiopia's determination to go ahead with the construction of the GERD.[47]

The report identified no basic flaws with the GERD but recommended the carrying out of two more in-depth studies, one on water resources/hydropower system simulation model and the other on transboundary environmental and socioeconomic impact assessment.[48] Consequently, Egypt demanded that construction of the GERD be suspended until the studies are completed. Ethiopia, on the other hand, claimed that the Panel did not recommend such suspension and that the construction of the GERD and the carrying out of the studies can, and will, proceed concomitantly. Another impasse ensued, but the three parties continued to talk to each other and agreed to meet at the ministers of water resources level to discuss their differences. Henceforth, the two studies would become, and continue to be, the focal issue of the differences and discussion on the GERD, despite the continued efforts to resolve them. The attempts to resolve the dispute over the studies, the GERD, and indeed the Nile itself have led to the conclusion of the first ever trilateral agreement on the Nile between Egypt, Ethiopia, and Sudan, as discussed below.

---

[46] International Panel of Experts (2013).

[47] It is clear that Ethiopia chose May 28 for diverting the Nile because that is the day the current ruling party came to power in Addis Ababa in 1991. The GERD is being flagged as the success story of the government and its ruling party, and as an indicator of Ethiopia's national pride.

[48] A year and a half after the report of the International Panel of Experts was issued in May 2013, the Massachusetts Institute of Technology (MIT) issued in November 2014 its Report, *The Grand Ethiopian Renaissance Dam: An Opportunity for Collaboration and Shared Benefits in the Eastern Nile Basin – An Amicus Brief to the Riparian Nations of Ethiopia, Sudan and Egypt, from the Eastern Nile Working Group* (convened at the Massachusetts Institute of Technology on 13–14 November 2014). The report identified no major flaws with the GERD, and made some important recommendations such as the need for coordination between the GERD, the AHD and Roseiris dam. See MIT report (2014).

# 7 The Agreement on Declaration of Principles on the GERD and the Two Studies

The three parties continued with their on-and-off meetings on the GERD and the two studies after the Panel issued its report in May 2013, and throughout 2014. However, it was the summit between the two top political leaders of Egypt and Ethiopia in June 2014 that led to the breakthrough.[49] Following extensive meetings and deliberations thereafter, the three parties concluded, on March 23, 2015, the agreement titled "Agreement on Declaration of Principles between the Arab Republic of Egypt, the Federal Democratic Republic of Ethiopia, and the Republic of the Sudan on the Grand Ethiopian Renaissance Dam Project (GERDP)."[50] It was signed in Khartoum by the two presidents—Abdel Fattah El-Sisi and Omer Hassan Ahmed Elbashir—and Prime Minister Hailemariam Desalegn, themselves, giving it the much-needed strong legal and political clout and visibility. Indeed, as mentioned earlier, the Declaration is the first agreement ever on the Nile to be concluded by three Nile riparian countries.[51]

The Agreement on Declaration of Principles (DoP) on the GERD consists of a preamble and ten principles, four of which relate to the GERD, while the other six deal with some basic principles of international water law. The preamble confirms the significance of the Nile River as a source of livelihood and development for the people of the three countries, thus restating a basic principle of international water law of equality of all the riparians in the sharing and uses of the common river.

Article 1 of the DoP deals with the principle of cooperation based on common understanding, mutual benefits, good faith, and the principles of international law, as well as understanding upstream and downstream water needs in its various aspects. Article 2 stipulates clearly the recognition of Egypt and Sudan of the purpose of the GERD as power generation, contribution to economic development, promotion of transboundary cooperation, and regional integration through generation of reliable and sustainable energy.

Articles 3 and 4 deal with the obligation not to cause significant harm and the principle of equitable and reasonable utilization, respectively. It is noteworthy that

---

[49] The African Union meeting in Malabo, Equatorial Guinea, in June 2014 provided an opportunity for the new President of Egypt, Field Marshall Abdel Fattah El-Sisi, and the Ethiopian Prime Minister Hailemariam Desalegn to meet face to face without a third-party intervention. The meeting went well and the two leaders agreed on general principles of cooperation in a number of fields, including the Nile waters and the GERD. It was further agreed that the tripartite meetings should resume soon. *See:* AU Meeting (2014).

[50] The Agreement on the Declaration of Principles (2015).

[51] It may be argued that the Minutes of the Dar-es-Salam meeting establishing the NBI should be considered the first such instrument as the Minutes were signed by nine countries. However, the Minutes have been viewed more as a declaration or a statement, and they were signed by Ministers or deputy ministers. The Declaration was signed by the highest political figures in the three countries, and related to the most controversial project in the history of the Nile Basin. Moreover, the Declaration included some basic principles of international water law, while the Minutes related only to the establishment of the NBI.

the DoP, unlike the UN Watercourses Convention,[52] and the CFA[53] started with the obligation not to cause significant harm rather than with the principle of equitable and reasonable utilization. This reversal of the order was perhaps a concession to Egypt, which believes that harm can only be caused by upstream riparians to the downstream ones.

This belief, actually, is not correct. In fact, it is now widely acknowledged that downstream riparians can also harm upstream riparians by foreclosing their future uses of water through the prior use of and the claiming of rights to such water.[54] Ethiopia understands and subscribes fully to this concept,[55] and Sudan has embraced it, believing that it will help protect its existing rights *vis-à-vis* Egypt's existing and increasing uses of the Nile waters.

Article 5 deals with the principle of cooperation in the first filling and operation of the dam. It deals with implementation of the recommendations of the International Panel of Experts and calls for respect of the final outcomes of the Tripartite National Committee (TNC) final report on the joint studies recommended by the Panel throughout the different stages of the dam project. Article 5 also asks the three countries to utilize the final outcomes of the studies to agree on the guidelines and rules for the first filling of the GERD. However, the article clarifies that this will take place "in parallel with the construction of the GERD." The article also asks the three parties to agree on guidelines and rules for the annual operation of the GERD but subjects this to adjustments that the owner of the dam may take from time to time. It then requires Ethiopia to inform the two other countries of any unforeseen circumstances requiring adjustments in the operation of the GERD.[56]

Following conclusion of the DoP, the three parties started discussing the modalities for the two studies, which were recommended by the International Panel of

---

[52] Convention on the Law of the Non-navigational Uses International Watercourses, adopted by the United Nations General Assembly on May 21, 1997, and entered into force on August 17, 2014. *See* Salman (2015).

[53] *See* Wouters et al. (2009), pp. 97–135.

[54] For a detailed analysis of this matter, *see* Salman (2010a), p. 1. *See* also Salman (2009).

[55] For discussion of Ethiopia's understanding of the concept of foreclosure of future uses, *see* Waterbury (2000), p. 84. There, Professor Waterbury referred to Ethiopia's Note Verbale of March 20, 1997, addressed to Egypt, on the Toshka or New Valley Project which Egypt was constructing, and which draws water from the Nile River. The Note Verbale stated: "Ethiopia wishes to be on record as having made it unambiguously clear that it will not allow its share to the Nile waters to be affected by a *fait accompli* such as the Toshka project, regarding which it was neither consulted nor alerted." Commenting on this paragraph of the Note Verbale, Professor Waterbury stated "The creation, de novo, of projects that use significant amounts of water may, and probably will, become the basis for asserting new acquired rights founded in established use. Egypt's action in the New Valley (or in the Sinai through the Peace Canal), in Ethiopia's view, preempts Ethiopia's right to harness the Nile water. If the principle of first in time, first in right prevails, then Ethiopia will have to forgo projects of its own in order to protect Egypt's use rights in the New Valley or in Sinai. Ethiopia will suffer appreciable harm in order not to cause harm to Egypt." *See id.*

[56] For a detailed discussion of the DoP, *see* Salman (2016a), p. 512; Salman (2016b), p. 203. *See* also Salman (2017c), p. 41.

Experts: one on hydrological modeling and the other on the impact of the GERD on Sudan and Egypt. It was agreed that international consultants would carry out the studies, under the overall supervision of the Tripartite National Committee (TNC).[57] Subsequently, the TNC recommended the French firm BRLi Group, to be assisted by the Dutch firm Deltares, to undertake the studies, and the recommendation was endorsed by the subsequent tripartite ministerial meeting.

However, differences emerged among the three parties on the detailed terms of reference of the two studies, as well as the role of each of the two firms in the carrying out of the studies. The differences soon moved to the two firms themselves. Deltares rejected the secondary role assigned to it and demanded an equal role with BRLi in the carrying out of the studies. The issue occupied the meetings of the TNC and the two tripartite meetings of the six ministers that took place in May and August 2015. In September 2015, Deltares announced that it was withdrawing and would not participate in the carrying out of the two technical studies.[58]

The TNC continued to meet to try to address the issues and differences related to the two studies and reach a compromise thereon. Indeed, the meetings continued despite Ethiopia's announcement on December 25, 2015, that it had returned the Blue Nile to its natural and main course of flow after it had completed the construction of the cement and steel work of the GERD. The announcement angered the Egyptians since it confirmed the completion of the physical works of the GERD. It should be recalled that Ethiopia diverted the Blue Nile on May 28, 2013, so as to start constructing the GERD. Thirty-one months later, the work was completed, and the river was returned to its natural course. That announcement indicated that the GERD has become, for all practical purposes, a *fait accompli*. Instead of complicating the NTC meetings, it could, however, be argued that this development has in fact pushed the parties in the direction of another agreement on the two studies, as discussed below.

## 8 The Saga of the Two Studies Continues: The Khartoum Document

The search for a solution to the saga of the two studies continued despite periodic public announcements by Egypt of its major concerns about the GERD, notwithstanding its signature of the DoP. On December 27, 2015, the ministers of water resources and the ministers of foreign affairs of the three countries held another meeting in Khartoum. After 2 days of intensive discussions, the six ministers signed

---

[57] Sometimes the Committee is referred to as the Tripartite National Committee (TNC), while at others it is referred to as the Technical National Committee (TNC). In some occasions, the Committee is called the Tripartite Technical National Committee, but still with the acronym (TNC).

[58] See *Deltares Withdraws from GERD Studies* (2015).

on December 28, 2015, a document titled "Summary and the Outcomes of the Meeting" (referred to hereinafter as the "Khartoum Document").[59]

The Khartoum Document consists of six provisions and three annexes. The Document has confirmed "the sincere and full commitment of the three countries to adhere to the Agreement on Declaration of Principles (DoP)," putting an end to the rumors about Egypt's imminent move to withdraw from the DoP.

The first paragraph of the Document records the endorsement of the six ministers of the choice by TNC of the French Firm Artelia to replace the Dutch Firm Deltares.[60] Thus, the two French firms—BRLi Group and Artelia—will be the firms that will carry out the two studies on water resources/hydropower system simulation model and on transboundary environmental and socioeconomic impact assessment. The Khartoum Document has also endorsed the selection of the British law firm Corbett and Co. to draft the contracts with the two firms and to supervise the implementation of the legal obligations under the contracts. The three parties agreed that the cost of the three firms will be shared equally by the three countries.

Annex C of the Document dealt with the roadmap for carrying out the two studies and set forth certain dates for completion of actions thereon.[61] The signature of the contracts with the two French firms and the launching of the studies would take place, as per this Annex, in Khartoum on February 1, 2016.

Despite this clear stipulation, the TNC and the three ministers of water resources did not meet until February 7, 2016, and the contracts were not signed then. The meeting took place in Khartoum, and lasted until February 10, 2016. The Press Release issued on the last day of the meeting indicated that "the TNC deliberated on the clarification issues on the updated technical proposal, financial proposal of the consultant, draft contract document, and agreed to resolve the pending issues through communications among the TNC, the consultant and the legal adviser."[62] The Press Release added that the TNC had agreed to hold its 11th meeting in Addis Ababa, Ethiopia to sign the contract for the two studies based on the completion of the pending issues to be resolved through communication. However, the Press Release did not specify the date of the 11th meeting or the new date for signature of the contract.

After a series of meetings of the TNC, the contracts were finally signed with BRLi Group and Artelia on September 20, 2016, more than 7 months from the originally agreed-upon date. The contract stipulated that the two studies on "Water Resources/Hydropower System Simulation Model" and "Transboundary Environmental and Socio-economic Impact Assessment" would be completed within 11 months, that is, by August 2017.

---

[59] A copy of the Khartoum Document is on file with author.

[60] See *Egypt, Ethiopia, Sudan replace Dutch firm with French Artelia for GERD impact study* (2015).

[61] Annex A of the Khartoum Documents listed the attendees of the meeting, while Annex B included the agenda for the meeting.

[62] See Press Release of the 10th Tripartite National Committee (2016).

However, the signature of the contracts and commencement of work on the two studies would actually bring about more serious substantive issues and differences regarding the baseline hydrological data upon which the studies would be based. It would also reveal the irreconcilable views of Egypt and Sudan regarding the concepts of current uses and rights, as discussed below.

## 9   Current Uses and Current Rights and the Baseline Data for the Two Studies

Although BRLi Group and Artelia agreed in September 2016 to complete the two studies on simulation modeling and transboundary impact by August 2017, that actually did not happen. The TNC continued to meet during this period but issued no statement regarding the status of the studies, and Ethiopia continued its full speed construction of the GERD.

On November 11, 2017, the TNC held its 17th meeting in Cairo, attended also by the three ministers of water resources. The meeting was supposed to discuss the inception report prepared by BRLi and Artelia on the two studies. This report, it was explained, was a preliminary inception report and not a final one. However, the meeting ended abruptly on November 12 without any joint statement as to what went on, or even an agreement on the date for the next TNC meeting. Egypt Minister of Water Resources indicated that he had endorsed the inception report, which his Ethiopian and Sudanese counterparts rejected.[63]

However, the Sudanese Minister of Water Resources indicated that the talks on the GERD were waiting for the Egyptian side, which has asked for more time to consult with its country's leadership after reservations on many issues on the report.[64] The Ethiopian side kept quiet, knowing very well that the differences over the studies are now becoming an Egyptian Sudanese matter.

It turned out that the inception report raised the issue of the baseline hydrological data that the two firms would need to use to measure and determine the impact of the GERD on Sudan and Egypt. Egypt insisted that the baseline data to determine the impact should be its current uses of the Nile waters, while Sudan demanded that the firms' use the 1959 Agreement and the allocations stated therein for measuring the impact of the GERD on Sudan and Egypt. Clearly, Egypt is now claiming that its existing uses include every drop of water that has crossed into the AHD lake, including whatever Sudan has failed throughout the years in using.[65] On the other

---

[63] For the Egyptian Minister's statement (2017).

[64] For the Sudanese Minister's statement (2017a).

[65] As indicated before, Egypt has not specified any figure as its current uses. It should be added that the figure of 84 BCM, the annual flow of the Nile measured at Aswan, is no longer a globally accepted figure. The United Nations Development Programme (UNDP) indicated that the average annual flow of the Nile since 1960 is actually 109 BCM; *see* United Nations Development Programme (2013), p. 13.

hand, Sudan wants the allocation of the Nile waters under the 1959 Nile Waters Agreement between the two countries of 55.5 BCM and 18.5 BCM to form the baseline hydrological data for determining the impacts of the GERD on each of the two countries. Clearly, the Egyptian Sudanese alliance of close to 60 years against other Nile countries finally has to face its real moment of truth.

The Sudanese Minister divulged some information about the meeting when he stated that "Sudan and Ethiopia expressed reservation over some essential points in the inception report on the GERD's economic, social and environmental impact. At the top of these points was the nature of the baseline data from which any studies relating to the operation of the dam start, a point over which the Egyptian side expressed reservation."[66] The Minister underscored Sudan's position of existing rights by stating that "There is no way for relinquishing Sudan's share in the Nile water as approved in the 1959 agreement."[67]

Furthermore, the Sudanese Minister clarified that the differences over the inception report related to three issues: first, getting an explanation from the two firms on the expansion of their terms of reference beyond those agreed with the three countries; second, recognizing the 1959 Nile Waters Agreement as the baseline for determining the impact of the GERD on Sudan and Egypt; and, third, the fact that any data used in the final report will not create rights for any of the three countries.[68]

As if this was not enough, the Sudanese Minister of Foreign Affairs told the Television Channel, Russia Today, that Sudan will soon stop its water loan to Egypt. The Egyptian Minister of Foreign Affairs responded, saying that Sudan has been using its full share of the Nile waters and that in the few instances when Sudan failed to use part of its share, that part created problems with storage in the AHD lake and had to be diverted to Toshka to avoid such problems.[69] While the Sudanese Minister was talking about the water loan, his Egyptian counterpart was talking about the amount of Nile waters that Sudan failed to use. Clearly, Sudan and Egypt, the long-time Nile allies, are no longer able even to talk about the same Nile agenda item.

On December 26, 2017, 6 weeks after the abrupt ending of the November meeting of the TNC, the Egyptian Foreign Minister visited Addis Ababa to discuss the impasse over the DERD studies. It was reported during the visit that "Egypt has

---

It should be added the 1959 Nile Waters Agreement stipulates that any increase in the Nile annual flow above 84 BCM would be divided equally between the two countries. However, with Sudan being unable to use its original share of 18.5, there has been no call from the Sudan to divide the increase over 84 BCM that reached 109 BCM, as per the UNDP (2013). Thus, Egypt is clearly using a far larger amount of the Nile waters than 55.5 or even 62 BCM, and is refusing to divulge the actual figure.

[66] See the Sudanese Minister's statement (2017a).
[67] Sudanese Minister's statement (2017a).
[68] The Arabic version of the Sudanese Minister's statement (2017b).
[69] *See* Salman (2017d).

Toshka is a project that was planned, and its execution started, during former President Hosni Mubarak era, west of the AHD. The project is being irrigated by water diverted from the AHD Lake. For more information *see* Toshka project (2012).

recommended the World Bank as a technical mediator with a neutral and final opinion on the issue of Ethiopia's under-construction mega dam on the shared Nile River."[70] It was also reported that Ethiopia promised to study the proposal and reply as soon as possible and that Egypt would convey the proposal to Sudan in the coming few days.[71]

As discussed earlier in this article, it was the World Bank that facilitated the establishment of the NBI, as well as the negotiations of the CFA that collapsed in 2009. The Bank has also facilitated the preparation of a report, published in 2008, on opportunities for cooperation between the three countries on the Eastern Nile.[72] However, since the collapse of the CFA negotiations in 2009, the Bank has shrunk considerably its involvement in the Nile Basin.

One day after the disclosure of the Egyptian proposal regarding the involvement of the World Bank in the GERD studies, Ethiopian newspapers reported that the Minister of Foreign Affairs of Egypt had suggested to Ethiopia to exclude Sudan from the GERD talks, arguing that "the case Egypt has with Sudan is completely different from Ethiopia's case, and it is necessary to differentiate the two."[73] Some reports went further and suggested that "The Egyptian proposal (was) sent by President Abdel Fattah El-Sisi to Hailemariam Desalegn, Ethiopia's prime minister...."[74]

Egypt denied making the suggestion of excluding Sudan from the GERD talks.[75] The uproar and anger in Sudan over the report was formidable, and despite this denial, the relationship between the two countries continued to deteriorate and sank into a new low level.

If it is confirmed that the proposal to exclude Sudan from the GERD talks was really made by Egypt to Ethiopia, it would contravene both the 1959 Nile Waters Agreement, as well as the 2015 Agreement on the Declaration of Principles on the GERD (DoP).

With regard to the 1959 Nile Waters Agreement, as discussed earlier, the Agreement has established the Permanent Joint Technical Committee as a bilateral entity to facilitate cooperation between the two countries. The Agreement stipulates that in case any question connected with the Nile water needs negotiations with the governments of any other Nile riparian, the two parties would agree beforehand on a unified view in accordance with the investigations of the problem by the Committee. This unified view would henceforth form the basis of instructions to be followed by

---

[70] For a reference to the Egyptian proposal *see: 'Egypt seeks World Bank as technical mediator in Ethiopia's dam issue'* Xinhua News (2017).

[71] *'Egypt seeks World Bank as technical mediator in Ethiopia's dam issue'* Xinhua News (2017).

[72] In 2008, the Bank commissioned, at the request of the Eastern Nile Council of Ministers, an independent report on cooperation on the Eastern Nile; *see* Blackmore and Whittington (2008).

[73] *See 'Egypt proposes to exclude Sudan from dam talks' Fortune News* (2017).

[74] *See 'Egypt wants 'Sudan out' of contentious dam talks'* Aljazeerah News (2018).

[75] *See 'Egypt denies demanding Sudan exclusion from talks with Ethiopia over dam project (ST)'* Statenaw News (2018).

the Committee in the negotiations with the governments concerned.[76] Egypt had clearly failed to consult with Sudan before making the proposal, as the Agreement requires. In fact, the Committee has not played any role with regard to the disputes over the GERD, indicating the clear differences between the two countries and the waning role of the Committee itself.

With regard to the DoP, this Agreement has been concluded with a view to establishing a cooperative *modus operandi* by the three countries on the issues related to the GERD.[77] Article 1 of the DoP deals with the principle of cooperation, which should be based on common understanding, mutual benefits, good faith, and the principles of international law, as well as understanding upstream and downstream water needs in its various aspects.

Moreover, Article 9 of the DoP requires the three countries to cooperate on the basis of sovereign equality, territorial integrity, mutual benefit, and good faith in order to attain optimal utilization and adequate protection of the Nile. Article 5 confirms the agreement of the three countries to respect the final outcomes of the Tripartite National Committee (TNC) final report on the joint studies recommended by the International Panel of Experts. As clarified earlier, the TNC consists of two experts from each of the three countries.

Additionally, Article 10 on peaceful settlement of disputes states that the three countries will settle disputes arising out of interpretation or implementation of the DoP amicably, through consultation or negotiation, in accordance with the principle of good faith. The article goes on to state that if the parties are unable to resolve the dispute through consultation or negotiation, they may jointly request conciliation or mediation or refer the matter for the consideration of the heads of state/head of government.

Thus, the proposal to exclude Sudan from the GERD negotiations would clearly violate the spirit and letter of the DoP, as well as the provisions on the role and responsibilities of the Permanent Joint Technical Committee established by Egypt and Sudan under the 1959 Nile Waters Agreement.

Ethiopia must be watching the widening rift between Egypt and Sudan with great interest. Ironically, Egypt and Sudan were the ones that totally ignored Ethiopia's requests to participate in the Nile waters negotiations that led to the 1959 Agreement.[78] Ethiopia has made it clear to Egypt and Sudan that it is not concerned with the 1959 Agreement as it is not a party to it, leaving the battle over it to the countries that concluded the Agreement. Sudan has endorsed Ethiopia's position when it stated that any data used in the final report will not create rights for any of the three countries.

Sudan, which is now facing the embarrassment, dilemma, and consequences of its failure to use its share of the Nile waters under the 1959 Agreement, is demanding full compliance with the very same agreement that it has been criticizing as unfair and one sided. Egypt, on the other hand, is emphasizing current uses over

---

[76] *See* Nile Waters Agreement, Para Five (I).
[77] *See* Agreement on the Declaration of Principles (2015).
[78] *See* Salman (2013).

current rights so as to claim Sudan's unused share, but at the same time, Egypt wants to keep the 1959 Agreement alive and binding. The rift between Egypt and Sudan over the Nile waters widened, and the war of words escalated when Sudan accused Egypt of reluctance to adhere to the 1959 Nile Waters Agreement.[79] Ironically, and as discussed amply before, it is the 1959 Nile Agreement that bonded the two countries together that is now drifting them apart.[80]

On January 22, 2018, it was widely reported that Ethiopia has rejected Egypt's proposal of involving the World Bank in the GERD and its two studies. Ethiopia insisted that "There is an opportunity for the three countries to resolve possible disputes by themselves."[81]

Thus, the two suggestions attributed to Egypt with regard to the GERD—exclusion of Sudan from the GERD talks and involvement of the World Bank in the GERD studies—are no longer on the agenda for discussion by the parties. Egypt denied making the first suggestion, and Ethiopia rejected the second one. What is clearly left for the three parties—Egypt, Ethiopia, and Sudan—is to return to the negotiating table to try to resolve, by themselves, their differences over the GERD and its studies, as they have been doing since 2013. The effects of these developments on the negotiations between the three parties remain to be seen. However, one conclusion can be reached—further deterioration of the Egyptian–Sudanese relations, concomitant with strengthening of the Ethiopian–Sudanese ties.

## 10 Conclusion

Inauguration of the Sennar Dam in 1925 marked a new era in the modern history of Sudan. The dam was the first one in the entire sub-Saharan Africa constructed with European technology. Although its reservoir had a limited capacity of below one billion cubic meters and the hydropower generated was small, the Sennar Dam still

---

[79] See 'Sudan: Egypt refused new agreement for Nile waters" Middleestmonitor News *(2017)*.

[80] It should be added that the dispute over the Halaib triangle presents another thorny issue to the Egyptian Sudanese relations, and is no doubt exacerbating the Nile water dispute. The triangle, which faces the Red Sea, was occupied in 1992, and formally annexed in 1995, by Egypt which claims it as an Egyptian territory. This claim is totally rejected by the Sudan which insists that Halaib is a Sudanese territory, and has been recognized so by Egypt upon independence of Sudan in 1956. Sudan has asked for negotiations of the dispute or resort to mediation, arbitration or the ICJ, but Egypt has totally rejected these proposals. The dispute has been discussed by the Security Council in 1958 at the request of Sudan, and Sudan keeps renewing its complaint annually. What angers Sudan is the repeated demand by Egypt for arbitration of the GERD dispute, and Egypt adamant refusal to discuss the Halaib dispute with Sudan; *See* "Press conference to address the Hala'ib Triangle land dispute between Sudan and Egypt" Boundary News, (2016). It is interesting to note that the most recent row between Sudan and Egypt over Halaib erupted over Egypt's plans to build a dam in Halaib for collecting and storing rain and flood water for use in the dry season, and to replenish groundwater, *see:* "Egypt's dam plan in Halaib upsets Sudan" Arab News (2016).

[81] See "Ethiopia refuses World Bank arbitration over Nile River dam" Associated Press (2018).

had no competitor in the entire continent at the time of its completion in 1925, except for the Aswan Dam in Egypt.[82]

The Sennar Dam has no doubt brought Sudan from the middle ages to the twentieth century. It made the dream of the Gezira Scheme a reality and provided electricity to Khartoum for the first time ever. The Scheme turned out as a major development project that improved tremendously the living conditions of a large segment of the Sudanese people and provided the government with the desperately needed funds for starting basic services—education, health, roads, water supply—for the entire country. People flooded to the Scheme from all over Sudan and from as far as West Africa, looking for opportunities to improve their economic conditions.

The Gezira Scheme soon became a shining example for socioeconomic development, achievements, and success. By the early 1950s, it received the distinction of being the largest cotton farm in the world under one administration. Researchers arrived from all over the developed and developing world to study the Scheme and its success.

With more than 12 million feddans of irrigable land, and with two thirds of the Nile Basin falling within Sudan, the country was poised to be the bread basket of the Arab world, as many observers and experts thought in the 1950s. By that time, the size of the Scheme reached one million feddans, with additional 800,000 feddans ready and waiting for irrigation water. Sudan's plans in 1957 indicated that its water requirements were in the range of 23 BCM.

However, negotiations with Egypt over the sharing of the Nile waters that started in 1954 dragged for 5 years until the Nile Waters Agreement was finally concluded in November 1959. The formula of a dam for a dam, which was agreed upon by the British colonial administration in the 1920s (Sennar and Jebel Aulia dams), was insisted upon by Egypt and eventually accepted by the Sudanese politicians and bureaucrats in the 1950s (Roseiris and AHD). Moreover, the Sudanese negotiators granted Egypt far more concessions in the 1959 Nile Waters Agreement than under the 1929 Agreement. Although the 1959 Agreement established a close alliance between Egypt and Sudan, it also sealed the hydrohegemony of Egypt over Sudan and its Nile waters.

Sudan demanded 23 BCM during the negotiations with Egypt in the 1950s and at the end gave all possible concessions to Egypt to get 18.5 BCM under the 1959 Agreement. Ironically, Sudan ended using no more than 12 BCM annually for the last 60 years since the Agreement was concluded in 1959.

The failure of the Sudanese politicians and bureaucrats in the water sector could not possibly be bigger. Storage in the Sudanese dams has been no more than 10 BCM, compared to 162 BCM in Egypt. This is an embarrassing figure for a country that started water storage close to a century ago, with about one billion cubic meters in 1925. Sennar and Roseiris dams have lost more than half of their storage and hydropower generating capacities because of the accumulation of sediments carried

---

[82] The Aswan Dam was completed in 1902. Although its height was increased twice, its storage capacity remained limited, and it was eventually replaced by the Aswan High Dam (AHD) that was completed in 1970; United Nations Development Programme (2013).

by the Blue Nile from the Ethiopian highlands and the failure of the successive Sudanese governments to deal with this matter. The Gezira Scheme has deteriorated considerably during the last three decades because of poor management and the clogging of the irrigation canals with sediments. Gravity irrigation is gradually being replaced by the costly and environment-unfriendly pump irrigation.

Cotton lost its distinction as the flagship of the Gezira Scheme. Under the banner of crop choice put in effect by the Gezira Scheme Act in 2005, cotton is no longer a mandatory crop, or even a secondary crop, in the Gezira Scheme.[83] Sudan has lost most of its global cotton markets that need reliable and dependable annual supply. Egypt must have been quite happy to fill the vacuum in the cotton markets resulting from the departure of Sudan, just as it is happy with Sudan's failure to use its full Nile water allocation under the 1959 Nile Waters Agreement. Notwithstanding these facts, Egypt and Sudan remained allies against the other Nile riparians, at least publicly, and until recently.

However, the Egyptian–Sudanese alliance, which the 1959 Agreement established, has been fraught with contradictions from the time the Agreement was concluded, and it was clearly a matter of time before the alliance would start cracking. Uses by Egypt of the Nile waters started to include, from the start, all the Nile waters that Sudan failed to use as a part of Sudan's allocation under the 1959 Agreement, as well as those that Sudan failed to claim as a result of an increase in the flow of the Nile. Such current uses by Egypt have been clashing beneath the surface with the claims of Sudan for what it considers its current lawful rights under the 1959 Agreement. As such, Sudan is using no more than 12 BCM but insists on its full rights of 18.5 BCM under the Agreement.

On the other hand, Egypt claims as its current uses whatever it is actually consuming, notwithstanding the figure of 55.5 BCM in the 1959 Nile Agreement, and Egypt will not disclose the exact figure of its actual current uses. Thus, the 1959 Agreement may seem to have become an academic exercise with regard to the figures it has stipulated, which have no relevance to the new facts on the ground in each of the two countries. Still, each country wants to maintain the binding effect of the Agreement since it is the only point of reference they have, against each other and against the other Nile riparians that have rejected the Agreement. Indeed, when it comes to the 1959 Agreement, each of the two countries wants to stick to the Agreement and at the same time to have the ability to operate outside the Agreement. This approach has become clearer since the negotiations over the CFA faltered in 2008.

The Egyptian and Sudanese teams to the CFA negotiations must have realized the major differences, and indeed contradictions, over the two notions of "current uses" and "current rights" and, thus, the clear variance on their approaches. However, the two parties needed each other against the other Nile riparians and had to keep their eyes closed to these simmering differences. They needed to appear and behave as close allies notwithstanding those basic and major contrasts.

However, the issues around the GERD are far bigger, and the stakes far higher, than the CFA. Indeed, the differences over the GERD have overshadowed from the

---

[83] *See* Salman (2010b).

start those over the CFA. Sudan has concluded that the GERD is really its AHD without the financial, social, and environmental costs.

Egypt has realized from the very beginning that the main problems and challenges of the GERD to Egypt are the benefits accruing to Sudan and not the GERD *per se*. Regulation of the flow of the Blue Nile will enable Sudan to have two or three crop rotations as Egypt currently has. As a result, Sudan will need more Nile water than the currently used amount of 12 BCM, which will mean that Sudan could be able to use its entire allotted share of 18.5 BCM, or a good part of it. This is not to dismiss the concerns of Egypt about the period of filling the GERD reservoir, which is, no doubt, a legitimate concern.[84] However, this concern and the filling period required can be negotiated with Ethiopia.

It is widely expected that the studies by BRLi and Artelia will highlight this positive impact of the GERD on Sudan. The baseline hydrological data needed for the studies will point at the share of the Sudan Nile waters that has been going to Egypt since 1959. Other hydrological data that will have to be disclosed include the annual flow of the Nile—is it 84 BCM or 109 BCM or something in between? How much water is Egypt actually using: 55.5, 62, or 70 BCM? Is Sudan using 12 BCM, or is the figure even lower than that, as suggested by some experts?

It remains to be seen how Egypt and Sudan will end up addressing these complex and challenging differences over current uses and current rights and how the three countries will eventually deal with the two studies and other GERD issues. However, the fact remains and has been abundantly reconfirmed by recent developments—the GERD and other hydropower projects on the Nile in Ethiopia and Uganda are nonconsumptive and present no real challenges to Egypt and Sudan. The water supply projects in Tanzania are too small to have any serious impact on the waters of the White Nile eventually reaching Sudan and Egypt. Whatever projects and programs South Sudan may have for the Nile waters, they will be largely met and covered from the waters of the swamps there. The remaining upper riparians of Burundi, Rwanda, Kenya, Eritrea, and the Democratic Republic of Congo have little uses, stakes, and interests in the Nile waters. This leaves Egypt and Sudan as the only real competitors for the Nile waters.

Indeed, the first actual dispute on the Nile started a century ago between Egypt and Sudan on the consumptive and large uses of the Nile waters for irrigation in the two countries. Despite the 1959 Nile Waters Agreement, controversies over which of the two counties is using how much Nile waters have kept recurring. Being the two largest users of the Nile waters, disputes on the sharing and using of the Nile will remain for the foreseeable future, mostly and largely between Egypt and Sudan.

The GERD could and, indeed, should have been a jointly financed, owned, and operated project by Ethiopia, Egypt, and Sudan. Joint ownership would have addressed the concerns of Egypt and Sudan, which the two studies have been trying to address since 2013. Moreover, the benefits of the GERD—hydropower and water storage—would have been shared by the three countries. In fact, one can even argue that the GERD should have been built in the 1960s as a joint trilateral project in lieu of the AHD and Roseiris. That would have achieved the same benefits from the

---

[84] *See* Wheeler (2017), p. 193.

AHD and Roseiris and at the same time prevented the catastrophic social and environmental consequences of the AHD in Sudan and Egypt, including the huge evaporation losses of 10 BCM annually. Unfortunately, both opportunities for profound cooperative actions by the three countries were missed.

Needless to say, the sustainable and equitable sharing and managing of the Nile waters require genuine and good faith cooperation, not only between Egypt, Ethiopia, and Sudan but also among all the Nile eleven riparian countries. Such cooperation is the only way out of the disputes, confusion, and inefficient use of the Nile waters that have plagued the Nile Basin since the beginning of the last century. Indeed, such cooperation is desperately and urgently needed to pull the 250 million inhabitants in the Nile Basin eleven countries from their poverty, hunger, and darkness.

## References

Agreement (with Annexes) between the United Arab Republic and the Republic of the Sudan for the Full Utilization of the Nile Waters. 1959, and Protocol to the Agreement concerning the Establishment of the Permanent Joint Technical Committee; 453 United Nations Treaty Series 64 (1963). https://www.internationalwaterlaw.org/documents/regionaldocs/UAR_Sudan1959_and_Protocol1960.pdf

Agreement on Declaration of Principles between the Arab Republic of Egypt, the Federal Democratic Republic of Ethiopia, and the Republic of the Sudan on the Grand Ethiopian Renaissance Dam Project (GERDP). https://www.internationalwaterlaw.org/documents/regionaldocs/Final_Nile_Agreement_23_March_2015.pdf

Alsahafa newspaper, Issue No. 6487, Wednesday August 10, 2011, page 3. Khartoum, Sudan (in Arabic)

AU Meeting (2014) http://english.ahram.org.eg/NewsContent/1/64/257124/Egypt/Politics-/Egypts-Sisi-to-meet-Ethiopian-PM-on-sidelines-of-A.aspx

Blackmore D, Whittington D (2008) Opportunities for cooperative water resources development on the Eastern Nile; risks and rewards. World Bank. http://dalewhittington.web.unc.edu/files/2015/12/Blackmore-Whittington-EN-Scoping-Study-Final-2009.pdf

Braima A (2014) Sudan continues relinquishing a growing portion of Nile water share. http://sudanow-magazine.net/pageArch.php?archYear=2014&archMonth=11&Id=3311

Brunnee J, Toope S (2002) The changing Nile Basin regime – does law matter? Harv Int Law Rev 43:105

Collins R (1996) The waters of the Nile. Markus Wiener Publishers, Princeton

Collins R (2002) The Nile. Yale University Press, New Haven

Dafalla H (1975) The Nubian Exodus. C. Hurst & Company, London

*Deltares Withdraws from GERD Studies* (2015) https://www.deltares.nl/en/news/deltares-withdraws-from-gerd-studies. Accessed 15 Jan 2018

'Egypt denies demanding Sudan exclusion from talks with Ethiopia over dam project (ST)' Statenaw News (2018) http://www.satenaw.com/egypt-denies-demanding-sudan-exclusion-talks-ethiopia-dam-project/. Accessed 15 Jan 2018

*'Egypt proposes to exclude Sudan from dam talks' Fortune News* (2017) https://addisfortune.net/articles/egypt-proposes-to-exclude-sudan-from-dam-talks/. Accessed 15 Jan 2018

'Egypt wants 'Sudan out' of contentious dam talks' Aljazeerah News (2018) http://www.aljazeera.com/news/2018/01/egypt-sudan-contentious-dam-talks-180102123313038.html. Accessed 15 Jan 2018

Egyptian Minister's statement (2017) http://www.egypttoday.com/Article/2/32422/17th-round-of-GERD-tripartite-talks-hits-wall-in-Cairo. Accessed 15 Jan 2018

Exchange of Notes between Great Britain and Northern Ireland and Egypt in Regard to the Use of the Waters of the River Nile for Irrigation Purposes (1929) https://www.internationalwaterlaw.org/documents/regionaldocs/Egypt_UK_Nile_Agreement-1929.html. Accessed 15 Jan 2018
Gaitskill A (1959) Gezira: a story of development in the Sudan. Faber and Faber, London
Garstin W (1904) Report upon the basin of the Upper Nile, with proposals for the improvement of the river. Harrison & Sons Ltd., London
'GERD increases installed generation capacity to 6,450MW' Fana News (2017) http://www.fanabc.com/english/index.php/news/item/8243-gred%E2%80%99s-installed-generation-capacity-increased-by-additional-450mw. Accessed 25 Dec 2017
Gibb A (1953) A study of the Managil extension of the Gezira scheme. Alexander Gibb, London
Howell P, Lock M, Cobb S (1988) The Jonglei canal – impact and opportunity. Cambridge University Press, Cambridge
Ibrahim A (2012) The Nile Basin Cooperative Framework Agreement: the beginning of the end of Egyptian hydro-political hegemony. Mo Environ Law Policy Rev 18:283
International Panel of Experts, Grand Ethiopian Renaissance Dam, Final Report, Addis Ababa, Ethiopia, 31 May 2013. https://www.internationalrivers.org/sites/default/files/attached-files/international_panel_of_experts_for_ethiopian_renaissance_dam-_final_report_1.pdf. Accessed 15 Jan 2015
Krishna R (1988) The legal regime of the Nile River basin. In: Starr J, Stoll D (eds) The politics of scarcity, water in the Middle East. Routledge, London
Mahgoub F (2014) Current status of agriculture and future challenges in Sudan. Current African Studies, No. 57. The Nordic Africa Institute
Massachusetts Institute of Technology (MIT) (2014) The Grand Ethiopian Renaissance Dam: an opportunity for collaboration and shared benefits in the Eastern Nile basin – an Amicus brief to the riparian nations of Ethiopia, Sudan and Egypt, from the Eastern Nile Working Group. https://jwafs.mit.edu/sites/default/files/documents/GERD_2014_Executive_Summary.pdf
Mekonnen Y (1984) The Nyerere doctrine of state succession and the new states of East Africa
Mekonnen DZ (2010) The Nile Basin Cooperative Framework Agreement negotiations and the adoption of a 'water security' paradigm: flight into obscurity or a logical cul-de-sac? Eur J Int Law 21:421
Meseret E (2018) Ethiopia refuses World Bank arbitration over Nile River dam. Associated Press: http://www.foxnews.com/world/2018/01/21/ethiopia-refuses-world-bank-arbitration-over-nile-river-dam.html
Nelson SS (2012) Mubarak's dream remains just that in Egypt's desert. https://www.npr.org/2012/07/10/155027725/mubaraks-dream-remains-just-that-in-egypts-desert. Accessed 20 Nov 2017
Nile Basin Cooperative Framework Agreement 2010 (CFA). http://www.nilebasin.org/images/docs/CFA%20-%20English%20%20FrenchVersion.pdf. Accessed 1 Jan 2018
Nile Basin Initiative. http://www.nilebasin.org/newsite/. Accessed 15 Jan 2018
Press Release of the 10th Tripartite National Committee – *TNC Meeting on the Grand Ethiopian Renaissance Dam (GERD)* (2016). On file with author
Salman SMA (2008) Water resources in the Sudan north-south peace process – past experience and future trends. Afr Yearb Int Law 16:299
Salman SMA (2009) The World Bank policy for projects on international waterways – an historical and legal analysis. Martinus Nijhoff, The Hague
Salman SMA (2010a) Downstream riparians can also harm upstream riparians: the concept of foreclosure of future uses. Water Int 35:1
Salman SMA (2010b) The World Bank and the Gezira scheme in the Sudan - political economy of irrigation reforms. The World Bank. http://www.salmanmasalman.org/wp-content/uploads/2014/06/GeziraSchemeReportSalman2June2010.pdf. Accessed Sept 2017
Salman SMA (2013) The Nile Basin Cooperative Framework Agreement – a peacefully unfolding African spring? Water Int 38:17

Salman SMA (2014) Water resources in the Sudan north south peace process and the ramifications of the secession of South Sudan. In: Weinthal E, Troell J, Nakayama M (eds) Water and post-conflict peace building. Environmental Law Institute, Washington DC

Salman SMA (2015) Entry into force of the UN Watercourses Convention – why should it matter? Int J Water Resour Dev 31(1)

Salman SMA (2016a) The Grand Ethiopian Renaissance Dam: the road to the declaration of principles and the Khartoum document. Water Int 41:512

Salman SMA (2016b) The declaration of principles on the Grand Ethiopian Renaissance Dam: an analytical overview. Ethiopian Yearbook of International Law

Salman SMA (2017a) Sudan and the Nile waters. Sudan Research Center, Fairfax. (Arabic)

Salman SMA (2017b) The Nile Basin Cooperative Framework Agreement – disentangling the Gordian knot. In: Yihdego Z, Rieu-Clarke A, Cascao AE (eds) The Grand Ethiopian Renaissance Dam and the Nile Basin: implications for transboundary water cooperation. Earthscan, London

Salman SMA (2017c) Agreement on declaration of principles on the Grand Ethiopian Renaissance Dam: levelling the Nile Basin playing field. In: Yihdego Z, Rieu-Clarke A, Cascao AE (eds) The Grand Ethiopian Renaissance Dam and the Nile Basin: implications for transboundary water cooperation. Earthscan, London

Salman SMA (2017d) The Grand Ethiopian Renaissance Dam and the Riddle of the Sudanese Water Loan to Egypt. https://www.alrakoba.net/news-action-show-id-292389.htm. Accessed 10 Jan 2018

Sudanese Minister's statement (2017a) http://news.xinhuanet.com/english/2017-11/20/c_136764448.htm. Accessed 15 Jan 2018

Sudanese Minister's statement (2017b) Arabic version. https://www.alrakoba.net/news-action-show-id-292485.htm. Accessed 15 Jan 2018

Treaty between Ethiopia and the United Kingdom relative to the frontiers between the Anglo-Egyptian Sudan, Ethiopia, and Eritrea (1902) http://treaties.fco.gov.uk/docs/pdf/1902/TS0016.pdf. Accessed 15 Dec 2017

Tvedt T (2004) The River Nile in the age of the British: political ecology and the quest for economic power. IB Tauris, London

United Nations Development Programme (2013) Water governance in the Arab region – managing scarcity and securing the future. UNDP, Regional Bureau for the Arab States. http://www.undp.org/content/dam/rbas/doc/Energy%20and%20Environment/Arab_Water_Gov_Report/Arab_Water_Gov_Report_Full_Final_Nov_27.pdf. Accessed 25 Oct 2017

Waterbury J (2000) The Nile Basin—national determinants and collective action. Yale University Press

Wheeler K (2017) Managing risks while filling the Grand Ethiopian Renaissance Dam. In: Yihdego Z, Rieu-Clarke A, Cascao AE (eds) The Grand Ethiopian Renaissance Dam and the Nile Basin: implications for transboundary water cooperation. Earthscan, London

Wouters P, Vinogradov S, Magsig B (2009) Water security, hydrosolidarity, and international law: a river runs through it. Yearb Int Environ Law

Yihdego Z (2017) The fairness "dilemma" in sharing the Nile waters: what lessons from the Grand Ethiopian Renaissance Dam? Int Water Law 2

**Salman M. A. Salman** is Fellow with the International Water Resources Association (IWRA); and Editor-in-Chief of International Water Law Journal published by Brill. Until 2009 Dr. Salman was the World Bank advisor on water law. www.salmanmasalman.org.

# The Challenge of Overlapping Regional Economic Communities in Africa: Lessons for the Continental Free Trade Area from the Failures of the Tripartite Free Trade Area

**Melaku Geboye Desta and Guillaume Gérout**

**Abstract** The Tripartite Free Trade Area (TFTA) was launched with several objectives, an important one being to address the challenge of too many regional economic communities (RECs) with too many overlapping memberships in the eastern half of the continent. This article attempts to describe the genesis of the problem in the continent since the Abuja Treaty of 1991, articulates how the inability to address the relationship between the TFTA and its preexisting RECs derailed the TFTA project, and makes detailed recommendations on how to avoid the same mistakes in the CFTA negotiations. The key message of this article is very simple: TFTA's fate was sealed when the negotiators abandoned the original objective of forming a customs union by merging the constituent RECs into one. To succeed, the Continental Free Trade Area (CFTA) will need to avoid that mistake, aim to become a continental customs union and eventually a common market, and ensure the progressive merger of all RECs into one through a detailed program of integration over a realistic implementation period.

---

M. G. Desta (✉)
Leicester De Montfort School of Law, Faculty of Business and Law, De Montfort University, Leicester, UK

United Nations Economic Commission for Africa, Addis Ababa, Ethiopia
e-mail: melaku.desta@dmu.ac.uk

G. Gérout
African Trade Policy Centre, United Nations Economic Commission for Africa, Addis Ababa, Ethiopia

## 1 Introduction

The desire to build a strong, diversified and meaningfully united African economic space has been formally recognized at least since the creation of the Organization of African Unity (OAU) in 1963.[1] Several significant steps have been taken to translate this ambition into reality, one of the most recent being the launch of the Tripartite Free Trade Area (TFTA) at Sharm El Sheikh, Egypt, on June 10, 2015, by the heads of state and government of 26 countries that are members of three partly overlapping regional economic communities in Eastern and Southern Africa—the Common Market for Eastern and Southern Africa (COMESA), the East African Community (EAC), and the Southern African Development Community (SADC). The 26 countries represent just over 47% of the African Union (AU) membership and about half of the continental GDP and population.[2] An even more interesting aspect of the TFTA Agreement that is rarely mentioned is its Article 41, which provides for accession not only by the Member States of COMESA, EAC, and SADC but also by "other member states of the African Union," thus potentially making it a continental instrument.[3] News of the launch was greeted with varying degrees of enthusiasm and expectation.[4]

The TFTA idea was born out of the need to rationalize and speed up the African economic integration process by, among others, "resolv[ing] the challenges of overlapping memberships of the Tripartite Member/Partner States to the three Regional Economic Communities"[5] and the preference to do so through the establishment of "a single Customs Union beginning with a Free Trade Area."[6] The Tripartite initiative—of which the TFTA is only the first step in the effort to speed up the integration of the three RECs "into a larger integrated market"[7]—is thus a collective response to the challenge of overlapping membership that has bedevilled the African

---

[1] For a detailed discussion of the evolution of the concept and policy of creating an integrated African economic space, see AUC (2009).

[2] See Luke and Mabuza (2015).

[3] Art. 41 of the Agreement Establishing a Tripartite Free Trade Area Among the Common Market for Eastern and Southern Africa, the East African Community and the Southern African Development Community (hereafter referred to as the TFTA Agreement), 10 June 2015, Sharm el Sheikh, provides: "1. This Agreement shall remain open for accession by any Member/Partner State of COMESA, EAC or SADC. 2. The Agreement shall also remain open for accession to other member states of the African Union. 3. The Tripartite Council of Ministers shall adopt accession regulations." See COMESA-EAC-SADC (2015).

[4] To mention just a few examples, for Disparte and Bugnacki, this was the "crucial inflection point" for the continental integration process (see Disparte and Bugnacki (2015) while for Luke and Mabuza this was "a milestone for Africa's regional integration process." (See Luke and Mabuza (2015).

[5] See para. 9 of the preamble of the TFTA Agreement.

[6] See para. 3 of the preamble of the TFTA Agreement.

[7] See para. 3 of the preamble Declaration Launching the Negotiations of the Establishment of the Tripartite Free Trade, 12 June 2011, Johannesburg.

integration agenda since its early days.[8] Overlapping REC membership—or membership of a single country in several RECs at the same time—causes several problems, the most obvious being the extra difficulties to meet national contributions and obligations to the various regional economic communities, low implementation of integration programs, poor level of participation in decision-making forums, and "duplicated or conflicting programme implementation."[9] It is thus hardly surprising that, even at continental level, overcoming "the challenges of multiple and overlapping memberships" was identified as one of the five major objectives of the Continental Free Trade Area (CFTA) project.

This article is an attempt to assess the potential of the TFTA to overcome this hurdle for the eastern half of the continent. To this end, the article (1) briefly recounts the story of African integration starting from the onset of decolonization and the establishment of the OAU all the way to today's efforts to establish the CFTA; (2) describes and analyzes the challenge of overlapping membership broadly, as well as within the particular regional context of what has now come to be known as the TFTA; (3) examines the text of the TFTA Agreement and its potential implications for its constituent RECs, as well as for the CFTA; and (4) draws conclusions, provides perspectives on the way forward, identifies the major lessons that the CFTA negotiators may learn from the TFTA experience.

## 2  The African Regional Integration Agenda in Brief

African leaders have long dreamt about creating a continent that is integrated politically and economically, a dream that served as a motto during the struggle against colonial rule and as an organizing principle since independence. Soon after the first sub-Saharan African country, Ghana, gained its independence in 1957, leaders of then independent African countries initiated a process that led to the signing of the Charter of the Organization of African Unity (OAU) in 1963 and its establishment in 1964.[10] The OAU Charter was as much the formal manifestation of that dream as the beginning of a long process toward its realization.

A key mission of the OAU was, of course, political—to bring the independence of the continent to completion guided by the principle of "absolute dedication to the total emancipation of the African territories which are still dependent."[11] But the

---

[8] As the High-Level Panel observed, the RECs, "which are expected to serve as building blocks in the integration process, have been constrained by several factors, particularly the overlapping memberships, the insufficient inter-RECs co-operation and lack of coordination and harmonisation at the continental level." See High-Level Panel, *Audit of the African Union* (report submitted to the AU Assembly, 18 December 2007). Available at http://www.aprmtoolkit.saiia.org.za/component/docman/doc_view/277-atkt-au-audit-report-2007-en, p. xv, para. 16.

[9] See UNECA (2006), p. xvii, (hereafter ARIA II).

[10] See Charter of African Unity, 25 May 1963a, Addis Ababa (hereafter referred to as the OAU Charter).

[11] See Art. III:6 of the OAU Charter.

OAU founders went further and agreed to "coordinate and harmonize their general policies" in the fields of politics, economics, diplomacy, culture, as well as defense and security.[12] Indeed, one item on the agenda of the OAU inaugural summit on May 25, 1963, was entitled "Areas of Co-Operation in Economic Problems," under which the summit resolved to appoint a preparatory economic committee to study such questions as "(a) the possibility of establishing a free trade area between the various African countries; (b) the establishment of a common external tariff to protect the emergent industries and the setting up of a raw material price stabilization fund; [and] (c) the restructuralization of international trade."[13] It is thus evident that the seeds of the African economic integration project were planted from the day the OAU was launched in 1963. The ambition to create free trade areas and customs unions, the latter implicit in the ambition to establish a common external tariff, "between the various African countries" was explicitly tied to the industrialization imperative on the one hand and the challenges posed to public finances due to fluctuating commodity prices and therefore foreign currency revenues on the other. It is not accidental that these same imperatives still sit at the top of African economic policy discourse to this day.

The period since 1963 has been one of constant, at times frustrating, efforts to further these objectives in every front.[14] Among the notable steps taken are

1. the 1976 Kinshasa Declaration to promote regional economic and technical cooperation (which expressed the ambition to establish the African Common Market and the African Economic Community (AEC) within a period of 15 to 20 years);
2. the 1979 Monrovia Declaration, where members declared their commitment "to promote the economic integration of the African region in order to facilitate and reinforce social and economic intercourse" and "pave the way for the eventual establishment of an African common market leading to an African Economic Community";
3. the 1980 Lagos Plan of Action (LPA), which aimed to create an African Common Market through a progressive elimination of trade barriers among all African countries by, first, establishing subregional preferential trade areas, FTAs, and customs unions and, second, the reduction and eventual elimination of barriers to trade among the subregional entities[15];

---

[12] See Art. II:2 of the OAU Charter. Then Nigerian Minister of Justice and a participant in the negotiations for the OAU charter recalled in 1965 that a proposal by Ghana and a couple of other countries for the establishment of a political union of Africa was "firmly rejected" by the conference. See Elias (1965), p. 245.

[13] See OAU Secretariat, Resolutions Adopted by the First Conference of Independent African Heads of State and Government (Addis Ababa, Ethiopia, 22–25 May 1963b, CIAS/PLEN.2/REV.2).

[14] For a list of important decisions taken by the OAU between the 1960s and the 1980s, see *Abuja Treaty*, Preamble.

[15] The ambition of the Lagos Plan of Action (LPA) was such that it aimed to exempt trade in "all food products originating from member countries ... from the application of regulatory

4. the Final Act of Lagos annexed to the LPA, which reaffirmed the commitment to set up the African Economic Community by the year 2000;
5. the 1991 Abuja Treaty Establishing the AEC, which translated the long-held dream into binding legal obligations on African countries in their role as parties to the treaty, as well as to subregional economic integration organizations[16];
6. the 2000 Constitutive Act of the AU, which was designed to, *inter alia*, accelerate the implementation of the Abuja Treaty[17];
7. the 2007 Accra Declaration on the Union Government of Africa, where the AU Assembly agreed "to accelerate the economic and political integration of the African Continent, including the formation of a Union Government for Africa with the ultimate objective of creating the United States of Africa"[18];
8. the January 2012 AU Assembly Decision to fast-track the establishment of a CFTA[19];
9. Agenda 2063, often described as the continent's "collective vision and roadmap for the next fifty years," committed to "speed-up actions to fast-track the establishment of the Continental Free Trade Area by 2017"[20]; and
10. the June 2015 AU Assembly Decision on the Launch of Continental Free Trade Area Negotiations.[21]

Of these, the Abuja Treaty has been the keystone of the African economic integration process, to which we now turn.

## 2.1 The Abuja Treaty

Formally known as the *Treaty Establishing the African Economic Community*, the Abuja Treaty is the single most important legal instrument on African economic integration. The Treaty adopted a "trade-led mainstream economic integration

---

non-tariff barriers except health requirements, *effective from January 1982.*" See Chapter VII of OAU (1980).

[16] See OAU (1991).

[17] It is notable that talk of accelerating implementation of the AEC project started already before the actual adoption of the Abuja Treaty text on 3 June 1991. For example, when the so-called Kampala Document was adopted on 22 May 1991 launching the *Conference on Security, Stability, Development and Cooperation in Africa* (CSSDCA), the cooperation calabash observed that economic integration "should be intensified and a shortened timetable for the African Economic Community should be agreed upon." See Kampala Document (1991) available at https://slideblast.com/oau-african-union-summit_595a55381723dde9bcd9d736.html.

[18] See Accra Declaration on the Union Government of Africa Accra, Ghana, 3 July 2007, available at: http://www.dirco.gov.za/docs/2007/ghan_decl0706.htm.

[19] See AU (2012b) Decision on Boosting Intra-African Trade and Fast-tracking of the CFTA, Assembly/AU/Dec.394(XVIII), 29–30 January 2012.

[20] See AU, Agenda 2063: the Africa We Want (Popular Version, 2015a), para. 72(h), p. 17.

[21] See AU (2015b) Decision on the Launching of the Negotiations of the Establishment of the Continental Free Trade Area, Assembly/AU/Dec.569(XXV), 15 June 2015.

model"[22] but also recognized the particular challenges of establishing a common market for a continent of more than 50 predominantly small economies.[23] To overcome this, members decided early on to use regional economic communities (RECs) as the building blocks of the AEC,[24] which required strengthening existing RECs, establishing new ones where they did not exist in a region, and/or consolidating them where there were more than one in a region. In all cases, the policies of all RECs would need to be harmonized and brought to a point of convergence progressively.

On that basis, the Treaty laid out a detailed 34-year plan[25] by which the RECs would gradually evolve into a continental common market through six successive stages:

1. strengthening of existing RECs and establishing new ones in regions where they do not exist (5 years);
2. stabilization of tariffs and other trade barriers within RECs and coordination and harmonization of activities among existing and future communities (8 years);
3. establishment of free trade areas and customs unions at the level of each REC (10 years);
4. establishment of the continent-wide customs union with a common external trade regime (2 years);
5. establishment of an African Common Market (ACM) with common monetary, financial, and fiscal policies; free movement of people within the continent, including rights of establishment; and common policies in such areas as agriculture, transport and communications, industry, energy and scientific research (4 years); and

---

[22] See UNECA (2006).

[23] For a useful summary of the varying sizes of African economies, see Hartzenberg (2011) Regional Integration in Africa Trade, WTO Staff Working Paper ERSD-2011-14 (October 2011), available at https://www.wto.org/english/res_e/reser_e/ersd201114_e.pdf, p. 3.

[24] However, the Treaty does not even name these regional organizations; it simply assumed that the RECs would be a different version of the five official sub-divisions of the continent determined by the OAU in 1976—Central Africa, East Africa, North Africa, Southern Africa and West Africa. A 1976 OAU Council of Ministers meeting declared that "there shall be FIVE regions of the OAU, namely, Northern, Western, Central, Eastern and Southern." See Resolution CM/Res. 464(XXVI) of the 27th Ordinary Session of OAU Council of Ministers (1976), paragraph 2(a), quoted in draft report of the Ministerial Meeting on Rationalization of RECs, Ouagadougou, Burkina Faso, 27–31 March 2006, available at https://au.int/web/sites/default/files/decisions/9591-council_en_23_february_1_march_1976_council_ministers_twenty_sixth_ordinary_session.pdf.

[25] Note however that the Fourth Extraordinary Session of the Assembly of Heads of State and Government of 8–9 September 1999 at Sirte, Libya, has decided to "shorten the implementation periods of the Abuja Treaty" but no decision has yet been taken on the specifics. See OAU (1999) Sirte Declaration, oc. EAHG/Draft/Decl. (IV) Rev.1, available at https://issafrica.s3.amazonaws.com/site/uploads/SUMDECLUNREF.PDF.

6. consolidation and strengthening of the structure of the ACM through the free movement of people, goods, capital, and services and institution building (5 years).[26]

Although it has been ratified by nearly all African countries[27] and entered into effect in 1994, member countries have not always conducted themselves in accordance with the terms of the Abuja Treaty. Incidentally, if the Abuja program had been implemented in full, 2017 would have seen the completion of its third stage; i.e., free trade areas and customs unions would have been established at the level of each REC. This, however, is far from reality; only the EAC and Economic Community of West African States (ECOWAS) can claim to have a functioning customs union on the continent today.[28]

The factors that may explain this gap between commitment and implementation are likely to be many, but this article seeks to closely examine only one of them—the role of the flaw in the original design of the AEC as a structure that stands on five RECs as its supporting pillars, or building blocks as they are often described. When members established the AEC, they left the actual task of establishing these building blocks, the RECs, for the future. In reality, however, the number and shape of these RECs became such that "rationalisation and reconfiguration of the RECs ... proved much slower and more complicated than may have been anticipated."[29] Perhaps the most authoritative articulation of this challenge came from the UNECA in 2006, when it observed that countries failed to take seriously their otherwise binding legal commitments under the Abuja Treaty:

> In the 15 years since the Abuja Treaty was signed African countries have introduced numerous initiatives in regional integration without coordinating them at the continental level. Integration outcomes clearly show that the continental blueprints for integration have served only as loose frameworks — not as rule-based points of reference — for the regional integration agenda. Coordinating mechanisms with a legal basis — essential in enforcing standards and commitments to integration at all levels — are lacking. And this has led to overlapping memberships and ineffective coordination and harmonization of programmes among the regional economic communities.[30]

This is a finding of fundamental importance about the meaning and effect of the legal obligations contained in the Abuja Treaty. When the authors said "coordinating

---

[26] Adapted from Article 6 of the AEC Treaty. A substantial part of the Treaty is devoted to an elaboration of the expectations and obligations of the parties at each of these six stages and the modalities for the final realization of the AEC. See in particular, Articles 28–66 of the Treaty.

[27] Forty-nine of the 55 AU Member States are parties to the Abuja Treaty—the remaining six being Djibouti, Eritrea, Madagascar, Morocco, Somalia, and South Sudan. See list of countries that have signed, ratified/acceded to the Abuja Treaty, available at https://au.int/sites/default/files/treaties/7775-sl-treaty_establishing_the_african_economic_community_1.pdf, consulted on 3 September 2017, updated 15 June 2017.

[28] See UNECA (2017), p. 20 (noting further that COMESA, SADC, and ECCAS have only an FTAs).

[29] See High-Level Panel (2007), p. 12, para. 30.

[30] See ARIA II (2006), p. 91.

mechanisms with a legal basis ... are lacking," they were not suggesting that the Abuja Treaty is not a "law"; they meant that the "law" in the treaty books would amount to little unless it is implemented as a binding instrument—either wilfully obeyed by its subjects (the states parties in our case) or enforced through some institutional mechanisms such as a court.[31] Many African countries did not live up to the letter and spirit of their legal commitments under the Abuja Treaty. Perhaps the most critical verdict of this propensity to ignore otherwise binding decisions came from Rwandan President Paul Kagame when he recently concluded, among others, that "the chronic failure to see through African Union decisions has resulted in a crisis of implementation."[32] The President further observed:

> The Assembly has adopted more than 1,500 resolutions. Yet there is no easy way to determine how many of those have actually been implemented. By consistently failing to follow up on the implementation of the decisions we have made, the signal has been sent that they don't matter. As a result, we have a dysfunctional organisation in which member states see limited value, global partners find little credibility, and our citizens have no trust.[33]

Membership of African countries in multiple RECs, i.e. one and the same country joining two or more RECs at the same time, thus emerged as a particularly problematic manifestation of this challenge to implement agreed commitments in the area of regional and continental economic integration.

## 3  The Challenge of Multiple Membership in RECs and Successive Attempts to Address It

As indicated earlier, the challenge posed by overlapping RECs to the continental project has its roots in the design of the AEC project. When the Abuja Treaty was signed in 1991, the OAU had 51 Member States of different sizes, shapes, strengths, and so on. What was clear at the time, and just as clear even today, is that the economy and market size in each country were simply too small and too weak to support independent development. From this perspective, therefore, the decision for these countries to form part of one unified body, the AEC, was the product of economic necessity rather than mere choice. The only issue left was about the mechanics of achieving it—what would be the most feasible strategy to bring about the desired level of closer integration among over 50 countries that were at different stages of development?

The strategy that won the day was for all the countries to first organize themselves into five regional clusters based essentially on physical proximity or neighborliness

---

[31] For interesting reflections on the meaning and role of international law, see Harold (1997).

[32] See Kagame (2017), p. 4 (hereafter Kagame Report).

[33] Kagame Report (2017), p. 5. For a more positive assessment, see Gathii (2010), p. 573 (arguing that African RTAs are in fact consciously designed as "flexible regimes of cooperation as opposed to containing rules requiring scrupulous and rigorous adherence").

in the form of RECs.³⁴ Once established, each REC would follow a continentally agreed route plan, with distinct milestones on the way, and ultimately merge into one continental economic entity in the form of the AEC. We can thus picture the AEC as a house that stands on five pillars or building blocks. For such a project to materialize, common sense would suggest that (1) the five building blocks each be of reasonable strength and stability; (2) each block be of comparable strength; (3) each block evolve in a synchronized fashion, move in the same direction and at broadly the same pace; and, finally, (4) each constituent country only belong to one block.

The Abuja Treaty has provided for all these requirements in some detail, but, in practice, almost each of the above elements was disregarded. Instead of building five strong and stable RECs, new ones continued to be created, including in regions where more than one REC already existed prior to the Abuja Treaty.³⁵ The AEC was not equipped to provide the necessary centralized and effective leadership from above, allowing different RECs to follow their own route maps in disregard of what others were doing and contrary to the detailed plans and milestones set out in the Abuja Treaty.

When individual countries became members of more than one, in some cases up to four, RECs at the same time, its impact was highly detrimental to the common project. A country that is a member of both COMESA and SADC, for example, would stifle the ability of each REC to move at a pace it may deem appropriate to its regional context while remaining within the broad agenda laid down in the Abuja Treaty; that country effectively conjoins the two RECs in a manner akin to the Siamese twins, with all the handicap associated with it.

The reality is not far from the above scenario. Countries pursued their individual interests in multiple groupings, leading to the creation of too many RECs,³⁶ with overlapping membership and duplicative mandates. Moreover, Member States implemented their obligations under the REC treaties to varying degrees, including on such core commitments as the pace of trade liberalization to achieve agreed milestones. As a result, by the time the TFTA idea emerged in 2008, all TFTA countries were involved in at least one AU-recognized REC, while most participated in

---

³⁴ The decision to divide the continent into five regions was taken by the OAU Council of Ministers at its Twenty-Sixth Ordinary Session in Addis Ababa, Ethiopia, from 23 February to 1 March 1976 (CM/Res. 464 (XXVI)), where it decided: "there shall be FIVE Regions of the OAU namely, Northern, Western, Central, Eastern and Southern."

³⁵ A good example may be the Western African Monetary Zone, a regional grouping involving six countries members of both CEN-SAD and ECOWAS—namely Gambia, Ghana, Guinea, Liberia, Nigeria and Sierra Leone—that was created in 2000 to establish a second monetary union within the ECOWAS region. It is expected that WAMZ would merge with WAEMU to form a single monetary union at some point in the future. See http://www.wami-imao.org. It is to be noted that the ECOWAS Treaty also provides for the establishment of a monetary union, under Art. 55 of the ECOWAS Treaty.

³⁶ Although the assumption of the Abuja Treaty in 1991 was the division of Africa into five regions, today Africa has as many as 14 RECs that officially aspire to evolve into FTAs, customs unions and so on. For an excellent analysis of the state of African RECs and the AEC project, see ARIA II (2006).

several RECs with different and inconsistent levels of commitments toward regional integration.

To measure regional integration, three pan-African institutions (AfDB, AUC, and UNECA) created an African regional integration index based on five dimensions of regional integration.[37] According to this index, the trade integration dimension obtains the highest score, which is understandable considering that this has been a "longstanding regional integration priority across the regions."[38] But the index also shows disparities between the RECs, with some of the lowest scorers on trade integration achieving high marks in other dimensions of the index. It is also notable that countries that belong to various RECs[39] also achieved uneven scores depending on the REC within which their performance was considered.

In summary, what comes out clearly is that poor design from the outset allowed Member States to frustrate the Abuja program of integration, while lack of adequate follow-up and coordination mechanisms meant that countries did so without suffering any meaningful consequences in economic, political, reputational, or other terms. Resolution of this design flaw thus became the sine qua non of success in the continental integration project. The initial OAU/AU approach was to keep that original design and make it work by, first, denying recognition to new RECs and, second, attempting to rationalize the RECs that it was prepared to recognize. These strategies no doubt helped to mitigate the gravity of the problem but did not resolve it completely. From this perspective, the decision to progressively merge the three RECs into the COMESA-EAC-SADC Tripartite was a welcome step toward resolving the issue of overlapping memberships, which appears to be a belated acknowledgment that the Abuja design was not taking us anywhere in practice. In the next section, we will consider the regional context within which the TFTA initiative was taken, starting with a brief introduction to the constituent RECs and their overlapping membership.

## 3.1 The Three RECs: COMESA, EAC, and SADC

**COMESA FTA** The Common Market for Eastern and Southern Africa (COMESA) is one of the major regional economic communities, made up of 19 Member States,[40] recognized as a building block for the African Economic Community (AEC) as per the Abuja Treaty. Established in COMESA (1994) as a successor to the Preferential Trade Area (PTA) for Eastern and Southern Africa, which had been in existence

---

[37] See AfDB, AUC and UNECA (2016), p. 7.
[38] See AfDB, AUC and UNECA (2016), p. 7.
[39] To give a few examples, Kenya belongs to four RECS (CEN-SAD, COMESA, EAC and IGAD).
[40] COMESA members are: Burundi, Comoros, DR Congo, Djibouti, Egypt, Eritrea, Ethiopia, Kenya, Libya, Madagascar, Malawi, Mauritius, Rwanda, Seychelles, Sudan, Swaziland, Uganda, Zambia and Zimbabwe.

since 1981, COMESA successfully established an FTA[41] on October 31, 2000, and launched its Customs Union in June 2009, "which is yet to be operational." COMESA also "envisages becoming a Common Market by 2017, and full Economic Community by 2025."[42]

The COMESA Treaty was first notified to the World Trade Organization (WTO) Committee on Trade and Development in May 1995 as a Treaty that "provides for the establishment of a customs union, including a common external tariff, within a transitional period of ten years and for free movement of persons and the right of establishment of business by nationals of COMESA in any member States."[43] This notification does not make reference to the legal basis for its existence, but the fact that it was submitted to the WTO Committee on Trade and Development, rather than the Committee on Regional Trade Agreements (RTAs), appears to indicate that COMESA probably, and rightly, sought to be justified under the Enabling Clause.[44] This position is confirmed by Egypt's most recent notification of the COMESA Treaty in January 2017 to the same WTO Committee on Trade and Development, where it used Paragraph 4(a) of the Enabling Clause for the legal justification of an RTA at the WTO.[45] In terms of the depth of liberalization, Article 46(1) of the COMESA Treaty indicates that Member States of the COMESA FTA shall apply duty-free treatment to goods originating in other COMESA FTA Member States:

> Member States shall reduce and ultimately eliminate by the year 2000 [...] customs duties and other charges of equivalent effect imposed on or in connection with the importation of goods which are eligible for Common Market tariff treatment.[46]

As indicated earlier, while COMESA aims at creating a customs union among its 19 Member States, only 16 are participating in the COMESA FTA today. The difference in the membership of COMESA on the one hand and its FTA on the other indicates that different Member States implemented the COMESA trade agenda differently. COMESA regularly calls upon non-FTA members to join the FTA,[47] while it is also exploring options to better monitor and report on the state of implementation of its trade liberalization programs.[48]

---

[41] So far only 16 Member States are participating in the COMESA FTA, with Ethiopia, Eritrea and Swaziland not fully implementing the FTA.

[42] See COMESA Secretariat, Medium Term Strategic Plan 2016–2020: In pursuit of Regional Economic Transformation and Development, p. 7.

[43] See WTO (1995) Notification of the Common Market for Eastern and Southern Africa, WT/COMTD/N/3 (29 June 1995).

[44] See WTO (2017a), available at: http://rtais.wto.org/UI/PublicMaintainRTAHome.aspx.

[45] See WTO, WT/COMTD/N/51 (9 January 2017).

[46] Art. 46.1 of the COMESA Treaty.

[47] See COMESA (2016) Communique of the Nineteenth Summit of the COMESA Authority of Heads of State and Government. In: COMESA. Available in COMESA. http://www.comesa.int/wp-content/uploads/2016/10/Summit-Communique-19.10.16-2.pdf.

[48] See Gakunga (2016).

**EAC** The EAC is another AU-recognized regional economic community made up of six partner states.[49] Five of these, i.e. except South Sudan, are parties to a fully-fledged customs union, with the latter expected to become a full member by 2019. The Republic of South Sudan joined the EAC on April 15, 2016, as its sixth member with a three-year transition period to become a full member of the customs union.[50]

Like COMESA, the EAC Treaty was notified to the WTO Committee on Trade and Development under the Enabling Clause in 2000.[51] Unlike the notification of COMESA, however, members of the EAC explicitly referred to the Enabling Clause as the legal basis on which they concluded the Treaty, whose objectives included as follows:

> to develop policies and programmes aimed at widening and deepening co-operation among the Partner States in political, economic, social and cultural fields, research and technology, defence, security and legal and judicial affairs, for their mutual benefit. In pursuance of those objectives, the Parties have agreed to establish among themselves a Customs Union, a Common Market, subsequently a Monetary Union and ultimately a Political Federation in order to strengthen and regulate the industrial, commercial, infrastructural, cultural, social, political and other relations of the Partner States. To that end, there shall be accelerated, harmonious and balanced development and sustained expansion of economic activities, the benefit of which shall be equitably shared.[52]

All five full members of the EAC (i.e., except South Sudan) are also members of the customs union and the common market, thereby obviating the need for a distinction between the REC, the EAC in this case, on the one hand and its FTA or customs union on the other. No tariffs apply to intra-EAC trade among the five members, making the EAC the most advanced REC in the continent in terms of the depth of trade liberalization.[53]

**SADC FTA** SADC is yet another AU-recognized REC that was established by the Treaty of 1992, signed in Windhoek, Namibia, with a number of objectives that could be described as the achievement of regional integration and poverty alleviation within the Southern African region encompassing 15 Member States.[54] To achieve these goals, SADC Member States have entered into a number of legally binding agreements, known as protocols, in several areas, including trade in goods and services, movement of persons, finance and investment, energy and natural

---

[49] These are Burundi, Kenya, South Sudan, Rwanda, Tanzania and Uganda.

[50] Under its terms of accession, South Sudan will be a full member of the EAC customs union in 2019. See EAC Secretariat, EAC Permanent/Principal Secretaries and Officials from the Republic of South Sudan discuss integration of the new Partner State into EAC (25 October 2016), available at http://www.eac.int/news-and-media/press-releases/20161025/eac-permanentprincipal-secretaries-and-officials-republic-south-sudan-discuss-integration-new.

[51] See WTO (2000) Notification of the East African Customs Union, WT/COMTD/N/14 (11 October 2000).

[52] See WTO (2000).

[53] See AfDB, AUC and UNECA (2016), p. 16.

[54] They are Angola, Botswana, Democratic Republic of Congo (DRC), Lesotho, Madagascar, Malawi, Mauritius, Mozambique, Namibia, Seychelles, South Africa, Swaziland, Tanzania, Zambia and Zimbabwe.

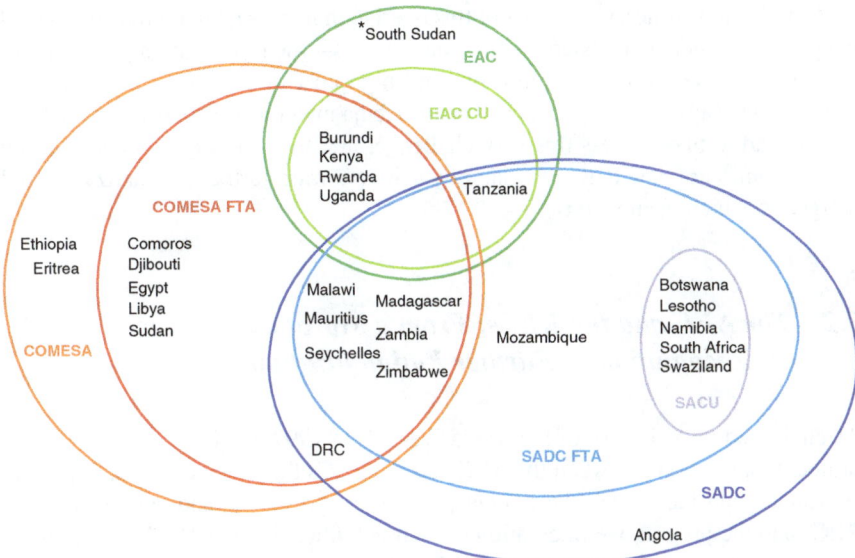

**Fig. 1** Overlapping membership of the three RECs forming part of the TFTA. * *South Sudan is not a TFTA Member/Partner State, though eligible for accession*

resources, etc. The Protocol on Trade, which governs the SADC FTA, is implemented by all Member States[55] except Angola and DRC. In other words, like in COMESA, there is a need to distinguish between SADC and its FTA as the latter does not enjoy the full membership of the former. The SADC FTA has eliminated tariffs on more than 93% of all tariff lines including South Africa and on more than 98% of tariff lines excluding South Africa.[56]

Unlike COMESA and the EAC, SADC was notified to the WTO under the provisions of GATT Article XXIV in August 2004.[57] The notification described the aim of the SADC Protocol on Trade and the Amending Protocol as "establishing a free trade area within the meaning of Article XXIV of the GATT 1994, in accordance with a plan and schedule which considers the differences in development, trade and financial status of the signatories."[58]

In summary, while these three RECs are at different stages of advancement on the path of integration, what is also clear is that their membership compositions overlap significantly, which is represented well in Fig. 1.

---

[55] The members of SADC are: Angola, Botswana, Democratic Republic of Congo (DRC), Lesotho, Madagascar, Malawi, Mauritius, Mozambique, Namibia, Seychelles, South Africa, Swaziland, Tanzania, Zambia and Zimbabwe.

[56] See WTO (2017b).

[57] See WTO (2004) Notification of the Protocol on Trade in the Southern African Development Community, WT/REG176/N/1 (9 August 2004). To note that all RTA that South Africa is party to are notified under Art. XXIV GATT.

[58] See WTO (2004).

As indicated earlier, the impact of this overlap in membership on the continental integration agenda manifested itself in many forms—the proliferation of incompatible obligations, regulatory confusion, and high cost of participation being only some of the examples. In order to rescue the Abuja integration agenda, the OAU and the AU had to first address this very challenge, first by imposing a moratorium on the recognition of new RECs and later by a drive toward further rationalization and merger, to which we now turn.

### 3.2 The AEC and the RECs: From a Moratorium on Recognition to Further Rationalization

As envisaged in Article 88 of the Abuja Treaty,[59] in 1997, the OAU came up with a protocol on relations between the AEC and the RECs that was designed, in part, to coordinate and harmonize the policies, measures, programs, and activities of the RECs and the progressive integration of their activities into the ACM "as a prelude to the African Economic Community."[60] The Inter-Governmental Authority on Development (IGAD), COMESA, ECOWAS, and SADC signed the Protocol in 1998, along with the OAU. However, this did not stop countries in these regions from creating new RECs or from adopting diverging policy directions.

The first concrete and meaningful step to stem the proliferation of RECs was taken in 2006, when the Conference of African Ministers of Economic Integration (CAMEI) requested the AU Assembly "to halt the recognition of new RECs" and limit this status to the eight RECs that had already been recognized by then: the Arab Maghreb Union (AMU), the Community of Sahel-Saharan States (CEN-SAD), COMESA, EAC, the Economic Community of Central African States (ECCAS), ECOWAS, IGAD, and SADC.[61]

---

[59] Article 88 provides as follows: "Relations between the Community and Regional Economic Communities. 1. The Community shall be established mainly through the co-ordination, harmonisation and progressive integration of the activities of regional economic communities. 2. Member States undertake to promote the co-ordination and harmonisation of the integration activities of regional economic communities of which they are members with the activities of the Community, it being understood that the establishment of the latter is the final objective towards which the activities of existing and future regional economic communities shall be geared. 3. To this end, the Community shall be entrusted with the co-ordination, harmonisation and evaluation of the activities of existing and future regional economic communities. 4. Member States undertake, through their respective regional economic communities, to coordinate and harmonize the activities of their sub-regional organisations, with a view to rationalising the integration process at the level of each region."

[60] See the Protocol adopted by the Thirty-Third Ordinary Session, OAU (1997) Decision on the African Economic Community.

[61] See COMAI (2006) Declaration of the First Conference of African Ministers of Integration (COMAI), adopted on 30–31 March 2006, Ouagadougou, Burkina Faso COMAI/Decl.(I). available at http://www.africa-union.org/Economic%20Affairs/RECS%20Rationalization/AU%20site5/Reports/Ouagadougou%20DECLARATION%2031%20March%202006.pdf.

The Assembly accepted the request at its seventh ordinary session in July 2006 in Banjul,[62] where it also reiterated that these recognized RECs must "coordinate and harmonize their policies among themselves and with the Commission with a view to accelerating Africa's integration process."[63] As a follow-up, a revised protocol on the relations between the AU and the RECs was signed in February 2008.[64] However, the Assembly once again avoided the hard decision to streamline the RECs along the five regions, limiting itself to an exhortation that the parties to the Protocol "coordinate their policies, measures, programs and activities *with a view to avoiding duplication thereof.*"[65] Furthermore, the revised Protocol called upon the RECs to review their treaties to ensure that they created an "organic link" with the AU with particular emphasis on (1) strengthening their relations with the AU, (2) aligning their programs, policies and strategies with those of the AU, (3) ensuring the implementation of the Protocol on the relations between the AU and RECs, and (4) providing for the "eventual absorption" of the REC into the AEC when reaching step 5 of the modalities laid down under Article 6 of the Abuja Treaty.[66]

However, and despite their commitments under the revised Protocol, the RECs largely stuck to their own established paths and responded differently to this call for alignment. Either the REC treaties did not make any explicit link with provisions of the revised Protocol on relations between the AU and RECs,[67] or, if they did, the commitments remained merely on paper without implementation.[68] It is thus clear that most RECs have not taken the steps necessary to align their objectives with the Abuja program of integration as reaffirmed by the 1998 Protocol and its 2006 revision. This does not mean that the integration efforts at the REC level were necessarily

---

[62] See AU (2006) Decision on the Moratorium on the Recognition of Regional Economic Communities (RECs).

[63] See paras. 3–4 of the Decision on the Moratorium on the Recognition of Regional Economic Communities (RECs).

[64] See AU decision adopted by the Ninth Ordinary Council of the Assembly of the African Union (1–3 July 2007, Accra, Ghana), Assembly/AU/Dec.166–167 (IX); Assembly/AU/Decl.1(IX), available at http://www.africa-union.org/root/AU/Conferences/2007/june/summit/doc/accra/Draft_Assembly_Decisions.pdf, hereafter referred to as the *Protocol on AU-RECs Relations* (2008).

[65] See Art. 4 of the AU Protocol on AU-RECs Relations (2008). AU (2008) Protocol on AU-RECs Relations.

[66] See Art. 5 of the Protocol on AU-RECs Relations.

[67] For example, Art. 24.1 of the SADC Treaty only refers to international instruments that may pursue the objectives of the SADC Treaty, which relegates the Abuja Treaty to a partner instrument to promote their own objectives: "Member States and SADC shall maintain good working relations and other forms of cooperation, and may enter into new agreements with other states, regional and international organisations, whose objectives are compatible with the objectives of SADC and the provision of this Treaty" (SADC 1992). In the case of the AMU Treaty, there is no reference either to the Abuja Treaty or the AU Constituent Act to this day.

[68] For example, Art. 7(i) of the IGAD Agreement provides that one of the aims and objectives of the IGAD shall be to "promote and realize the objectives of the COMESA and the African Economic Community" (See IGAD 1986). In practice, however, IGAD has not taken any decisive step to comply with the commitments under the Protocol on AU-RECs relations.

in vain; indeed, as we shall see further down, some RECs have succeeded in creating an increasingly integrated market over the years. The conclusion we are drawing here is limited to Abuja's broadly linear model of progression from a series of subregional free trade areas and customs unions all the way to a unified continental common market.[69] It is this path of integration program that was not adhered to by many RECs.

## 3.3 From Rationalization to Merger

An important question that arises at this stage is as to how individual African countries could maintain their membership in more than one REC and still achieve the required level of economic integration within the RECs while avoiding duplication. As indicated earlier, several approaches were proposed to achieve some degree of "rationalization," with the most radical one advocating for the merger and eventual absorption of all RECs (which were in existence when the Assembly took its 2006 Decision) into five—one each for Central, Eastern, Northern, Southern, and Western Africa. To illustrate with the help of a scenario for Eastern Africa, that would have meant the establishment of an East Africa Economic Community (EAEC), which would include

> Burundi, Comoros, Djibouti, Eritrea, Ethiopia, Kenya, Madagascar, Mauritius, Malawi, Rwanda, Seychelles, Somalia, Sudan, Tanzania, and Uganda. The secretariats of the Common Market for Eastern and Southern Africa (COMESA), the East African Community (EAC), and the Inter-Governmental Authority for Development (IGAD) would unite to form a new secretariat to serve this community.[70]

This approach would be in line with Article 88 of the Abuja Treaty and give Africa "the best hope of full integration,"[71] but it was also unlikely to happen over the short to medium term "because countries have political, historical, and other reasons" for belonging to the existing RECs.[72] As a result, the continental integration agenda was left clinging to the old strategy of policy harmonization and coordination among the RECs, an approach that had led nowhere for so long.[73] It was

---

[69] See Hartzenberg (2011).

[70] ARIA II (2006), pp. 116–117. It is notable that the expert meeting that preceded the First Conference of African Ministers of Economic Integration (CAMEI) observed, in 2006, that "although recognized as RECs, EAC, IGAD and CEN-SAD do not satisfy the criteria of 'region'...." See "First Conference of African Ministers of Economic Integration (CAMEI) Meeting of Experts 27–28 March 2006 Ouagadougou (Burkina Faso), CAMEI/Consol Report/(I), available at http://www.africa-union.org. Note that both CEN-SAD and EAC were created in 1999, i.e. after the protocol was signed in 1998.

[71] See ARIA II (2006), p. xxiv.

[72] See ARIA II (2006), p. 117.

[73] Note that harmonization and coordination of the activities of RECs have been at the centre of the Abuja Treaty from the beginning. To mention just one example, Article 28:2 provides: "Member States shall take all necessary measures aimed at progressively promoting increasingly

after all this that Africa signaled a significant turn away from the original blueprint of building the AEC on five RECs to the megaregional solution.

At a meeting held on October 22, 2008, in Kampala, Uganda, the heads of state and government of the eastern and southern half of the continent adopted the decision to merge COMESA, EAC, and SADC into one Tripartite REC.[74] The AU Summit that was held in January 2012 took these several steps further through two highly significant decisions. In the first one, the Assembly extended an invitation to the ECOWAS, ECCAS, CEN-SAD, and AMU "to draw inspiration from the tripartite arrangement ... and create a second pole of integration so as to speed up the establishment of the African Economic Community."[75] In the second decision taken at the same meeting, the Assembly agreed that

> the CFTA should be operationalized by the indicative date of 2017 ... with the following appropriate milestones:
>
> i) Finalization of the East African Community (EAC) – the Common Market for Eastern and Southern Africa (COMESA) – Southern African Development Community (SADC) Tripartite FTA initiative by 2014;
> ii) Completion of FTA(s) by Non-Tripartite RECs, through parallel arrangement(s) similar to the EAC-COMESA-SADC Tripartite Initiative or reflecting the preferences of their Member States, between 2012 and 2014;
> iii) Consolidation of the Tripartite and other regional FTAs into a Continental Free Trade Area (CFTA) initiative between 2015 and 2016;
> iv) Establishment of the Continental Free Trade Area (CFTA) by 2017 with the option to review the target date according to progress made.[76]

These same milestones were repeated, almost verbatim, in the *Declaration on Boosting Intra-African Trade and the Fast-Tracking of the Continental Free Trade Area (CFTA)*, which was adopted on the same date.[77] It was thus clear that the TFTA was not just a megaregional solution to the problem that faced the eastern half of the continent; it was also hoped to inspire the other half of the continent to do the same so as to lead to the establishment of the AEC on two legs. The above Decision also made it clear that the CFTA was to be launched only after the completion of the TFTA and its counterpart for the western half of the continent; indeed, the CFTA was to be a mere "consolidation" of these two halves rather than the creation of a new entity from scratch. Not surprisingly considering the level of ambition contained in

---

closer co-operation among the communities, particularly through co-ordination and harmonisation of their activities in all fields or sectors in order to ensure the realisation of the objectives of the Community."

[74] The 1st Tripartite Summit resolved "that the three RECs should immediately start working towards a merger into a single REC with the objective of fast-tracking the attainment of the African Economic Community." See the COMESA-SADC-EAC (2008) Final communiqué of the 1st Tripartite Summit, paragraph 13.

[75] See paragraph 7 of the AU (2012a) Decision on African integration, of the 18th Ordinary Session of the AU Summit, ref. Assembly/AU/Dec.392(XVIII).

[76] See AU (2012) Decision on Boosting Intra-African Trade and Fast Tracking the Continental Free Trade Area, Doc. EX.CL/700(XX), the 18th Ordinary Session of the AU Summit, ref. Assembly/AU/Dec.394(XVIII), para. 4.

[77] See Assembly/AU/Decl.1(XVIII).

the above Decision, its milestones were missed; the TFTA was launched in 2015 but not really completed until recently, while the western half of the continent took no concrete steps to emulate the tripartite example. At the same time, however, the ambition to establish the CFTA in 2017 is still alive and well; only its configuration had to be rethought.

## 4 The Tripartite Initiative and Its Unfulfilled Promise

As pointed out already, the TFTA—the first of three pillars of the Tripartite project—was launched on June 10, 2015, i.e. just 5 days before the launch of the CFTA negotiations on June 15, 2015.[78] With the CFTA negotiations set to conclude by the end of 2017, the continental economic integration project is still looking within reach, albeit in a roadmap different from that envisaged in the Abuja Treaty and in a configuration distinct from what the 2012 AU Assembly Decision contemplated. Neither the departure from the Abuja roadmap nor the modifications from the configuration envisaged in the 2012 Decision necessarily change the intended destination, which remains the full economic integration of the continent.[79] However, as will be demonstrated shortly, the potential of the TFTA to contribute to this goal has diminished significantly because of its reluctance to address the challenge of overlapping FTA membership in the eastern half of the continent.

The seeds of the TFTA were planted when the joint COMESA-SADC taskforce was enlarged in 2005 to allow for EAC participation.[80] The first Tripartite Summit that was held in Kampala, Uganda, on June 22, 2008, issued the *Kampala Communiqué*, in which it "approved the expeditious establishment of a Free Trade Area (FTA) encompassing the member/partner States of the 3 RECs with the ultimate goal of establishing a single Customs Union."[81] The Summit further noted that the TFTA was not an end in itself but "a crucial building bloc [*sic*] towards achieving the African Economic Community as outlined by the Treaty of Abuja."[82]

The recommendations of the Tripartite Taskforce included the establishment of a Tripartite FTA; steps to ease the movement of business persons in the TFTA region[83];

---

[78] See 25th Ordinary Summit Decision on the launch of the CFTA, ref. Assembly/AU/Dec.569(XXV).

[79] Indeed, in the words of a 2007 AU Assembly declaration, "the ultimate objective of the African Union is the United States of Africa with a Union Government as envisaged by the founding fathers of the Organization of African Unity. ..." See Accra Declaration, http://www.africa-union.org/ConceptNote.html.

[80] See para. 6, COMESA-EAC-SADC (2008) 1st Tripartite Summit Working Document on Trade and Infrastructure, p. 3.

[81] See para. 14(j) of the COMESA-EA-SADC (2008) Final communiqué of the 1st Tripartite Summit.

[82] COMESA-EA-SADC (2008), para. 11.

[83] COMESA-EA-SADC (2008), para. 44.

the harmonization of development plans in information and communication technologies, energy, and transport; the establishment of a single upper air space[84]; and the creation of Tripartite institutions.[85]

Acting on these recommendations, the first Tripartite Summit resolved that "the three RECs should immediately start working towards a merger into one single REC."[86] To this end, the Summit decided to anchor the merger on three pillars, namely market integration (through the establishment of the Tripartite FTA (TFTA), which will evolve into a customs union), infrastructure development, and industrial development.[87] Pursuing those objectives, the Member States decided, during their second Summit held in June 2011 in Johannesburg, South Africa, to launch the negotiations of the TFTA "covering [the] three regional economic communities in order to ensure the integration of the three regional economic communities into a larger integrated market."[88] At this same Summit, a memorandum of understanding (MoU) was signed by the three RECs on June 12, 2011, to set a framework of cooperation pertaining to the Tripartite initiative.[89]

This MoU recalled the continental integration objectives of the AU Constitute Act, as well as those of the Abuja Treaty, but it was remarkably silent on the first Tripartite Summit Decision, possibly signaling doubts about the proposal to merge the three RECs contained in that Decision.[90] It was revealing that while trade liberalization, customs cooperation, and the establishment of a free trade area are among the objectives of the MoU, it makes no reference to the goal of addressing overlapping memberships,[91] which had been one of the objectives of the Tripartite until then. Nor does the MoU refer to the eventual merger of the three RECs in the longer term; on the contrary, it requires for work plans to "be developed on a short and longer-term basis for planning and implementation of activities of common interests,"[92] which clearly presupposes the coexistence of the TFTA alongside its constituent RECs for some time to come.

A look at the evolution of the draft language of the objectives of the TFTA Agreement also appears to suggest that the idea of the tripartite customs union was alive and well until just before the 2011 summit. For example, the objectives of the 2010 revised draft—which served as a basis for the text-based negotiations—reads as follows:

---

[84] COMESA-EA-SADC (2008), para. 100.
[85] COMESA-EA-SADC (2008), para. 104.
[86] See COMESA-EA-SADC (2011a), para. 13.
[87] See Communiqué of the Second COMESA-EAC-SADC Tripartite Summit (2011a), Johannesburg: COMESA-EAC-SADC; see also paras. 14, 16 and 17 Communiqué of the 1st Tripartite Summit, 2008, pp. 3–4.
[88] See Recital no. 3 of the Declaration Launching the Negotiations for the Establishment of the Tripartite Free Trade Area, 12 June 2011. See COMESA-SADC-EAC (2011b).
[89] See COMESA-EAC-SADC (2011c).
[90] See Art.6.1(a) of the Tripartite MoU.
[91] See Art. 1.3(a) of the Tripartite MoU.
[92] See Art. 9 of the Tripartite MoU.

Article 3: ... The general objectives of the Tripartite Free Trade Area shall be:

1. to promote the rapid social and economic development of the region through job and wealth creation and the elimination of poverty, hunger and disease through building skills, innovativeness and hard and soft infrastructure; and through improving the location of factors for sustainable generation of national, regional and foreign investment and of trade opportunities.
2. to create a large single market with free movement of goods and services and business persons, and eventually to establish a customs union.
3. to resolve the challenges of multiple membership and expedite the regional and continental integration processes;
4. to build a strong people-based Tripartite Free Trade Area; and
5. to promote close cooperation in all sectors of economic and social activity among the Tripartite Member States.[93]

However, the same article under the signed version of the TFTA Agreement (renumbered as Article 4) had deleted the reference to the objectives of dealing with multiple memberships and the long-term goal to establish the customs union, limiting itself to the broad aspiration to enhance the regional and continental integration processes:

Article 4: ... The general objectives of the Tripartite Free Trade Area shall be to:

a. promote economic and social development of the Region;
b. create a large single market with free movement of goods and services to promote intra-regional trade;
c. enhance the regional and continental integration processes; and
d. build a strong Tripartite Free Trade Area for the benefit of the people of the Region.[94]

It is thus hardly surprising that the final text of the TFTA Agreement effectively abandoned the initial plan to establish a TFTA customs union. Indeed, the concept of a customs union appears only once in the whole Agreement, in a preambular reference to the Kampala Communiqué in which the Tripartite Summit "agreed, inter alia, to establish a single Customs Union beginning with a Free Trade Area."[95] Considering the gradual move away from the earlier commitment to merge the three RECs, the abandonment of the customs union idea was almost inevitable. The TFTA Agreement does not make any provision even on the relationship between the TFTA and its constituent RECs.

This leads to the question of whether the TFTA can still deliver on its promises. There are several reasons why this question is even raised. Firstly, although the launch of the TFTA in 2015 was warmly welcomed as an important step in the effort to speed up the process of regional economic integration on the continent, it has yet to see the light of day. As of November 2017, 21 of the 26 participating countries

---

[93] Revised 2010 draft TFTA Agreement, available at: https://www.tralac.org/images/Resources/Tripartite_FTA/Draft%20Agreement%20Establishing%20Tripartite%20FTA%20Revised%20Dec%202010.pdf.
[94] Art. 4 of the TFTA.
[95] See para. 3 of the preamble of the TFTA.

have signed the Agreement, while only two, Egypt and Uganda, have ratified it.[96] Considering that the Agreement requires 14 ratifications to enter into force,[97] the slow pace of this process is a cause for concern. Secondly, although some of the most important outstanding agreements, such as on rules of origin, trade remedies, and dispute settlement, were concluded recently,[98] the national schedules of tariff liberalization commitments have yet to be finalized. Thirdly, considering that the CFTA itself, encompassing all African countries, is set to be launched by the end of 2017, the question of whether the TFTA will have a chance to serve as a building block for continental integration is looking increasingly unlikely.[99]

When these considerations are put together, even the most optimistic observer will be challenged to see any institutional role for the TFTA going forward. The almost inescapable conclusion appears to be that the TFTA started with the worthy ambition to address some of the most fundamental obstacles to the Abuja program of continental integration, including the multiplicity of RECs, their overlapping memberships, and duplicative mandates, by merging the three RECs into a single customs union has been abandoned. Instead, the TFTA Agreement has limited its ambition to the establishment of a free trade area, which appears to have the potential to exacerbate the problem of overlapping membership rather than remedy it. The western half of the continent that was supposed to follow the model of the TFTA was left without a model to follow. As a consequence, the CFTA that was meant to stand on two legs representing the eastern and western halves of the continent has had to be reconfigured to build itself essentially on all the AU member countries becoming part of the free trade area individually and directly. The next question to consider therefore is what exactly went wrong between the launch of the TFTA negotiations in 2008 and the conclusion of the TFTA Agreement in 2015 and what lessons can be learned from that experience for the ongoing CFTA negotiations, to which now turn.

## 4.1 What Went Wrong with the TFTA Vision?

Our research shows that the major turning point in the TFTA negotiation process occurred around June 2011, when Member States decided to adopt a number of apparently inconsistent "principles of negotiations,"[100] which were later carried into

---

[96] For the latest information on the status of signatures and ratifications, see TRALAC, https://www.tralac.org/resources/by-region/comesa-eac-sadc-tripartite-fta.html.

[97] Article 39 of the TFTA Agreement requires that it "shall enter into force on the Thirtieth day after the deposit of the fourteenth instrument of ratification by Member/Partner States of COMESA, EAC and SADC."

[98] For more information on this, see Mangeni (2017a).

[99] For comments on the relationship between the TFTA and the CFTA, see Erasmus (2016); see also Mangeni (2017b).

[100] See COMESA-SADC-EAC (2011a) Guidelines for Negotiating the Tripartite Free Trade Area among the Member/Partner States of COMESA, EAC and SADC (12 June 2011), available at https://www.tralac.org/files/2011/06/Annex-1-T-FTA-Negotiating-Principles-etc.pdf.

the TFTA Agreement as "principles governing this Agreement."[101] We shall discuss three principles that we believe can serve to explain this issue here: (1) building on the acquis of the existing REC FTAs, (2) variable geometry, and (3) MFN treatment.

*The Principle of Preservation of the Acquis* This is a reference to the REC acquis,[102] i.e. the desire to use the depth of tariff liberalization already achieved at the level of each participating REC as a basis for the TFTA negotiations. Applied plainly, this principle would ensure that the ambition of liberalization at the TFTA level would exceed the level attained by any one of the individual RECs. In practice, however, this can be an impossible standard to meet. For example, COMESA and EAC have, in principle, agreed to eliminate tariffs on all intraregional trade, thus implying that the TFTA has to use this level of commitment as its floor. Indeed, the TFTA would struggle to meet even the more limited level of liberalization attained by the SADC FTA. The TFTA negotiation modalities on the other hand have put a liberalization ambition of 60 to 85% over a period of 5 to 8 years and with 15% of tariff lines allowed as exclusions from liberalization.[103] Reconciling the principle of preservation of the acquis, as described earlier, with this relatively limited TFTA ambition thus appears to be inconsistent.[104] Perhaps because of that realization, the negotiating principle itself was later "clarified"[105] to mean that those countries that already participate in existing FTAs would continue to trade on the bases of those FTAs and "would not negotiate additional trade liberalization schedules," while the negotiations between countries that do not participate in existing RECs could lead to the establishment of "new FTAs in their own right."[106] The effect of this "clarification" for the TFTA's original objective of addressing overlapping memberships was merely to exacerbate it. Not only does this leave the old problem of multiple REC FTAs with overlapping memberships intact; it also appears to further complicate it through the new arrangements that may be established between countries that are not parties to existing RECs. As we shall see further down, this understanding also erodes the role of the most-favored-nation (MFN) treatment as the guardian of nondiscrimination.

---

[101] See Art. 6 of the TFTA Agreement.

[102] "Building on the *acquis* of the existing REC FTAs in terms of consolidating tariff liberalisation in each REC FTA," para. 3(v) of the TFTA negotiating principles, 1st Tripartite Summit, 2011.

[103] See Update on the Tripartite Free Trade Area Negotiations: Statement by Mr Sindiso Ngwenya, Secretary General of COMESA, available at https://www.tralac.org/news/article/6974-update-on-the-tripartite-free-trade-area-negotiations-statement-by-mr-sindiso-ngwenya-secretary-general-of-comesa.html.

[104] For more details, see Luke and Mabuza (2015).

[105] See Erasmus (2013).

[106] See Erasmus (2015).

*The Principle of Variable Geometry* This principle is intended to allow two or more countries participating in an existing REC to integrate their economies faster than other countries in the same REC, if they so wish. Article 1 of the TFTA Agreement defines "variable geometry" to mean "the principle of flexibility which allows for progression in cooperation amongst members in a larger integration scheme in a variety of areas and at different speeds." While this principle may have been brought into the TFTA negotiation process out of necessity, it is also likely to further complicate the resulting regulatory framework for trade in the Tripartite region.[107] Indeed, as Erasmus rightly cautioned, this principle may "allow the co-existence of different trading arrangements which have been applied within COMESA, EAC and SADC Member States and any trading arrangements that may be reached during the negotiations."[108] Needless to say, the introduction of variable geometry into the TFTA process would have undermined the original intention to merge the three RECs engaged in the TFTA process.

*The MFN Principle* Some of the problems identified under the sections on preservation of the REC acquis and on variable geometry come out clearly in the section of the TFTA dealing with the MFN principle, which has been given a *sui generis* meaning not commonly found elsewhere in international trade law. The TFTA Agreement thus provides:

Article 7

Most-Favoured-Nation Treatment

1. Tripartite Member/Partner States shall accord to one another the Most Favoured-Nation Treatment.
2. Nothing in this Agreement shall prevent a Tripartite Member/Partner State from maintaining or entering into new preferential trade agreements with third countries provided that any advantage, concession, privilege or favour granted to a third country under such agreements are offered to the other Tripartite Member/Partner States on a reciprocal basis.
3. Nothing in this Agreement shall prevent two or more Tripartite Member/Partner States from entering into new preferential agreements which aim at achieving the objectives of this Agreement among themselves, provided that any preferential treatment accorded under such agreements is extended to the other Tripartite Member/Partner States on a reciprocal and non-discriminatory basis.
4. Any agreement entered into under paragraph 2 and 3 shall be notified to the Tripartite Sectoral Ministerial Committee responsible for Trade, Finance, Customs, Economic Matters and Home/Internal Affairs.

The meaning and scope of this provision require careful elucidation. The MFN principle is one of two fundamental manifestations of the principle of nondiscrimi-

---

[107] See European Parliament (2015), p. 4 (noting that application of the principle of variable geometry "will lead to an increase in the complexity of regional integration arrangements, instead of their simplification, as originally intended. Ultimately, there will not be a single TFTA but a complex structure of multiple trade agreements").
[108] See Erasmus (2015).

nation, national treatment being the other one. As such, the MFN principle requires that each party to a particular trading arrangement benefits from the best possible terms of trade that its partner may have given for the benefit of a third party. By making such benefit available immediately and unconditionally, the MFN principle also extends the scope of application of the most liberal outcome in any negotiations to all trading partners that benefit from an MFN obligation. The MFN principle thus serves the twin objectives of nondiscrimination and liberalization at one and the same time.[109]

Considered from this fundamental understanding of the MFN principle, the TFTA Agreement breaks new ground in many senses. Firstly, Article 7(1) of the Agreement provides—in conventional-sounding language—that "Tripartite Member/Partner States shall accord to one another the Most Favoured-Nation Treatment." On the surface, there is little that is remarkable about this provision; it appears to fit in with the traditional conception of the MFN principle. Indeed, Article 1 of the TFTA Agreement also defines the MFN principle in a language that is substantially common to most other trade agreements:

> "Most Favoured Nation treatment" (MFN) means that advantages that any Tripartite Member/Partner State offers to third countries would be offered to other Tripartite Member/Partner States. The purpose is to ensure that Tripartite Member/Partner State trade amongst each other on terms as good as or better than that offered to non-FTA partners.

However, this definition is further qualified by the following:

> These advantages would be extended on reciprocity.

By adding this last qualification, the TFTA Agreement has effectively denied legal content to the otherwise binding-sounding obligation in Article 7(1) of the Agreement that "Tripartite Member/Partner States shall accord to one another the Most Favoured-Nation Treatment." The essence of the MFN principle lies in its ability to extend new trading opportunities to old partners, not because of any measure they have taken but merely because their trading partner has given better terms of trade to a third party. The TFTA, by making the new trading opportunities conditional on reciprocity, has ensured that whatever benefits a country may acquire cannot be the same as those enjoyed by the partner that is most favored; on the contrary, they will be as good or as bad as the TFTA country's ability to "pay for" them, i.e. by their ability to reciprocate.

The concerns raised on the basis of the definitional provision of the TFTA Agreement are not allayed by the rest of the operative provisions of Article 7. Indeed, the reciprocity condition contained in the definitional provision finds its expression under the two remaining substantive provisions of Article 7. While Article 7(2) recognizes the right of a Tripartite Member/Partner State to conclude preferential trade agreements with third countries, its obligation to extend the resulting advantages, concessions, privileges, or favors to TFTA members is subject to the reciprocity condition. Likewise, and in clear application of the principle of variable

---

[109] For a discussion of the MFN principle in terms of its application at the multilateral level, see Van den Bossche and Werner (2013).

geometry discussed above, Article 7(3) also recognizes the right of two or more TFTA Member States to enter into new preferential agreements among themselves, their obligation to extend the terms of this new preferential arrangement to other TFTA Member States being once again dependent on reciprocity.[110] To illustrate these two points, consider the following hypotheticals:

1. if a TFTA Member State, say Ethiopia, enters into a bilateral arrangement with a non-African country, say Yemen, and gives the latter tariff-free access to its market for 100% of tariff lines, all Ethiopia is required to do under Article 7(2) of the TFTA Agreement is offer all TFTA Member States the same right as those granted to Yemen on the condition that each of them is prepared to do the same for the benefit of Ethiopian goods. In this hypothetical scenario, and despite the supposed presence of an MFN provision in the TFTA Agreement, Ethiopia could easily end up creating as many tariff schedules as the number of TFTA countries that are willing to reciprocate at varying but acceptable levels. Such an outcome cannot serve anybody's interests, and the practical difficulty and cost of administering such a complex system would be enough to argue against it; and
2. if, on the other hand, Ethiopia enters into a deeper preferential agreement with another TFTA Member State, say Sudan, the MFN obligation here would apply to both Ethiopia and Sudan to extend the same terms of trade to all other TFTA countries—but, again, on the condition that those other countries are prepared to do the same for the benefit of these two countries.

From this, it is reasonable to conclude that the MFN principle, as applied in Article 7 of the TFTA Agreement, is at best ineffective and at worst counterproductive. It is ineffective in the sense that the provision does not have the prospect of enabling TFTA Member States to automatically benefit from future liberalization moves that may be undertaken by a smaller group of TFTA countries inter se or between any one or more TFTA member and any third state. Where it becomes potentially counterproductive, by not disciplining the application of variable geometry, it exacerbates the complications of an already complicated "spaghetti bowl" in the megaregion.

In summary, as the Preamble to the TFTA Agreement clearly demonstrates, the TFTA process was launched with a number of worthy objectives, perhaps the most prominent one being the commitment to resolve "the challenges of overlapping memberships of the Tripartite Member/Partner States to the three Regional

---

[110] Curiously, this time the condition of reciprocity is supplemented with that of non-discrimination, but the practical implication of this addition remains unclear. Two questions arise: firstly, if the benefits of the new—deeper—preferential agreement are to be extended to the other TFTA members on a reciprocal basis, would that not inevitably require country-by-country negotiations to determine whether the new benefits have been adequately reciprocated? If yes, would that not almost certainly mean different countries would be prepared to "pay for" the new benefits? If yes, would that not mean the countries that have formed the new—deeper—preferential regime will be unable to treat the other TFTA members the same way, making discrimination a practical necessity? Secondly, what does the presence of a non-discrimination condition in para. 3 of Article 7, and its absence in para. 2 of the same provision, imply?

Economic Communities."[111] Not only has "overlapping membership" bedevilled the continental economic integration agenda for too long; the only provision that is couched in the strong language of "resolving challenges" in the whole Preamble is dedicated to this subject. However, the introduction of such principles as preservation of the REC acquis, variable geometry, and the like into the negotiation process and the subsequent creative but ill-advised adaptation of the established principle of MFN, purportedly to accommodate it, appear to have frustrated its original and worthiest goals.[112] This is a serious missed opportunity. The only hope for the moment appears to lie with the CFTA itself, for which some lessons from the TFTA experience need to be outlined.

## 4.2 What Can the CFTA Learn from the TFTA Experience?

That the CFTA faces the same challenges as the TFTA in terms of overlapping memberships and related issues, as well as the means to address them—i.e., definitions of guiding principles—is beyond dispute. If the TFTA aimed to bring together 26 countries that were clustered around three RECs under one roof and is struggling because of their multiple and overlapping membership in those RECs, the CFTA faces that same problem, only about twice as hard. In an instructive joint Issues Paper they prepared to inform the policy discourse leading to the launch of the CFTA in 2012, the AU Commission and the UNECA identified some well-known challenges that "can as well impede the creation of the CFTA," including the following:

> Overlapping membership to RECs continues to pose a big challenge towards negotiating and establishing a CFTA. Specifically, some countries belong to customs unions yet continue to negotiate towards establishing other customs unions. It is hoped that establishing a grand CFTA would serve as an effective route to resolve the issue of multiple and overlapping membership.[113]

This wise counsel, if heeded, could have helped the TFTA negotiators to stay on the course they had charted in Kampala in 2008 to progressively merge the three RECs and achieve their initial objective of making the TFTA a building block for continental integration. As we have seen throughout this article, however, those initial objectives of the TFTA negotiations were abandoned midway, thereby effectively depriving the TFTA of its very raison d'être. There are signs that the CFTA might follow a similar course to the TFTA in terms of the adoption of potentially incompatible negotiating principles that are likely to complicate the process. See objectives and principles proposed by HATC,Fn which were adopted by the Summit launching the negotiations.[114]

---

[111] See para. 9 of the preamble of the TFTA Agreement.
[112] Cf. Erasmus (2013, 2015), Kalenga (2016) and European Parliament (2015).
[113] See AUC and UNECA (2012), p. 13.
[114] See AU (2015c).

For example, among the "overarching principles" guiding the CFTA negotiation process are (1) reservation of the acquis, (2) variable geometry, and (3) MFN treatment.[115] Considered on their own, there is of course nothing wrong with these principles; they become problematic only when they are interpreted and applied in a manner that would make them incompatible with the intermediate objective to create a single economic area out of the many and contribute to the ultimate objective of continental economic integration. It is ominous that the definitions adopted by the CFTA Negotiating Forum for these principles appear to have been inspired by the "clarified" TFTA negotiating principles.[116] The lesson for the CFTA negotiators should be clear by now; unless they are careful, the CFTA project may also fall into the same trap as the TFTA.

## 5 Concluding Remarks and Lessons for the CFTA Negotiators

The Pan-African ideal of a continent of free and independent states, progressively harmonizing their socioeconomic policies, creating ever larger markets through the removal of regulatory and infrastructural bottlenecks to cross-border economic transactions, forging common positions on issues of common interest in international affairs and defending them in one voice, and ultimately of forming a politically united Africa has been the most powerful driver behind the multipronged, challenging, and decades-old integration effort on the continent. The issue discussed in this article, i.e. overlapping RECs due to multiple membership of countries therein, is one of the thorniest issues that has bedevilled the Abuja program of integration from its early days. A number of serious attempts have been made to address this issue once and for all, including (1) a freeze on the recognition of new RECs, (2) rationalization of the recognized RECs along the five regions of the continent, (3) the creation of two megaregional RECs representing the eastern and western halves of the continent, and finally (4) the creation of a CFTA made up of all African countries regardless of the level of integration achieved by the RECs to which each country is a party.

The TFTA initiative was meant to be the merger of the major RECs in the eastern half of the continent, which was to become the eastern leg on which the CFTA would stand, while the western leg would be created from the merger of the RECs in that half of the continent, i.e. AMU, CEN-SAD, ECOWAS, and ECCAS. However, when the TFTA negotiators abandoned the idea of merging the three RECs, and

---

[115] CFTA Negotiations Guiding Principles, Annex to the Report of the 2nd Meeting of the CFTA-Negotiating Forum and African Ministers of Trade, 16–24 May 2016.
[116] Indeed, the African Union Commission prepared the Draft Terms of Reference of the CFTA Negotiating Forum "based on best practices in the RECs and the Tripartite." See CFTA Negotiations Guiding Principles, Annex to the Report of the 2nd Meeting of the CFTA-Negotiating Forum and African Ministers of Trade, 16–24 May 2016.

with that the goal of forming a customs union for the Tripartite region, the vision to erect the CFTA on two legs became the first casualty. The CFTA project was thus forced to start almost from scratch, just like what the TFTA did before it, trying to build a free trade area based principally on individual countries regardless of regional configurations, hence the need for CFTA negotiators to study the lessons of the TFTA particularly to avoid its pitfalls.

Three key lessons emerge from our research. Firstly, the CFTA negotiators need to have a clear position on what the CFTA's relationship with RECs is going to be in the immediate-to-long term. In the short term, the CFTA Agreement will need to provide for detailed provisions to accommodate those RECs that have already formed customs unions while requiring others to either evolve toward that goal over a fixed transition period or phase themselves out. As a free trade area itself, the CFTA cannot meaningfully apply such cardinal principles as MFN treatment if it allows subregional FTAs to coexist with it. In the long term, the CFTA Agreement will need to provide for its own evolution to a customs union and a common market in the form of a binding time frame with detailed milestones at each stage, at which point the preferential economic regimes contained in each of the existing RECs will need to be phased out. In other words, if any REC is to have life after the continental customs union/common market has been established, its mandate will have to be restricted to cooperation on issues of regional concern that fall outside the substantive scope of the CFTA, such as issues of regional security and the like.

Secondly, the CFTA negotiators need to avoid the mistake of the TFTA negotiation process in translating such agreed negotiating principles as reservation of the acquis, MFN treatment, and variable geometry into actual legal commitments. To cite a few examples, at their meeting in Niamey, Niger, in June 2017, Members States agreed on the CFTA negotiating modalities for goods and services where they set an ambition "to liberalize 90 per cent of tariff lines with flexibility accorded in the remaining 10 per cent for sensitive and excluded products."[117] While this is clearly an encouraging sign, whether the concept of "reservation of the acquis" adds any practical value to the negotiation process needs careful scrutiny. Likewise, the principles of variable geometry and MFN treatment under the CFTA would sit well together only if the pace and scope of allowable progression at REC level is properly regulated by the CFTA Agreement so that the RECs, in exercising their rights under the principle of variable geometry, would follow an agreed path that leads to a single point of convergence where they all merge to form the continental customs union and eventually a common market. In other words, the MFN provision of the CFTA Agreement will need to provide for carefully circumscribed and time-bound exceptions for existing RECs to continue to maintain more preferential terms of intra-REC trade compared to other CFTA members during an agreed transition period provided the CFTA institutions exercise supervisory and regulatory powers over the RECs.

Finally, the approach of the TFTA Agreement where the MFN treatment obligation was subjected to reciprocity needs to be avoided in the CFTA. As we showed in the analysis above, by requiring reciprocity as a condition of MFN, the TFTA Agreement effectively stripped this cardinal principle of any meaningful content.

---

[117] See AUC (2017).

Our recommendation here is for the CFTA Agreement to allow an exception from the MFN only for RECs that are or working toward becoming a customs union. In this light, the Agreement should recognize and accommodate the right of existing REC customs unions to exist and admit new members or allow existing RECs that are not yet customs unions to evolve into one within an agreed time frame. Only this approach will introduce the parameters by which the issue of overlapping RECs and multiple membership of countries therein will be resolved once and for all within an agreed time frame.

In summary, what comes out clearly is that poor design from the outset allowed Member States to frustrate the Abuja program of integration, while lack of adequate follow-up and coordination mechanisms meant that countries did so without suffering any meaningful consequences in economic, political, reputational, or other terms. Resolution of this design flaw has been the sine qua non of success in the continental integration project for a long time. The initial OAU/AU approach was, first, to deny recognition to new RECs and, second, to attempt to rationalize the RECs it recognized. These strategies no doubt helped to mitigate the gravity of the problem but did not resolve it completely. From this perspective, the decision to progressively merge the three RECs into the COMESA-EAC-SADC Tripartite was a welcome step toward resolving the issue of overlapping RECs. However, that promise was not translated into actual commitments in the text of the final TFTA Agreement. Indeed, instead of resolving the problem of overlapping RECs through the multiple membership of member countries, the TFTA ended up creating yet another layer of complexity as it attempted to coexist with the three RECs it was meant to replace and even envisage the creation of many more layers of preferential arrangements among its members. The ongoing negotiations to establish the CFTA provide another opportunity to resolve this perennial problem by bringing all African countries under one free trade area regardless of the level of advancement of the integration process at the level of their respective RECs. However, to seize the CFTA opportunity, its negotiators need to learn from the experience of the TFTA process.

## References

AfDB, AUC and UNECA (2016) African Regional Integration Index. UNECA, Addis Ababa
AU (2006) Decision on the Moratorium on the Recognition of Regional Economic Communities (RECs)
AU (2007) Audit of the African Union
AU (2008) Protocol on AU-RECs Relations
AU (2012a) Decision on African integration
AU (2012b) Decision on Boosting Intra-African Trade and Fast-tracking of the CFTA
AU (2015a) Agenda 2063: The Africa We Want (Popular version)
AU (2015b) Decision on the Launching of the Negotiations of the Establishment of the Continental Free Trade Area
AU (2015c) Report of the Chairperson of the High Level African Trade Committee (HATC) to the Twenty-Fifth Ordinary Session Assembly of the Union
AUC (2009) *Minimum Integration Programme*. Available at http://www1.uneca.org/Portals/ctrci/6th/MinimumIntegrationProgrammeEng.pdf

AUC (2017) The AUC and Ministers of Trade share the Report and Outcomes of the African Union Ministers of Trade Meeting with President Issoufou Mahamadou. In: AU Press Release. Available at AU. https://au.int/en/pressreleases/20170620/auc-and-ministers-trade-share-report-and-outcomes-african-union-ministers

COMAI (2006) Declaration of the First Conference of African Ministers of Integration (COMAI)

COMESA (1994) Treaty Establishing the Common Market for Eastern and Southern Africa

COMESA (2016) Communique of the Nineteenth Summit of the COMESA Authority of Heads of State and Government. In: COMESA. Available in COMESA. http://www.comesa.int/wp-content/uploads/2016/10/Summit-Communique-19.10.16-2.pdf

COMESA-EAC-SADC (2008) 1st Tripartite Summit Working Document on Trade and Infrastructure

COMESA-EAC-SADC (2011a) Second COMESA-EAC-SADC Tripartite Summit

COMESA-EAC-SADC (2011b) Declaration Launching the Negotiations of the Establishment of the Tripartite Free Trade Area

COMESA-EAC-SADC (2011c) Memorandum of understanding on Inter-Regional Cooperation and Integration Amongst Common Market for Eastern and Southern Africa (COMESA), East African Community (EAC) and Southern African Development Community (SADC)

COMESA-EAC-SADC (2015) Agreement Establishing a Tripartite Free Trade Area Among the Common Market for Eastern and Southern Africa, the East African Community and the Southern African Development Community

COMESA-SADC-EAC (2008) Final communiqué of the 1st Tripartite Summit

COMESA-SADC-EAC (2011) Guidelines for Negotiating the Tripartite Free Trade Area among the Member/Partner States of COMESA, EAC and SADC

Disparte D, Bugnacki J (2015) TFTA: Africa's crucial inflection point. In: Huffington Post. Available via TRALAC. https://www.tralac.org/news/article/7891-tfta-africa-s-crucial-inflection-point.html

Elias TO (1965) The charter of the organization of African Unity. Am J Int Law 59:245

Erasmus G (2013) Redirecting the Tripartite Free Trade agreement negotiations? In: TRALAC Discussions. Available at TRALAC. https://www.tralac.org/discussions/article/5571-redirecting-the-tripartite-free-trade-agreement-negotiations.html

Erasmus G (2015) The continental FTA should develop its own REC acquis. In: TRALAC Discussions. Available at TRALAC. http://www.truckandbus.co.za/the-continental-fta-should-develop-its-own-rec-acquis/#64253547

Erasmus G (2016) One year after its launch: has the Tripartite Free Trade Area been overtaken by events?. In: TRALAC Briefs. Available at TRALAC. https://www.tralac.org/publications/article/9949-one-year-after-its-launch-has-the-tripartite-free-trade-area-been-overtaken-by-events.html

European Parliament (2015) The Tripartite Free Trade agreement: integration in Southern and Eastern Africa – Briefing. In: EPRS. Available at European Parliament http://www.europarl.europa.eu/RegData/etudes/BRIE/2015/551308/EPRS_BRI(2015)551308_EN.pdf

Gakunga M (2016) COMESA to publish annual assessments on implementation of Free Trade Area. In: COMESA News. Available in COMESA. http://www.comesa.int/summit2016/2016/10/16/comesa-to-publish-annual-assessments-on-implementation-of-free-trade-area/

Gathii JT (2010) African regional trade agreements as flexible legal regimes. N C J Int Law Commer Regul 35:571–668

Harold HK (1997) Why do nations obey international law? Yale Law J 106:2599–2659

Hartzenberg T (2011) Regional integration in Africa trade. In: WTO. Available at: Staff Working Paper ERSD-2011-14. https://www.wto.org/english/res_e/reser_e/ersd201114_e.pdf

IGAD (1986) Agreement Establishing the Inter-Governmental Authority on Development

Kagame P (2017) The imperative to strengthen our Union: report on the proposed recommendations for the institutional reform of the African Union. In: Graduate School of Development Policy and Practice. http://www.gsdpp.uct.ac.za/sites/default/files/image_tool/images/78/News/FInal%20AU%20Reform%20Combined%20report_28012017.pdf

Kalenga P (2016) Critical issues un the negotiations of the continental Free Trade Area. In: TRALC Working Papers. Available at TRALAC. https://www.tralac.org/publications/article/9172-critical-issues-in-the-negotiations-of-the-continental-free-trade-area.html

Luke D, Mabuza Z (2015) The Tripartite Free Trade Area agreement: a milestone for Africa's regional integration process. In: Bridges Africa. Available via ICTSD. http://www.ictsd.org/bridges-news/bridges-africa/news/the-tripartite-free-trade-area-agreement-a-milestone-for-africa%E2%80%99s

Mangeni F (2017a) The Tripartite Free Trade Area – a breakthrough in July 2017 as South Africa signs the tripartite agreement. In: TRALAC News. available at TRALAC. https://www.tralac.org/news/article/11860-the-tripartite-free-trade-area-a-breakthrough-in-july-2017-as-south-africa-signs-the-tripartite-agreement.html

Mangeni F (2017b) The relation between the tripartite FTA and the continental FTA. In: TRALAC News. Available at TRALAC. https://www.tralac.org/news/article/11511-the-relation-between-the-tripartite-fta-and-the-continental-fta.html

OAU (1963a) Charter of African Unity

OAU (1963b) Resolutions Adopted by the First Conference of Independent African Heads of State and Government

OAU (1980) Lagos Plan of Action

OAU (1991) Treaty Establishing the African Economic Community

OAU (1997) Decision on the African Economic Community

OAU (1999) Sirte Declaration on the African Union

SADC (1992) Treaty of the Southern African Development Community

UNECA (2006) Assessing regional integration in Africa II: rationalizing regional economic communities. UNECA, Addis Ababa

UNECA (2017) Economic report on Africa 2017: urbanization and industrialization for Africa's transformation. UNECA, Addis Ababa

Union Government of Africa (2007) Accra Declaration on the Union Government of Africa

Van den Bossche P, Werner Z (2013) The law and policy of the World Trade Organization. Cambridge University Press, New York

WTO (1995) Notification of the common market for Eastern and Southern Africa, WT/COMTD/N/3

WTO (2000) Notification of the East African Customs Union, WT/COMTD/N/14

WTO (2004) Notification of the Protocol on Trade in the Southern African Development Community, WT/REG176/N/1

WTO (2017a) Regional Trade Agreement Information System. http://rtais.wto.org/UI/PublicMaintainRTAHome.aspx. Accessed 2 September 2017

WTO (2017b) Tariff Analysis Online. https://tao.wto.org/. Accessed 2 September 2017

**Melaku Geboye Desta** is professor of International Economic Law, Leicester De Montfort University School of Law, De Montfort University, England, UK (currently on sabbatical), and Principal Adviser, Capacity Development Division, UNECA. Dr Desta has published widely in the fields of international Economic law and policy in general and agriculture and natural resources in particular. Dr Desta has consulted for a number of international organizations and national governments and served as arbitrator in international disputes. All view expressed in this article are exclusively personal to the author and do not in any way reflect or represent the views of any institution with which he is associated at any time.

**Guillaume Gérout** is a Trade Policy Consultant at the African Trade Policy Centre of the United Nations Economic Commission for Africa (ECA). He has previously been a fellow for the International Organization for la Francophonie, seconded at the ECA. He has also worked on free trade negotiations, especially the Economic Partnership Agreements, at the Development and Regional Integration Division of the Seychelles Ministry of Foreign Affairs and Transport. He holds degrees from Faculty of Economics and Law of the University of la Reunion and from the Institute of European Studies of the University of Paris III—Sorbonne-Nouvelle. All views expressed in this article are exclusively personal to the author and do not in any way reflect or represent the views of any institution with which he is associated at any time.

# Like Fish in a Stream? Considering the Agency of the UN Peacekeepers of the Global South: Rwanda and India as Case Studies

**Philip Roberts**

**Abstract** 'Blue Helmet' peacekeeping operations have come to characterise the UN's response to armed conflict. These operations have evolved from the 'simple' monitoring of ceasefires into complex 'peacebuilding' projects and interventionist 'peace enforcement' actions and employ considerable forces of peacekeepers, contributed by member states. The composition of these forces has also transformed over the period as the previously predominant troops from the developed Northern states have given way to the peacekeepers of the Global South. Peacekeeping scholarship is sharply divided between those who regard this sea change as indicative of a rising Global South and those who perceive its soldiers as exploited substitutes for the developed world, finessed into the role via a West-oriented UN. This paper asks if the current composition of troop-contributing countries to UN Blue Helmet peacekeeping operations reflects the changing identities, interests and ambitions of the Global South or just the continuing hegemony of the developed world. Do the Southern states have agency in respect of their participation, or are they merely 'fish in a stream', obliged by persistent hegemonic currents to conform to the agendas of the North? Using a case study of India and Rwanda, the article argues that Northern hegemony does still find expression in UN peacekeeping operations but is straining to contain the more assertive Southern states, which participate, largely, for their own carefully considered, often very disparate, reasons.

## 1 Introduction

In the years since the Cold War, so-called Blue Helmet peacekeeping operations have come to characterise the United Nations' responses to armed conflict, even though such operations have an indistinct legal foundation within the UN Charter.[1]

---

[1] There is debate as to whether 'the appropriate procedures or methods of adjustment' of Article 36,

P. Roberts (✉)
University of Aberdeen, Aberdeen, UK
e-mail: philip.j.roberts.15@aberdeen.ac.uk

These operations, initially limited to the 'simple' monitoring of ceasefires, have evolved into more holistic and complex 'peacebuilding' projects and interventionist 'peace enforcement' actions and employ considerable forces of peacekeepers, contributed by the member states.[2]

The composition of these forces, comprised of national contingents 'loaned' to the UN by member states, has also been transformed. The previously predominant troops from the developed Northern countries have been almost completely replaced by the soldiers, police officers, and civilian specialists of the Global South.[3] For example, while the leading troop contributors in 1990 included Northern peacekeeping stalwarts like Canada, Finland, Austria, Ireland, the UK, Sweden and Norway, the top 10 contributors of May 2017 were Ethiopia, India, Pakistan, Bangladesh, Rwanda, Nepal, Burkina Faso, Senegal, Ghana and Indonesia. The proportion of peacekeepers provided by the top 10 ranked Northern contributors went down from 72% to 6% over the same period, and by 2017 the total Northern contribution amounted to just over 7000 of the almost 97,000 peacekeepers engaged on the 23 extant UN missions.[4] In contrast, 80% of the UN's annual peacekeeping budget is supplied by 10 developed countries, headed by the US, thus constituting a 'tacit bargain in which developing world blood is paid for with developed world treasure'.[5]

The sea change in contributor composition has stimulated a considerable scholarly debate between those who regard it as a progressive trend on the part of a rising Global South and more sceptical commentators who perceive the soldiers of the South as exploited substitutes for the casualty-averse developed countries, finessed into the role via a West-oriented UN.[6] The Southern peacekeepers have been represented as the 'Askaris and Sepoys of the New World Order',[7] engaged in 'riot control' to keep the unruly peripheries of the (new) (UN) empire of the world in order—much as their predecessors did in colonial times—while the Global North is

---

Chapter VI of the United Nations Charter provide a basis for peacekeeping missions, alone or in conjunction with Article 42, Chapter VII. The latter allows for 'such action by air, sea, or land forces' necessary to maintaining or restoring international peace and security and, combined, Chapters VI and VII of the Charter seem to provide a foundation for both consensual and non-consensual peacekeeping. Howe et al. (2015), pp. 8, 9.

[2] Levin et al. (2016), p. 107; Gray (2016), p. 195.

[3] Global South' will be used here, following Dirlik (2007), p. 12, to refer to those societies, 'largely but by no means exclusively located in the geographical south, that…face difficulties in achieving the economic and political goals of capitalist modernity'. The term is generally accepted to include emerging Southern countries, such as Brazil and India, but to exclude Australia, New Zealand and Japan.

[4] The average strength of each mission is 4200, but only eight missions have more than 1000 personnel, and several of them have a post-conflict 'peacebuilding', rather than 'peacekeeping' role. Six African missions account for over 73,000 of the total. Providing for Peacekeeping (2017).

[5] Providing for Peacekeeping (2017); UN Financing (2017); Levin et al. (2016), p. 108.

[6] For an example of the positive view, see Amar (2012), pp. 1–13. For sceptics, see, Cunliffe (2013).

[7] Cunliffe (2013), p. 30.

happy to use the (financially and politically) cheaper manpower of the developing countries to perform this generally thankless task.[8]

This article asks if the current, imbalanced, composition of troop-contributing countries to UN peacekeeping operations reflects the changing identities, interests and ambitions of the Global South or just the continuing hegemony of the developed world. Do the Southern states have agency in respect of their participation, or are they merely 'fish in a stream', so to speak, obliged by persistent hegemonic currents to conform to agendas in which they have little or no input or interests of their own?[9]

The question has considerable significance. If the answer is in the negative, then the supply of peacekeepers is likely to dwindle as fast as the UN's credibility, with serious consequences for the management and prevention of conflict.

The article argues that while Northern hegemony still finds expression in the mandating, funding and resourcing of UN peacekeeping operations,[10] it is straining to contain the more assertive Southern states. These countries, informed by evolving perceptions of their international identities, roles and interests, are determined to challenge the 'pay but won't play' mentality of the developed states and participate in UN peacekeeping largely for their own, carefully considered, often disparate reasons.

The article employs a 'Most Different' comparative case study of India and Rwanda. These countries make attractive subjects because they are both from the South, albeit transitioning through differing stages of development; are amongst the most consistent contributors of UN peacekeepers; and yet differ in virtually every other relevant historical, social, economic and political respect. The Most Different approach lends itself to such disparity, as it 'homes in' on causal factors through a process of elimination, so that points of similarity are of greater significance for their rarity. The main sources for interpretative analysis will be the recorded comments and writings of national and UN politicians, military figures, national and international media sources and officials involved in peacekeeping.[11] This evidence, considered against the backdrop of some earlier scholarship, will be collated around a selection of key variables pertaining to the degree of agency and autonomy enjoyed

---

[8] The 'Global North' includes Australia, New Zealand and Japan, alongside the developed countries of the northern hemisphere. The latter includes, and is often most characterised by, the liberal North American and European democracies, usually collectivised as 'the West'. Dirlik (2007), pp. 12–14; Pugh (2004), p. 41.

[9] 'Agency' is construed in the sense that an 'agent performs activity that is directed at a goal… adopted on the basis of an overall practical assessment of his options and opportunities'. It assumes autonomy, as opposed to the control of others. Wilson and Shpall (2016).

[10] The term will be applied to the 'full spectrum of UN peace and security missions', variously denoted as 'peacekeeping', 'robust peacekeeping', 'peace enforcement' or 'peacebuilding'. More will be said about these expressions during the discussion, but the Capstone Doctrine describes them as operations deployed to prevent, manage, and/or resolve violent conflicts or reduce the risk of their recurrence'. Some regional organisations conduct peacekeeping operations, but this article is only concerned with UN missions. See UNDPKO (2008), p. 97; Gray (2016), p. 194.

[11] For explanations of the 'Most Different' model, the usage of case studies and interpretive analysis, see Peters (1998), pp. 36–41; Gerring (2004), pp. 342, 343; Lamont (2015), pp. 77, 78.

by India and Rwanda in relation to peacekeeping, with the intention of shedding light on the general phenomenon of Global South participation. It will be augmented by brief consideration of two analogous troop contributors, Indonesia and Ethiopia, to gauge the wider applicability of the learnings drawn from the detailed case study.

The article comprises three chapters. Section 2 establishes the theoretical framework of the discussion, while Sect. 3 presents the case study of India and Rwanda. An analysis of that research follows in Sect. 4, and the article concludes with a summary of findings.

## 2 Theoretical Framework

The relatively substantial literature on UN peacekeeping sets the scene for the paper and can be divided into explanatory, positive and sceptical outputs.

Bellamy and Williams' excellent study of the influences and difficulties that attend the provision of peacekeepers for UN missions examines patterns of contribution and the motivations of troop-contributing countries. It also explains the growing North/South divide in participation, mandating and funding, which could be summarised as 'The South plays, the North pays' and presents explanations for the increasing non-participation of the latter.[12] A rough consensus is achieved by several authors on the broad rationales that, to varying extents, motivate states to contribute to UN peacekeeping, and these can be sub-categorised into political, economic, security, institutional and normative drivers. The boundaries of these terms will be delineated during the discussion.[13]

An influential section of scholarship takes a sceptical view of the aims and consequences of UN peacekeeping and the involvement of Global South countries. It presents modern UN peacekeeping as an instrument for transforming colonial imperialism into 'imperial multilateralism' and disseminating neoliberal democracy across the world.[14] This utilises a 'peacebuilding consensus' through which the UN and a variety of other actors seek to address the root causes of conflict by (re)creating Western, neoliberal, development driven, political, judicial and cultural structures in affected states.[15] The UN regards this as a 'silver bullet' for resolving conflict and has effectively taken over the running of destabilised countries for this purpose, thereby diluting the inviolability of Westphalian state sovereignty so

---

[12] Bellamy and Williams (2013).

[13] Bellamy and Williams (2013), pp. 17–21; Nieto (2012), pp. 166, 167; Capie (2016), pp. 1–27; Hansel and Moeller (2014), pp. 141–157.

[14] 'Imperialism' here refers to any system of domination and subordination organised with an imperial centre and a periphery. It thus extends beyond actual military occupation or colonialism. See Said (1994), p. 9; Cunliffe (2013), pp. 20–26.

[15] The 'actors' can include NATO, the Council of Europe, the UN Commission on Human Rights, the European Court of Human Rights and the World Bank. Richmond (2004), pp. 83–92 and (2009).

intrinsic to its own charter.[16] Richmond decries this as 'benign colonialism' and the 'rehabilitation of imperial duty', but Chandler traces its roots to the UN's failure to arrest the mass slaughters of the 1990s in internal conflicts such as Rwanda and Bosnia.[17] The resultant policy reviews, including that of the Brahimi Panel, concluded that peacekeepers, confronted by 'obvious aggressors', were 'morally compelled'—and implicitly authorised—to use robust, even pre-emptive, force, especially in defence of civilians.[18] Brahimi also recommended the type of holistic, multidimensional peacebuilding process implemented in East Timor and Kosovo.[19] These approaches have since been encapsulated in UN policy, for instance in the 'Responsibility to Protect' (R2P) concept, despite their divergence from the organisation's long-standing 'Holy Trinity' of peacekeeping principles, i.e. impartiality, the consent of the warring parties and the use of force only in self-defence.[20] In any case, the foot soldiers of this new imperialism are, according to Cunliffe, the latter day 'Askaris and Sepoys' of the Global South, conditioned by the legacy of colonial military service to do the dirty work on behalf of the rich Western countries, the latter having 'outsourced' peacekeeping to the South after the humiliations of the 1990s.[21] These accounts emphasise a division of labour described as the 'crisis management of the haves and have nots', whereby the North participates in cohesive, well-equipped operations, typically touching on its own interests and led by NATO, e.g. Afghanistan, while the UN-commanded Blue Helmet operations are staffed primarily by forces from the South, labouring under different rules of engagement, dis-unified command structures and a lack of joint planning and training.[22] The clear inference of this section of scholarship is of a compliant Global South, just 'going with the flow' as they—wittingly or unwittingly—further this imperialistic agenda. There is little sense of agency on the part of these states or of their diverse nature, situations and aspirations.

Other writers, however, are far more positive. To them, the changing composition of troop-contributing countries demonstrates the increasing assertiveness and independence of the Global South as a trend to 'South to South' assistance grows.[23] However, much of this scholarship was inspired by the briefly hopeful aftermath of the Arab Spring of 2011, the emergence of the BRICS states and the rise of fiercely independent governments in Latin America. It appears overly optimistic now, and

---

[16] UN Charter (1945), Article 2(1)(4).

[17] Chandler discerns in this a switch to a people-centred, rather than a state-centred approach. See Chandler (2001), pp. 1, 2; Richmond (2004), pp. 83–101.

[18] UNPO (2000), paras. 48–50.

[19] UNPO (2000), paras. 35–47.

[20] Note, however, that R2P restricts coercive, external, interventions to a last resort, and emphasis the central responsibility of the affected state itself. WSO (2005), paras. 138, 139; Howe et al. (2015), p. 9.

[21] Cunliffe (2013), pp. 121–123.

[22] Tanner (2010), p. 211.

[23] Amar (2012), pp. 2, 3; Nieto (2012), pp. 162, 163; de Coning et al. (2013), pp. 135–152.

Amar's reference to 'an inverting (of) the essential pillars of global hierarchy' clearly demands reappraisal.[24]

In theoretical terms, this article shies away from the general liberal theories and postcolonial explanations that underlie the sceptical scholarship described above because, amongst other things, they tend to ignore the idiosyncratic nature of human decision making and confuse causation with correlation.[25] Instead, it will treat the deep-rooted asymmetry of the relationship between the Global North and South in terms of a neo-Gramscian hegemony, built not on coercion but on the self-interest of the subordinate states and/or a recognition of the hegemon's social legitimacy to lead.[26] The article will set hegemonic structural constraints against the evolution of the self-identities and interests of states and their resultant actions, which constructivists ascribe to the continuous social interaction of states in the international arena.[27] This will allow an assessment of the degree to which the hegemony restricts or even negates the modern-day sovereignty and autonomy of the Global South in the field of UN peacekeeping.

The article will continue, within this scholarly and theoretical framework, with a themed comparison of India and Rwanda, designed to identify behaviour indicative of either the weight of hegemony on the two countries or, alternatively, the exercise of agency on their own behalf. Their historical and political backgrounds will be compared, along with the rationales that explain their participation in UN peacekeeping and the barriers that threaten its continuance.

## 3 Case Study of India and Rwanda

The two states quickly impress as very different entities. India, the second most populous state on earth, has the biggest—pluralistic, vibrant, sometimes rowdy—democracy and the third highest national gross domestic product, while autocratic Rwanda has a fraction of India's land area and population and a very modest, though recovering, economy.[28]

Since securing its independence from British colonial rule in 1947, India has become a leading economic and political power in Asia and a member of the emergent BRICS group of nations, though plagued by persistent social inequality.[29] Its foreign policy is generally non-aligned, keeping it 'free of entanglement in conflicts

---

[24] Amar (2012), p. 3.

[25] See summary of democratic peace theory and liberal institutionalism, for instance, in Bellamy and Williams (2013), pp. 4–17.

[26] Clark (2011), pp. 6–8; Cox (1987, 1996).

[27] See Ruggie (1998), p. 856; Wendt (1992), pp. 392–394, both prominent proponents of social constructivism.

[28] International Monetary Fund (2017).

[29] Namely Brazil, Russia, India, China and South Africa.

or alliances',[30] and founded on a belief in the essential equality and sovereignty of states.[31] It also draws on a normative sense of being a good international citizen.[32] However, although India has certainly consistently demonstrated South-to-South solidarity, it has evolving regional and global imperatives of its own.[33] It maintains tense relationships with neighbours and regional rivals, Pakistan and China, but has begun to present itself as more than just an Asian heavyweight. In 2005, Prime Minister Singh announced that 'the 21st Century will be an Indian Century',[34] and the country relaxed its traditional multilateral, non-aligned, stance to engage with smaller groups of powerful nations on specific issues like climate change and UN reform, as it sought a greater global voice.[35] It has repeatedly argued that its size, economic prospects and possession of nuclear weapons—in defiance of international convention—qualifies it for Great Power status and a louder voice at the UN.[36]

Rwanda was also colonised, by Germany and then Belgium, until 1962. Both colonisers promoted the Tutsi minority at the expense of the Hutu majority, which contributed to a cycle of large-scale ethnic violence and, latterly, civil war, culminating in the 1994 genocide perpetrated against the Tutsi population.[37] Three months of slaughter were eventually ended by the Tutsi Rwandan Patriotic Army (RPA) rebel force, led by current president Paul Kagame, who has since overseen the social and economic revival of the country.[38] However, the disintegration of the 2500 strong in-country UN force at the start of the genocide, as most national contingents withdrew unilaterally, and subsequent inaction, engendered an enduring distrust of the UN and international community.[39]

Although India has demonstrated a similar tendency to communal violence in the past, Rwanda took a very distinctive political and constitutional path after the genocide. Although styled as a democratic republic, many commentators and international human rights/civil rights bodies regard it, effectively, as a one-party state under Kagame's Rwandan Patriotic Front (RPF), in which political debate and dissent is repressed by legislation purportedly designed to prevent a further slide into

---

[30] 2011 speech by Foreign Secretary Ranjan Mathai quoted in Hansel and Moeller (2014), p. 146.

[31] Acharya (2011), pp. 851–869; Hansel and Moeller (2014), p. 146.

[32] Hansel and Moeller (2014), p. 148.

[33] India concentrates most of its peacekeeping efforts in Asia and Africa and regards itself as an advocate of developing nations. Banerjee (2013a); Hansel and Moeller (2014), p. 148; Singh (2007), pp. 72–78.

[34] See Acharya (2011), p. 62, which also notes the support since afforded to the country's global ambitions by Presidents G.W. Bush and Obama.

[35] Mukherjee and Malone (2011), pp. 311–329.

[36] India has never acceded to the 1968 Non-Proliferation Treaty. Tannenwald (2013), pp. 299–317; Singh (2007), p. 80.

[37] Beswick (2014), p. 218.

[38] UN Outreach Programme (2017).

[39] UN Past Missions (2017).

genocide.[40] Ranked at 138 and designated an 'authoritarian state' in a 2016 democracy index (India came 32nd), Rwanda is very much dominated by Kagame's autocratic, highly personalised and apparently unassailable leadership.[41] Its foreign policy also bears the indelible marks of the genocide, in that it emphasises African solidarity and self-help, as opposed to any reliance on the international community.[42] Rwanda has become a very prominent and consistent UN troop-contributing country while also reserving the right to intervene, without UN mandate or approval, in the Democratic Republic of the Congo (DRC), allegedly committing its own atrocities as it attacks exiled Hutu forces.[43]

The Rwanda Defence Force (RDF) was created in 2002 by the merger of the RPA, the military wing of the RPF and victors of the civil war, with the established national army. It is very much RPF in ideology and spirit and sees itself as the successor of the Rwandan (in part mythical) national armies of the pre-colonial period. These were never co-opted for use by the colonial powers—a small riposte to Cunliffe—and still serve as a symbol of national cohesion and sovereignty.[44] It has a strength of 33,000 and is widely recognised as a professional and cohesive organisation, despite its factional origins. It is, however, very much under what Jowell calls 'subjective' control, in that it is 'linked to ruling political structures …and… deeply involved with state control, authority and decision making'.[45] Military figures, like Kagame himself, make up a significant proportion of the country's elite.

Conversely, India's massive armed forces are under 'objective' political control, which is to say they are separated from the political process and do not meddle in it.[46] India is well resourced for peacekeeping, possessing the world's third largest, very professional, military of over 1.3 million people; a considerable defence budget; and substantial civil police resources.[47]

Turning to that contribution, India was placed 2nd and Rwanda 5th in the May 2017 world rankings of UN contributors, with over 7000 and 6000 personnel respectively deployed on UN missions (compared to the UK's 693 and the USA's 77).[48] India's involvement goes back to 1950, since when it has contributed more personnel than any other country and has suffered the highest number of fatalities. Most of its missions have been in Africa and, less commonly, Asia, although it did send personnel to Haiti and Yugoslavia.[49]

---

[40] See Roth (2009); Wedgwood (2010); 'Game Over for Democracy in Rwanda' Freedom House (2015).

[41] Economist Intelligence Unit (2016).

[42] Beswick (2014), pp. 221–223.

[43] Beswick (2014), pp. 221–225.

[44] Jowell (2014), p. 284.

[45] Jowell (2014), p. 279.

[46] Jowell (2014), pp. 278, 279.

[47] Banerjee (2013a).

[48] UN Peacekeeping Resources (2017).

[49] Hansel and Moeller (2014), p. 141.

Internal turmoil and lingering insurgency precluded Rwanda's involvement until 2004, but it has since become a top troop contributor to both UN and African Union (AU) missions. Its UN contribution has not fallen below 3000 troops since 2007 and is currently consistently over 6000. Its peacekeeping is focused almost exclusively on Africa, where it has become particularly associated with Darfur and South Sudan, but it has made penny number deployments elsewhere. Both countries have solid reputations for the professionalism and aptitude of their peacekeepers, some of whom have occupied leadership positions on UN peacekeeping operations.[50]

Finally, the national processes employed to field UN requests for peacekeeping forces are noteworthy for their reflection of the differing characters of the states and their forces, democratic/objective versus autocratic/subjective. India uses a formal protocol, which requires assessment of the political and logistical implications by the relevant government and military departments, prior to a final decision by Cabinet. The rather 'opaque' Rwandan process, in contrast, involves only a few senior RPF and military officials, with President Kagame having the final say in each case.[51]

Thus far the two countries exhibit a few shared characteristics, aside from their commitment to peacekeeping, namely, a history of colonial occupation and communal violence; an evolution towards a more assertive foreign policy, born out of a shift in their perceived self-identities and roles in the world; and some consequent defiance of the UN and the established powers of the Global North, e.g. India's nuclear weapons and Rwanda's interventions in the DRC. These traits differ in degree and extent, but they do have some attraction to a constructivist, demonstrating how experiences and interactions with other states, negative and positive, can bring about a change in national direction, which somewhat confounds the more rigid structuralist. They also do not suggest states 'under the thumb' of the North.

The big question, of course, is what motivates India and Rwanda to participate in UN peacekeeping in the first place when they are under no compulsion to do so and it entails significant physical, political and reputational risk. The following discussion will demonstrate the complexity of the varying motivations involved.

In India's case, normative and political rationales take precedent. It 'bought in' to the stated purposes of the UN from the outset, regarding it as a vehicle for dismantling colonialism and promoting international peace and justice, in conformity with the principles of state sovereignty and equality.[52] Indeed, India formally assimilated these purposes into its Constitution of 1949, according to which

> The State shall endeavour to: promote international peace and security; maintain just and honourable relations between nations; foster respect for international law and treaty

---

[50] 'Beswick and Jowell (2014); 'UN Secretary-General praises India's peacekeeping contributions in remarks at New Delhi training centre' UN (2001); Banerjee (2013b), pp. 225–236; Banerjee (2013a); 'Ban Thanks India for Contribution to UN Peacekeeping Efforts' The Daily Pioneer (2014).

[51] Banerjee (2013a); Beswick and Jowell (2014).

[52] Banerjee (2013a).

obligations in the dealings of organised peoples with one another; and encourage settlement of international disputes by arbitration.[53]

This ethos is consistently invoked by Indian officials to explain the country's long-standing commitment to Blue Helmet missions, which they have described as a '...clear demonstration of the country's commitment to the objectives set out in the UN Charter. Not in terms of rhetoric and symbolism, but in real and practical terms, even to the extent of accepting casualties',[54] and

> one of the most visible manifestations of the solemn commitment we all made in 1945 when we signed the UN Charter and made the promise - "to save succeeding generations from the scourge of war" and to uphold fundamental human rights and dignities of every human being on this planet.[55]

Wrapped up in this is what a constructivist would call India's 'ideational self-image' as a moral force for good in the world and an advocate of developing nations.[56] The self-image of 'good citizen' all but dictates that India will behave like one, as interests and actions flow from identity.[57]

However, while this indicates a substantial degree of agency on India's part, it could, alternatively, be interpreted as the exercise of the 'socially legitimate' hegemony mentioned earlier, that legitimacy being dependent on the subordinate state's belief that the hegemon practices the principles it espouses.[58] The UN's initial success in convincing India that the organisation was 'the final arbiter of international peace and contributing to it (was) a necessary obligation'[59] could be construed in such terms. However, that only works if India regarded the UN as representative, or part, of the Global North, when the organisation's initial attraction for India was that of a fair-minded, anti-colonial 'honest broker', supportive of international equality, not hegemony. Alternatively, and with more justification, the UN could be seen as having successfully diffused the norm of peacekeeping to India through the constructivists' social interaction, rather than top-down hegemony, reliant on the power of the norm itself and its own influence to secure its adoption.[60] In this sense, the UN is an influential 'norm entrepreneur', even if its influence on India has since been somewhat diluted by the interventionist turn in UN peacekeeping policy.[61]

Economic, institutional (relating to the military) and security rationales do not figure large in India's commitment to UN peacekeeping. Unlike many smaller countries, the financial reimbursements paid by the UN to the country and to individual peacekeepers do not represent a big incentive. Repayments of equipment and

---

[53] The Constitution of India 1949, Article 51.
[54] Nambiar (2014).
[55] 'Inaugural Address by Preeti Saran' Ministry of External Affairs (2017).
[56] Hansel and Moeller (2014), p. 148.
[57] Wendt (1992), p. 398.
[58] Lebow (2003), p. 126; Gill (1993), pp. 42, 43.
[59] Banerjee (2013a).
[60] Fennimore (1996), p. 2.
[61] Bjorkdahl (2006), p. 215.

personnel costs—often long delayed—constitute only 0.6% of India's annual defence budget, and only a tiny proportion of India's large military and police forces ever serve on peacekeeping missions. It also takes a year to re-integrate returning peacekeepers into their regular roles, which further limits institutional benefits. Finally, since most Indian UN deployments are in Africa, they do not support any strategic security interest, these being concentrated much closer to home.[62]

Political considerations are far more relevant. India has long viewed peacekeeping as a means of assuming a leadership role in promoting Afro-Asian solidarity and currently regards it as a tool in its efforts to achieve a permanent seat on the United Nations Security Council and thereby enhance its global standing.[63] According to a leading Indian military authority on peacekeeping, 'large troop contributions undeniably reinforce our claim to a UNSC seat',[64] while External Affairs Minister Shri Krishna, speaking on India's election to a non-permanent seat on the Security Council, stated:

> We will utilize our tenure to provide a sense of satisfaction to all our partners and obtain their reaffirmation of the need for a permanent presence for India on the Security Council. India is fully committed to the principles and purposes of the UN… a major contributor to UN peacekeeping operations…(and) has excellent credentials to serve on the UN Security Council.[65]

This stance has received some support in the West, as well as in the developing world,[66] with India sometimes presenting it in the context of extending global power and influence beyond its established practitioners, to Africa as well as Asia.[67]

Rwanda's rationales for participation in UNKPOs have a quite different emphasis, reflecting the country's very individual identity and interests, stemming from its specific circumstances and, above all, its experience of genocide. They also reflect the autocratic nature of the state. No country is an absolute monolith, but the response to 1994, and all that caused it and resulted from it, takes a far more personalised form in Rwanda than in most countries. President Kagame is central to all that recent history and the decision-making process relating to peacekeeping operations. Consequently, normative, political and security rationales are predominant but are entwined with, and complemented by, economic and institutional motivators.

---

[62] 'UN owes India $55 Million for Peacekeeping Operations' The Hindu (2017); Hansel and Moeller (2014), p. 54; Banerjee (2013a).

[63] Banerjee (2013a).

[64] Lieutenant General Satish Nambiar, quoted in Hansel and Moeller (2014), p. 155.

[65] 'Speech by External Affairs Minister Shri S.M. Krishna' Ministry of External Affairs (2010). In similar vein, see 'India's Global Role, Speech by Foreign Secretary Shivshankar Menon' Ministry of External Affairs (2010).

[66] 'Africa vows to support India's permanent seat quest at UN Security Council' Asian Age (2011); 'US congressional resolution introduced backing India's UN Security Council Bid' Press Trust of India (2016).

[67] See for example Foreign Minister Sushma Swaraj's speech of October 2015. 'Sushma Swaraj Calls for Security Council Seat for India, Africa' Mint (2017).

In normative terms, the experience of genocide and the inglorious role of the international community in it have convinced Kagame that Rwanda cannot look to external actors, like the UN—'UNAMIR was here, armed...and people got killed while they were watching'[68]—to solve its problems in general or to prevent a recurrence in Africa.[69] Instead, the RPF has, in its view, the unquestioned moral authority, indeed the duty, to lead an African response to African security problems. This outlook underpins Rwanda's post-genocide commitment to peacekeeping, with its markedly African focus, and is frequently explicitly linked by Rwandan governmental figures to their country's own experience. The depth of this feeling was expressed by Minister of State Gasana in 2016:

> The 1994 Genocide against the Tutsi in Rwanda ...impressed upon us the conviction that we must take every measure necessary to secure the lives of civilians. This conviction coupled with our history fueled our desire to contribute to peacekeeping in a profound way.[70]

Mr Gasana was speaking in the context of the implementation of the so-called Kigali Principles, a set of non-binding rules championed by Rwanda, which reflect a distinctive feature of Rwandan peacekeeping policy not shared by India, namely enthusiastic acceptance of the perceived duty to intervene and use force against those who threaten civilians, even in internal conflicts.[71] India's discomfort with interventionist peace operations will be explored later, but Rwanda's very different response is unsurprising.

Aside from these normative aspects, peacekeeping serves the RPF's political interests in several ways. Domestically, it is a source of national pride and so a means of cohering the previously shattered nation around its leaders. It also enhances the international prestige of a state long associated with chaos but now seen by the developed world as a responsible force for good in the region and thus a more attractive candidate for strategic partnership, aid or investment. Kagame's 2016 comment, 'They called us a small failed state. But we refused to fail. We refused to be small', can be combined with that of an RPF colleague who ascribed much of Rwanda's progress to its international status, boosted by 'peacekeeping and its role in regional and continental integration'. Rwanda was 'a country whose achievements have been there for everyone to see'.[72] More objective support for these assertions is provided by Beswick, who agrees that peacekeeping has brought benefits in

---

[68] Then vice-president Kagame in a 1996 interview, in Gourevitch and Kagame (1996), pp. 174, 175; On a similar theme see 'Speech by H.E. Ambassador Valentine Rugwabiza, Permanent Representative to the United Nations and Member of Cabinet of the Government of Rwanda, at the 23rd Commemoration of the Genocide against the Tutsi' Permanent Mission of Rwanda to the United Nations (2017).

[69] Beswick (2014), pp. 222, 223.

[70] 'Statement by Minister of State Eugene-Richard Gasana' Permanent Mission of Rwanda to the United Nations (2016).

[71] Kigali Principles on the Protection of Civilians (2015).

[72] Paul Kagame and RPF cadre member Protais Musoni quoted in a report of the celebrations for the 22nd anniversary of Rwanda's liberation. See 'Rwanda celebrates 22 years of Liberation' The East African (2016).

the form of international prestige, Rwanda being 'a model country when it comes to professional peacekeeping'.[73] It has also afforded a degree of untouchability, the UN having been reluctant to apply pressure on Rwanda in respect of its own alleged transgressions in the DRC, for fear of provoking its withdrawal from UNKPOs.[74]

In Rwanda's case, security, economic and institutional rationales are closely linked and of much more significance than in India. The costs of maintaining the RDF have been considerably offset by UN reimbursements for peacekeeping expenses, to the tune of 70% of its total defence budget in some years.[75] Northern donors like the US, the EU, Germany and the UK also subsidise its peacekeeping activities. The supply of specialist training and logistical support is part of an emphasis on achieving African self-sufficiency in relation to peacekeeping and security while also securing reliable partners on the continent.[76] It is, consequently, the strongest military power in the region and a key ally of the US, which impacts very positively on Rwanda's regional standing and its own security *vis-à-vis* its neighbours in a frequently volatile area.[77] Further institutional benefits include the unifying and professionalising effect of peacekeeping duties on a military force, which includes former adversaries in its ranks, and the lucrative bonuses, drawn from UN allowances, which multiply the salaries of participating soldiers several-fold. It also ensures that ambitious officers have less time for political plotting. Taken together, these factors have contributed to the creation of a capable modern army that, to bring the rationales full circle back to the political, has become a key symbol and instrument of national unity and international relevance.[78]

As expected, there is a considerable divergence in the rationales of the two states, stemming from their distinctive experiences, identities and interests. However, the established regional power with global ambitions and the small, recovering, wounded state anxious to achieve internal cohesion and international security do share a desire to play a larger role internationally and to achieve the respect not always afforded to them by the established international elite. This chapter will go on to consider the factors that threaten India and Rwanda's continued participation in UN peacekeeping. From a theoretical perspective, it is probably only worth noting now that the remaining predominance of the Global North is certainly not, in Rwandan eyes, founded on any form of 'social legitimacy'. Memories of genocide and international inaction preclude this.

---

[73] The UN Assistant Secretary-General for Peace Building Support, quoted in Beswick (2014), p. 220.

[74] Allegedly in relation to reports of RPA/RDF genocide against Hutus in the DRC, it being claimed that Kagame had threatened to withdraw his forces from UN peace operations if unfavourable reports were not amended. See Beswick (2014), pp. 220, 221; Beswick and Jowell (2014).

[75] Wilen (2012), pp. 1332, 1333.

[76] Wilen (2012), p. 1331; Beswick (2014), p. 216; Jowell (2014), p. 288; US Department of State (2012).

[77] Waugh (2004), p. 98; Beswick and Jowell (2014).

[78] Beswick and Jowell (2014).

In terms of 'sticking points' threatening continued participation, India is less sanguine than Rwanda. Some of its complaints are commonplace in peacekeeping and, taken individually, are unlikely to derail its participation, e.g. the sometimes indistinct command and control arrangements of UN operations and the reputational damage caused by the occasional misconduct of its own peacekeepers.[79] Of far greater concern, however, are the trend to confrontational enforcement and the R2P doctrine, the lack of influence that India has over UN mandates and its perception of an international 'social' stigma attending its engagement in UN peacekeeping.

India's ambassador to the UN, Asoke Kumar Mukerji, succinctly expressed the country's unease with the interventionist approach adopted by the UN after the debacles of the mid-1990s:

> India is completely committed to peacekeeping provided peacekeeping is what we know it to be. The soldiers in the blue helmets, under the blue flag, are impartial. They are not supposed to be partisan. If somebody wants soldiers to go in and fight they should hire mercenaries, not take UN soldiers.[80]

As noted earlier, the equality and sovereignty of states have been an article of faith in India since independence, and it fears R2P's potential to become a thinly disguised excuse for the larger states to interfere in smaller ones whenever it suits them, as per colonial practice.[81] India was 'the worst of the recalcitrant'[82] in its opposition to the concept during the discussions leading to its endorsement by the UN at the 2005 World Summit on Genocide, and this scepticism has surfaced operationally.[83] In 2010, for example, New Delhi instructed the Indian commander of a sizeable peacekeeping force in the DRC to disobey a UN command to resist rebels threatening a civilian area.[84] However, India's verbally consistent stance on R2P over the years has often been belied by a pragmatic acceptance of confrontational mandates, which continue to be issued to this day. The government's enduring disquiet is strongly expressed in a 2017 speech by the Secretary for External Affairs:

> We also tell ourselves that little purpose is served if a UN Mission does not ensure the "protection of civilians" - no matter what the consequences. Yet …we do not adequately acknowledge that there are serious implications for the safety and security of our peacekeepers…when we ask them to ignore cardinal principles of effective UN peacekeeping – i.e., "consent of all parties", "neutrality", and resort to force only in self-defence – in pursuit of "robust mandates" that we set for them.[85]

---

[79] As in the DRC in 2008 when Indian peacekeepers were accused of sexual abuse. See Hansel and Moeller (2014), p. 154.

[80] 'What's the Point of Peacekeepers When They Don't Keep the Peace?' The Guardian (2015).

[81] Jaganathan and Kurtz (2014), p. 464.

[82] Unnamed Western diplomat quoted in Jaganathan and Kurtz (2014), p. 469.

[83] Jaganathan and Kurtz (2014), pp. 464–469.

[84] McGreal (2015).

[85] 'Inaugural Address by Preeti Saran' Ministry of External Affairs (2017).

Yet Indian forces continue to take part in 'robust', enforcement-oriented UN missions.[86] This highlights a common thread in Indian 'dissent': that the country's expressions of concern seem insufficient to affect any change in UN policy, possibly because India rarely follows through convincingly, such as by withdrawing from peacekeeping. Explanations for this will follow in Sect. 3, but it is becoming plain that one of India's normative rationales for engaging in peacekeeping, i.e. the UN's moral influence and principled authenticity, is wearing a little thin.

To add insult to India's injury, it has no input into the 'unwieldy' and 'unimplementable' mandates that 'put the credibility of the UN and the safety and security of peacekeepers at grave risk'. Instead, this remains the preserve of a 'fragmented' UN Security Council, the five permanent members of which contribute very few peacekeepers between them.[87] Head of the Army General Dalbir Singh Suhag has spoken of the 'right' of India, as one of the largest troop contributors, to participate in the decisions of the UN Security Council regarding the formulation of peacekeeping mandates and deployment of forces,[88] while Prime Minister Modi told a peacekeeping summit in 2015 that 'mandates are ambitious; but, resources are often inadequate …problems (in UN peacekeeping operations) arise to a large extent because troop contributing countries do not have a role in the decision-making process'.[89] India's frustration is all the greater because it has international law on its side. Article 44 of the UN Charter requires the UN Security Council to involve troop contributors in decisions relating to the deployment of forces under Article 43 (which envisaged a standing reserve to deal with breaches of the peace). Article 43 has never been implemented, but the legal principle is clear.[90] Finally, and perhaps most damagingly, there is a growing belief in India that its involvement is actually detrimental to its standing in the world. The 'cool kids' of the international community simply do not do UN peacekeeping any more, so that '…in public, governmental and UN perception around the world, India becomes bracketed with poor countries with bloated and antiquated defence forces desperate to earn foreign money'.[91]

All this contributes to a growing disillusionment amongst Indian commentators, who no longer see peacekeeping as a 'ticket to global power'. Singh remarked in 2007 that India should 'contribute only if and when there are at least some Western and industrialised countries also willing to shoulder the burden', but nothing has

---

[86] For example, the amended MONUSCO mandate of March 2014, which authorised 'targeted operations' to 'neutralise' armed groups threating civilians and state security in the DRC. See UNSCR (2014), p. 7; Hansel and Moeller (2014), pp. 146, 147.

[87] From a newspaper report of comments by India's Deputy Permanent Representative Tanmaya Lal, speaking at a General Assembly debate on peacekeeping operations. See 'India Slams UN for Unwieldy Peacekeeping Mandates' The Daily Pioneer (2016).

[88] 'India Has Right to Attend UNSC Decisions on Peacekeeping Ops' The Daily Pioneer (2015).

[89] 'Statement by Prime Minister at the Summit on Peacekeeping in New York' Ministry of External Affairs (2015).

[90] Gray (2016), p. 210.

[91] Thakur (2011), p. 900.

changed.[92] The North still does not do peacekeeping to any meaningful extent, and India, literally, soldiers on in its place.

Rwanda, on the other hand, seems a lot more sanguine. Crucially, it embraces the R2P principle while seldom missing an opportunity to remind the UN of its 'woefully inadequate' response to continuing atrocities against civilians.[93] Instead, the most serious barriers to its continued participation in UN peacekeeping are competing institutional preferences for crisis management, tensions with the UN over the DRC and restraints on finance and military capacity.[94]

While UN peacekeeping helps express Rwanda's self-identity as a leader and protector in Africa, the country's lingering anger with the UN—over 1994 and its censure of Rwanda's DRC interventions—could potentially cause an abandonment of UN peace operations in favour of AU missions, which would better fit with its belief in African solutions for African problems. Closer military partnership within East Africa has the same appeal, specifically in the form of the East African Standby Force (EASF), for which Rwanda is obliged to 'ring fence' a rapid deployment contingent.[95] However, Rwanda's dependence on foreign financial assistance incentivises its continuing focus on UN missions because neither the AU nor the EASF funds contributors.[96]

That said, the UN's notorious tardiness in reimbursing states could yet negate that advantage—Rwanda was owed $37 million in 2016—and the heavy burden placed on its military by UN (and AU) peacekeeping also threatens indefinite troop contributions.[97] Rwanda, like most troop contributors, operates a 'rule of thirds', whereby for every contingent on mission, one is being trained to replace it and a further one is recovering, retraining and re-integrating into its 'normal' functions, which imposes serious pressure on its overall operational capacity.[98] Rwanda's commitment to peacekeeping, and its utility as a regional ally, does attract foreign military capacity funding, but this is not a given. In 2012, for example, the US and the UK, amongst others, briefly suspended military and general aid to Rwanda in response to its support for the M23 rebel group, which UN forces were actually combatting at the time.[99]

---

[92] Singh (2007), p. 82.

[93] 'Statement by Rwandan UN Charge d'Affaires, a.i, Jeanne d'Arc Byaje' Permanent Mission of Rwanda to the United Nations (2016).

[94] Beswick and Jowell (2014).

[95] The EASF was established to provide a regional capability for rapid deployment of forces to carry out preventive deployment, rapid intervention, peace support/stability operations and peace enforcement. It, like the AU, is very much oriented towards the R2P doctrine); 'Remarks by President Paul Kagame' Government, Republic of Rwanda (2014).

[96] Wilen (2012), pp. 1332, 1333; Renwick (2015).

[97] 'UN Owes $80 million to India for Peacekeeping Operations' The Daily Pioneer (2013).

[98] Beswick and Jowell (2014).

[99] An example of robust 'peace enforcement' on the part of the UN. See Gray (2016), p. 205; Smith (2013b); 'USA Says Rwanda Army the Most Capable of World's Peacekeepers' News of Rwanda (2014); Beswick (2014), pp. 229, 230; Greening (2013).

In any case, the importance of peacekeeping to Rwanda, to President Kagame himself, and a favourable cost/benefits balance make its continuance in UN peacekeeping both likely and easily understandable. India's apparent determination to continue will take a little more explaining.

The points of coincidence emerging from the case study are strikingly few but significant in explaining the commitment of the two states to UN peacekeeping. India and Rwanda share the experience of colonisation (but not of colonial military service), subsequent internal turbulence, a strong political and moral sense of the extended role they should play in the wider world and a willingness to challenge the hegemony of the North to that end, albeit to varying degrees. They each maintain localised rivalries and share a South-to-South orientation. However, the many points of divergence also require attention. Beyond the broad brush of similarity, the particular national histories and circumstances have resulted in distinct identities and interests, motivations, concerns and emphases in peacekeeping activity. This finding is central to the argument here, in that it evidences the disparate and very individual nature of troop-contributing countries, which rather militates against the type of 'blanket' explanations provided by much of the related scholarship.

The following chapter comprises an analysis of the evidence amassed so far. It describes the nature and methodology of the hegemony of the Global North before assessing, with reference to India and Rwanda, the extent to which it accounts for the involvement of the Global South in peacekeeping or, conversely, the degree to which the two countries have been able to resist it and retain agency in their participation.

## 4 Analysis

As regards the nature of the hegemony enjoyed by the Global North, it is rooted in a centuries-old structural relationship between the two hemispheres, which, with or without formal colonialism, has always depended on asymmetrical economic arrangements in favour of the developed world. This has led indirectly to the 'political and cultural subordination' of the South.[100] The 'Open Veins of Latin America' resonates in Africa and Asia too, and, to Pugh, the imbalance is maintained in the modern age through 'the strategic imperatives of the post-industrialised capitalist world'.[101] Those imperatives work to further neoliberalism, which easily qualifies as 'the leading social force in a given historical structure', necessary to and constitutional of a neo-Gramscian hegemony.[102] The UN's place in all this is fiercely contested, but it suffices here to deny it the leading role ascribed by the sceptical

---

[100] That is, the 'dependency model'. Weisskopf (1981), pp. 327–336.

[101] Galeano (1973); Pugh (2004), p. 39.

[102] To neo-Gramscians like Cox, 'historical structure is 'a picture of a particular configuration of forces which imposes pressures and constraints'. Cox (1981), pp. 126–155.

scholarship.[103] Kennedy points out that 'the United Nations is not, and never has been, a large and centralized actor in world affairs'.[104] Rather, it was deliberately created, not as 'an embryonic world government, but an international corporation… with the nation-states as shareholders'. Consequently, it displays the dysfunctionality of its design, whereby the projection of Great Power rivalries and national interests and the voluntary nature of troop contributions render impossible the kind of command and control necessary for efficient orchestration, notwithstanding the UN's considerable normative influence. Cunliffe, for instance, may see imperialism behind every peacekeeper, but it is surely more plausible to regard the UN's switch to 'robust peacekeeping' and deep-rooted peacebuilding as a considered response to the failings of the past. In the 1990s, 'impartiality' and 'consent' meant standing aside for mass murderers and 'complicity with evil', while passive, 'traditional peacekeeping' has frequently served only to 'freeze' conflicts indefinitely.[105] These changes of tack by the UN might suit the neoliberalists, but it requires a rather unhealthy amount of cynicism to regard that as their main drivers. A final reference should perhaps be made to Pugh, who sees the UN as increasingly marginalised and 'neutered' by these capitalist forces, which operate through the exploitation of their hegemonic position by the national governments.[106]

In terms of methodology, the Northern countries are clearly conscious of their hegemonic advantage, which, in relation to peacekeeping, allows them the luxury of leaving it to others. Smith and Williams reference the US and the UK to present several reasons for this aversion to UN operations, including a focus on alternative strategic priorities and alliances, e.g. NATO in Afghanistan; a reluctance to submit to UN command and rules of engagement following negative experiences; and the perception that its expensively trained troops are overqualified for the task.[107] A lack of domestic political support, or demand, for peacekeeping also combines with various other, country-specific, political and situational qualms to encourage the Northern states to leave the 'coalface' aspects of missions to the Global South.[108] The developed countries, however, remain ostensible subscribers to the powerful UN peacekeeping norm and attempt to protect their standing as 'good international citizens' by financing the lion's share of the UN peacekeeping budget and providing logistical support, military funding and training, and token numbers of military specialists.[109] Incidentally, Smith and Williams make no mention of imperialism, and the general Northern conception of peacekeeping, if there is one, could be as easily summarised as a tedious but risk-prone chore, which the Northern states feel obliged

---

[103] Cunliffe (2013), p. 123.
[104] Kennedy (2006).
[105] UNPO (2000), p. ix; Richmond (2004), p. 86; Gray (2016), pp. 195, 196.
[106] Pugh (2004), pp. 39–44, 54.
[107] Williams (2013), p. 109.
[108] See Williams (2013), pp. 108–112; Smith (2013a), pp. 71–92.
[109] Coleman (2013), pp. 58, 59; US Department of State (2012).

to pretend some enthusiasm for while using their supporting role to further their own strategic or economic interests.[110]

In any case, Northern support makes peacekeeping possible for many of the Southern countries, which would be hard pressed to contribute without it. Rwanda, certainly, would be unable to achieve the rapid deployments it promotes without the US Air force, nor would its forces be as competent if denied American and European training.

Making something possible, however, is different from compelling or convincing someone to do it, and India does not require that level of outside support. To what extent, then, does Northern hegemony account for India's and Rwanda's participation in UN peacekeeping operations? In the neo-Gramscian construct, hegemony would require that the subordinate states share the peacekeeping norm and believe in the legitimacy of those that propagate it. Alternatively, they must believe that compliance is in their material or political interests. The 'legitimacy' scenario does not apply to either India or Rwanda. India is openly critical of the North's failure to deploy substantial forces to UN missions, and Rwanda has a generally low opinion of both the UN and international community. The UN had previously enjoyed some moral legitimacy with India, but this depended on its perceived impartiality rather than any hegemonic function and decreased markedly once the UN embraced R2P. Instead, both countries contribute to UN peacekeeping for their own specific and often quite different reasons but, essentially, because they think it is in keeping with their own sense of themselves and their national interests to do so. So in terms of the exercise of hegemony, the most the North can achieve with India and Rwanda is to persuade them to continue peacekeeping in its place in return for the rewards they seek from the relationship: for India, recognition as an equal by the developed countries and a place on the UNSC and, for Rwanda, the financial and military aid necessary for its Afro-centric peacekeeping, regional standing and security. This might qualify for the sort of narrow, self-interest, hegemony discussed earlier, but even then, only if India and Rwanda were being induced into a relationship from which they got less than they gave.

In that sense, there are strong indications that the North's hegemony is under strain. Rwanda is not at all deferential to it and seems to get the best of the bargain from this (roughly) symbiotic relationship. Its status as the USA's key ally in East Africa has benefitted its regional standing, and foreign funding and training has helped its peacekeepers gain international prestige, while the North exercises little control and influence over it in return. Wilen remarks that foreign donors contributed 95% of the funding for Rwanda's long drawn-out disarmament, demobilisation and re-integration programme but had no say in how it was implemented. In fact, she states that 'there are no external actors able to impose conditions on the Rwandan government'.[111] This contrasts sharply with the experience of the Latin American

---

[110] The UK, as an example, claimed a 'leading role' in UN peacekeeping in September 2016, when it had 343 troops committed to UN missions. See 'UK Bolsters Support to Peacekeeping in South Sudan' UK Ministry of Defence (2016).

[111] Wilen (2012), pp. 1330, 1331.

states fighting the US's proxy wars against drugs and terrorism in their own countries. There, funding is conditional on American dictation of the methods employed.[112] Similarly, the reinstatement, after only five months, of the foreign donor aid withdrawn following Rwanda's repeated incursions into the DRC suggests little heart to impose control on Kagame's regime. Wilen explains this by referring to Rwanda as a 'donor darling', benefitting from 'a legacy of international guilt' and thus 'attracting massive foreign aid, with surprisingly few conditions attached'.[113] This guilt, Rwanda's importance as a regional peacebuilder and its unrelenting calling out of the international community for the failures of 1994, has given it the upper hand in many senses in its relationship with the developed world, to the extent that it can easily be described as having successfully resisted its hegemony. Rwanda gives and gets from the relationship very much what it wants.

The balance is not as positive in India's case. It has had far less success in achieving an advantageous quid pro quo through peacekeeping or achieving redress for those aspects of UN operations that trouble it. In that sense, India is still suffering from the hegemony, even though it does not recognise any social legitimacy in the North's attempts to impose it. It has been unable to divert the UN from R2P interventionism and extended peacekeeping mandates, into which it still has no input; the North still 'pays but won't play'; and India's machinations to gain a permanent seat on the UNSC, secure more influence within the UN or otherwise move up the international hierarchy appear stalled, hindered, in the views of many, by its continued association with UN peacekeeping and the 'poor people' of the Global South.[114]

The case study sheds some light on this shortfall. Firstly, India's international ambitions are, on the face of it at least, far grander than Rwanda's and meet a correspondingly greater level of resistance from the established powers of the Global North, as they protect their predominance. Secondly, India lacks not just Rwanda's emotional leverage but also its conviction in pursuing its interests on the world stage. India makes frequent and frank criticism of the developed world and the UN but invariably fails to follow through on it, an example being the brief, ultimately fruitless, withdrawal of its helicopter fleet from UN operations in 2011 in protest at its disproportionate peacekeeping burden.[115] In Ramesh Thakur's words, 'Indian foreign policy has a habit of not letting national interests come in the way of abstract principles. Its leaders are easily seduced by praise and thrilled by a pat on the back.'[116] The North is happy to have India do more than its share of peacekeeping because it relieves it of an unwelcome job, while India continues out of a commitment to its perceived identity as a moral actor in the world, in the increasingly vain hope that doing its duty will secure its just reward. Unfortunately, it is unlikely that

---

[112] Even though these militarised approaches have impacted extremely detrimentally on host countries like Colombia and Mexico. Youngers and Rosin (2005), pp. 1–11, 45–47.

[113] Wilen (2012), p. 1326.

[114] Cunliffe (2013), p. 192; Hansel and Moeller (2014), p. 151.

[115] India quickly climbed down and began supplying helicopters again, in return for only one machine from the international community. Hansel and Moeller (2014), p. 151.

[116] Thakur (2011), p. 900.

India will ever gain the full attention, let alone the respect, of the developed countries on these issues unless it withdraws from UN peacekeeping. Even then, it would have to be joined by a substantial number of Southern states—a very unlikely occurrence—if the disinterested Global North was to be at all disturbed.

In addition, India's stated aspirations to a greater global role have become less convincing in recent years, belying that part of its claimed self-identity. Acharya, echoed by Mukherjee and Malone, remarks on India's lingering regional, rather than global, focus, despite its talk of greater ambitions, and notes that there 'do not seem to be any obvious Indian ideas or blueprints to inspire the reform and restructuring of the global multilateral order'.[117] Similarly, Jaganathan and Kurtz identify a disconnect between India's projection of itself as an 'emerging power' and its current abstention from significant diplomatic engagement beyond its region, which gives rise to the suspicion that India still has a regional, rather than a global, mindset.[118] If, as Wendt indicates, identity and interests are mutually constituted, this would go a long way to explaining why India has yet to fully shake off the hegemony of the Global North, although it has clearly started down that road.[119]

However, as the purpose of the case study is to shed light on the broader phenomenon of Global South peacekeeping, some thought must be given to the applicability of its learnings beyond India and Rwanda. Further in-depth case studies are impractical here, but a significant commonality in circumstances and motivations, both within and across the continental divide, is quickly apparent from a review of the approaches and practices of Ethiopia and Indonesia, 1st and 10th respectively in the rankings of UN troop-contributing countries of May 2017.

Populous, emerging Indonesia shares India's belief that peacekeeping will help it gain a louder voice in the UN, 'play a larger role on the world stage' and project its (comparatively nascent) democratic identity.[120] It also uses UN peacekeeping to rehabilitate its national image after bitter internal conflicts in Aceh and East Timor and to occupy and professionalise an army left virtually idle thereafter. Like Rwanda, it is partly motivated by UN reimbursements and allowances and owes much of its commitment to peacekeeping to a 'catalytic' individual, in its case former President and UN peacekeeper Yudhoyono.[121] Finally, Indonesia mirrors India's wariness concerning departures from traditional, 'Holy Trinity' peacekeeping missions while pragmatically endorsing forceful mandates in extreme instances.[122]

---

[117] Acharya (2011), p. 363; Mukherjee and Malone (2011), pp. 327–329.

[118] Jaganathan and Kurtz (2014), p. 461.

[119] Wendt (1992), p. 398.

[120] Capie (2016), pp. 5–7; Agensky and Barker (2012), p. 114. Indonesia has been contributing significant numbers of peacekeepers since 2004. In May 2017, it had 2719 UN peacekeepers deployed across nine missions, the biggest contingents being in Lebanon and Darfur. See UN Peacekeeping Resources (2017).

[121] Capie (2016), p. 7; Poole (2014), p. 47.

[122] See Capie (2016), pp. 8, 9 for Indonesian reservations regarding the use of force in the DRC and its encouragement for a forceful intervention in Syria.

Ethiopia, for its part, conforms to the Rwandan 'model' in many respects. While sharing India's normative belief in the international collective security system, it is recovering from decades of conflict and is chiefly motivated by political and security rationales and a consciousness of the international community's historical failure to assist in times of dire need.[123] Consequently, it too believes that, ideally, Africa should solve its own problems and demonstrates agency by confining its large-scale UN deployments to Darfur and South Sudan, where its own security and influence is at stake.[124] Its peacekeeping, like Rwanda's, brings financial, institutional and political benefits in the shape of foreign military aid and UN reimbursements, improving overall military capacity being particularly important to Ethiopia, as it too is threatened by the instability of its neighbours.[125]

Overall, the learnings gained from the India-Rwanda case study seem to hold good for Indonesia and Ethiopia and thus, potentially, for the wider Global South. Most significantly, both countries appear to have considerable agency in their participation as they address their specific situations and aspirations through peacekeeping. A much deeper study would be required to establish the extent to which they are constrained by hegemony, but there are indications that the experience of the latter pair of states approximates to that of the former, with Indonesia, like India, still further away from getting what it wants from the developed world.

## 5 Conclusion

This study has furnished two main conclusions relating to the research question and stated argument.

Firstly, the states of the Global North exert a long-established, but increasingly challenged, neoliberal hegemony over the Global South, the compliance of the latter being based largely on perceived self-interest rather than any sense of the North's legitimacy to lead. In relation to peacekeeping, the continued hegemony allows the North to restrict its involvement with UN peacekeeping to controlling mandates, funding and support functions, leaving the Global South to put their people in harm's way.

Secondly, UN peacekeeping is a vehicle by which the more assertive states of the Global South can challenge the Northern hegemony. The 'Most Different' case study served to highlight the widely varying rationales for the participation of two such countries. These emanate from their specific situations, evolving identities—their sense of their place in the world—and consequent changes to their perceived

---

[123] Principally, when Italy invaded the then Abyssinia in 1935–1936. Yihdego et al. (2016), pp. 3, 4.
[124] UN Peacekeeping Resources (2017). Ethiopia has been a regular troop contributor since the late 1990s and in May 2017 had a total of 8229 peacekeepers deployed across five UN missions. All but nine of this number were in South Sudan, Darfur or Abyei.
[125] E.g. Al Shabab incursions into Somalia. Firsing (2014), pp. 54–56; Dersso (2013); 'UK Supports Ethiopian Peacekeeping' Mareeg (2017).

interests. In this sense, points of difference are as significant as points of similarity, but both states are well aware of the agendas of the North and perceive peacekeeping as a means of advancing their claims to a more prominent role in international affairs. They increasingly reject subordination, but their experiences suggest that the extent to which a Southern state can resist Northern hegemony is in direct proportion to the degree of certainty and conviction invested in their sense of identity and its expression through national interests.

To conclude, this article has evidenced a degree of agency on the part of the Global South, which certainly does not conform to the sceptics' depiction of a uniform collection of brow-beaten states, bound by hegemonic structures to do the North's bidding. Or to return to the analogy of the title, the stream may still be running against the states of the Global South, but some, at least, are inclined, and able, to swim against the flow.

## References

Acharya A (2011) Can Asia lead? Power ambitions and global governance in the twenty-first century. Int Aff 87(4):851–869

Africa vows to support India's permanent seat quest at UN Security Council (2011) Asian Age (26 May 2011). https://search.proquest.com/docview/868595979?rfr_id=info%3Axri%2Fsid%3Aprimo. Accessed 3 July 2017

Agensky J, Barker J (2012) Indonesia and the liberal peace: recovering southern agency in global governance. Globalizations 9(1):107–124

Amar P (2012) Global South to the rescue: emerging humanitarian superpowers and globalizing rescue industries. Globalizations 9(1):1–13

Ban Thanks India for Contribution to UN Peacekeeping Efforts (2014) The Daily Pioneer (28 September 2014). http://www.dailypioneer.com/top-stories/ban-thanks-india-for-contribution-to-un-peacekeeping-efforts.html. Accessed 30 June 2017

Banerjee D (2013a) Peacekeeping contributor profile: India. Providing for Peacekeeping. http://www.providingforpeacekeeping.org/2014/04/03/contributor-profile-india/. Accessed 24 June 2017

Banerjee D (2013b) India. In: Bellamy A, Williams P (eds) Providing peacekeepers: the politics, challenges and future of United Nations peacekeeping contributions. Oxford University Press, Oxford, pp 225–245

Bellamy A, Williams P (2013) Introduction. In: Bellamy A, Williams P (eds) Providing peacekeepers: the politics, challenges and future of United Nations peacekeeping contributions. Oxford University Press, Oxford, pp 1–22

Beswick D (2014) The risks of African military capacity building: lessons from Rwanda. Afr Aff 113(451):212–231

Beswick D, Jowell M (2014) Peacekeeping contributor profile: Rwanda. Providing for Peacekeeping. http://www.providingforpeacekeeping.org/2015/03/30/peacekeeping-contributor-profile-/. Accessed 30 June 2017

Bjorkdahl A (2006) Promoting norms through peacekeeping: UNPREDEP and conflict prevention. Int Peacekeep 13(2):214–228

Capie D (2016) Indonesia as an emerging peacekeeping power: norm revisionist or pragmatic provider? Contemp Southeast Asia 38(1):1–27

Chandler D (2001) The people-centred approach to peace operations: the new UN agenda. Int Peacekeep 8(1):1–19

Clark I (2011) Hegemony in international society. Oxford University Press, Oxford

Coleman K (2013) Token troop contributions to United Nations peacekeeping operations. In: Bellamy A, Williams P (eds) Providing peacekeepers: the politics, challenges and future of United Nations peacekeeping contributions. Oxford University Press, Oxford, pp 47–68

Cox R (1981) Social forces, states and world orders: beyond international relations theory. Millennium: J Int Stud 10(2):126–155

Cox R (1987) Production, power and world order: social forces in the making of history. Columbia University Press, New York

Cox R (1996) Approaches to world order. Cambridge University Press, Cambridge

Cunliffe P (2013) Legions of peace: UN peacekeepers of the global south. Hurst, London

de Coning C, Karlsrud J, Breidlid I (2013) Turning to the south: civilian capacity in the aftermath of conflict. Glob Gov 19:135–152

Dersso S (2013) Peacekeeping contributor profile: Ethiopia. Providing for Peacekeeping. http://www.providingforpeacekeeping.org/2015/03/30/peacekeeping-contributor-profile-/. Accessed 30 June 2016

Dirlik A (2007) Global south: predicament and promise. The Global South:12–23

Economist Intelligence Unit (2016) Report, democracy index 2016. Economist Intelligence Unit Ltd, London

Finnemore M (1996) National interests in international society. Cornell University Press, New York

Firsing S (2014) Thinking through the role of Africa's militaries in peacekeeping: the cases of Nigeria, Ethiopia and Rwanda. S Afr J Int Aff 21(1):45–67

Galeano E (1973) Open veins of Latin America. Monthly Review Press, New York

Game Over for Democracy in Rwanda (2015) Freedom House. https://freedomhouse.org/blog/game-over-democracy-rwanda. Accessed 30 June 2017

Gerring J (2004) What is a case study and what is it good for? Am Polit Sci Rev 98(2):341–354

Gill S (1993) Epistemology, ontology, and the Italian school. In: Gill S (ed) Historical materialism and international relations. Cambridge University Press, Cambridge

Gourevitch P, Kagame P (1996) After genocide. Transition (72):162–194

Gray C (2016) The 2015 Report on *Uniting Our Strengths for Peace*. Chin J Int Law:193–213

Greening J (2013) Written statement to parliament on aid to Rwanda. UK Government. https://www.gov.uk/government/speeches/statement-from-justine-greening-on-aid-to-rwanda. Accessed 12 July 2012

Hansel M, Moeller M (2014) House of cards? India's rationales for contributing to UN peacekeeping. Glob Change Peace Secur 26(2):141–157

Howe B, Kondoch B, Spijkers O (2015) Normative and legal challenges to UN peacekeeping operations. J Int Peacekeep 19:1–31

Inaugural Address by Preeti Saran, Secretary (East) on the occasion of the Senior Mission Leaders Course conducted by Centre for UN Peacekeeping at Manekshaw Centre in New Delhi (2017) Ministry of External Affairs (20 March 2017). http://mea.gov.in/Speeches-Statements.htm?dtl/28189/inaugural+address+by+secretary+east+on+the+occasion+of+the+senior+missi on+leaders+course+conducted+by+centre+for+un+peacekeeping+at+manekshaw+centre+in+ new+delhi+march+20+2017. Accessed 11 July 2017

India Has Right to Attend UNSC Decisions on Peacekeeping Ops (2015) The Daily Pioneer (28 March 2015). http://www.dailypioneer.com/top-stories/india-has-right-to-attend-unsc-decisions-on-peacekeeping-ops.html. Accessed 11 July 2017

India Slams UN for Unwieldy Peacekeeping Mandate (2016) The Daily Pioneer (27 October 2016). http://www.dailypioneer.com/nation/india-slams-unsc--for-unwieldy-peacekeeping--mandates.html. Accessed 22 Dec 2016

India's Global Role, Speech by Foreign Secretary Shivshankar Menon. Cambridge (2010) Gateway House (20 September 2010). http://www.gatewayhouse.in/speech-foreign-secretary-mr-shivshankar-menon-india-and-international-security-inte/. Accessed 4 Sept 2017

International Monetary Fund (2017) World Economic Outlook Database. https://www.imf.org/external/pubs/ft/weo/2017/01/weodata. Accessed 23 June 2017

Jaganathan M, Kurtz G (2014) Singing the tune of sovereignty: India and the responsibility to protect. Conflict Secur Dev 14(4):461–487

Jowell M (2014) Cohesion through socialization: liberation, tradition and modernity in the forging of the Rwanda defence force. J East Afr Stud 8(2):278–293

Kennedy P (2006) UN: the World's Scapegoat. Edmonton Journal (28 August 2006)

Kigali Principles on the Protection of Civilians (2015) Global Centre for the Responsibility to Protect (29 May 2015). http://www.globalr2p.org/resources/985. Accessed 4 July 2017

Lamont C (2015) Research methods in international relations. SAGE, London

Lebow R (2003) The tragic vision of politics: ethics, interests and orders. Cambridge University Press, Cambridge

Levin J, MacKay J, Nasrirzadeh A (2016) Selectorate theory and the democratic peacekeeping hypothesis: evidence from Fiji and Bangladesh. Int Peacekeep 23(1):107–132

McGreal (2015) What's the point of peacekeepers when they don't keep the peace? The Guardian (17 September 2015). https://www.theguardian.com/world/2015/sep/17/un-united-nations-peacekeepers-rwanda-bosnia. Accessed 10 July 2017

Mukherjee R, Malone D (2011) From high ground to high table: the evolution of Indian multilateralism. Glob Gov 17(3):311–329

Nambiar S (2014) India and United Nations peacekeeping operations. Ministry of External Affairs. http://www.mea.gov.in/articles-in-indian-media.htm?dtl/22776/india+and+united+nations+peacekeeping+operations. Accessed 1 July 2017

Nieto W (2012) Brazil's grand design for combining global south solidarity and national interests: a discussion of peacekeeping operations in Haiti and Timor. Globalizations 9(1):161–178

Peters G (1998) Comparative politics, theory and method. New York University Press, New York

Poole A (2014) The foreign policy nexus: national interests, political values and identity. In: Roberts C, Habir A, Sebastian L (eds) Indonesia at home and abroad: economics, politics and security. Australian National University, Canberra

Providing for Peacekeeping (2017) Peacekeeping data: graphs. http://www.providingforpeacekeeping.org/peacekeeping-data-graphs/. Accessed 18 June 2017

Pugh M (2004) Peacekeeping and critical theory. Int Peacekeep 11:39–58

Remarks by President Paul Kagame During Summit on Strengthening International Peacekeeping on 26 September 2014 (2014) Government of Republic of Rwanda (13 November 2014). http://gov.rw/newsdetails2/?tx_ttnews%5Btt_news%5D=521&cHash=688a19ca739e0b5ff0fccf79f6dd2520. Accessed 12 July 2017

Renwick D (2015) Council on foreign relations: peace operations in Africa. 15 May. https://www.cfr.org/backgrounder/peace-operations-africa. Accessed 29 Aug 2017

Richmond O (2004) UN peace operations and the dilemmas of the peacebuilding consensus. Int Peacekeep 11(1):83–101

Richmond O (2009) Liberal peace transitions: towards a post-liberal peace in IR? E-International Relations. http://www.e-ir.info/2009/09/03/liberal-peace-transitions-towards-a-postliberal-peace-in-ir/. Accessed 25 May 2017

Roth K (2009) Human rights watch: the power of horror in Rwanda. https://www.hrw.org/news/2009/04/11/power-horror-rwanda. Accessed 27 June 2017

Ruggie J (1998) What makes the world hang together? Neo-utilitarianism and the social constructivist challenge. Int Organ 52(4):855–885

Rwanda celebrates 22 years of Liberation (2016) The East African (2 July 2016). http://www.theeastafrican.co.ke/Rwanda/News/Rwanda-celebrates-22-years-of-Liberation/1433218-3275894-12391uhz/index.html. Accessed 5 July 2017

Said E (1994) Culture and imperialism. Random House, New York

Singh S (2007) Peacekeeping in Africa: a global strategy. S Afr J Int Aff:71–85

Smith A (2013a) United States of America. In: Bellamy A, Williams P (eds) Providing peacekeepers: the politics, challenges and future of United Nations peacekeeping contributions. Oxford University Press, Oxford, pp 71–92

Smith (2013b) US blocks military aid to Rwanda over alleged backing of M23 child soldiers. The Guardian (4 October 2013). https://www.theguardian.com/global-development/2013/oct/04/us-military-aid-rwanda-m23-child-soldiers. Accessed 12 July 2017

Speech by External Affairs Minister Shri S.M. Krishna at Press Conference on India's election to UNSC, New Delhi, 12 October (2010) Ministry of External Affairs

Speech by H.E. Ambassador Valentine Rugwabiza, Permanent Representative to the United Nations at the 23rd Commemoration of the Genocide against the Tutsi (2017) Permanent Mission of Rwanda to the United Nations (17 April 2017). http://rwandaun.org/site/category/press-releases/. Accessed 12 July 2017

Statement by Minister of State in Charge of Cooperation, Eugene-Richard Gasana, at the High Level Meeting on Implementing and Endorsing the Kigali Principles, on 11 May 2016 (2016) Permanent Mission of Rwanda to the United Nations (11 May 2016). http://rwandaun.org/site/category/press-releases/. Accessed 31 Dec 2016

Statement by Prime Minister at the Summit on Peacekeeping in New York (2015) Ministry of External Affairs (29 September 2015). http://mea.gov.in/Speeches-Statements.htm?dtl/25856/statement+by+prime+minister+at+the+summit+on+peacekeeping+in+new+york. Accessed 24 Dec 2016

Statement by Rwandan UN Charge d'Affaires Jeanne d'Arc Byaje, at the Informal Dialogue on R2P (2016) Permanent Mission of Rwanda to the United Nations (8 September 2016). http://rwandaun.org/site/. Accessed 31 Dec 2016

Sushma Swaraj Calls for Security Council Seat for India, Africa (2015) Mint (27 October 2015). https://search.proquest.com/docview/1727429155/abstract/DD393B24E7044BFEPQ/1?accountid=8155. Accessed 3 July 2017

Tannenwald N (2013) Justice and fairness in the nuclear non-proliferation regime. Ethics Int Aff 27(3):299–317

Tanner F (2010) Addressing the perils of peace operations: toward a global peacekeeping system. Glob Gov 16(2):209–217

Thakur R (2011) India and the United Nations. Strateg Anal 35(6):898–905

The Constitution of India (1949) Article 51

UK Bolsters Support to Peacekeeping in South Sudan (2016) UK Ministry of Defence (8 September 2016). https://www.gov.uk/government/news/uk-bolsters-support-to-peacekeeping-in-south-sudan. Accessed 29 July 2017

UK Supports Ethiopian Peacekeeping (2017) Mareeg (28 February 2017). https://mareeg.com/uk-supports-ethiopian-peacekeeping/. Accessed 4 Sept 2017

UN Charter (1945) Charter of the United Nations. United Nations. http://www.un.org/en/charter-united-nations/index.html. Accessed 15 May 2017

UN Financing (2017) Financing peacekeeping. United Nations. http://www.un.org/en/peacekeeping/operations/financing.shtml. Accessed 21 June 2017

UN Outreach Programme (2017) Outreach programme on the Rwanda genocide and the United Nations: a brief history of the country. United Nations. http://www.un.org/en/preventgenocide/rwanda/education/rwandagenocide.shtml. Accessed 26 June 2017

UN Owes $80 million to India for Peacekeeping Operations (2013) The Daily Pioneer (11 October 2013). http://www.dailypioneer.com/world/un-owes-80-million-to-india-for-peacekeeping-operations.html. Accessed 22 Dec 2016

UN Owes India $55 million for Peacekeeping Operations (2017) The Hindu (5 May 2017). http://www.thehindu.com/news/international/un-owes-india-usd-55mn-for-peacekeeping-operations/article18389547.ece. Accessed 11 July 2017

UN Past Missions (2017) Completed peacekeeping missions: Rwanda. United Nations. http://www.un.org/en/peacekeeping/missions/past/unamir.htm. Accessed 27 June 2017

UN Peacekeeping Resources (2017) Contributor statistics. United Nations. http://www.un.org/en/peacekeeping/resources/statistics/contributors.shtml. Accessed 19 June 2017

UN Secretary-General praises India's peacekeeping contributions in remarks at New Delhi Training Centre.United Nations (2001) United Nations Statements and Messages (15 March 2001). http://www.un.org/press/en/2001/sgsm7741.doc.htm. Accessed 9 Aug 2017

UNDPKO (2008) United Nations peacekeeping operations: principles and guidelines (Capstone Doctrine). United Nations, New York

UNPO (2000) Report of the Panel on United Nations Peace Operations (17 August 2000). UN Doc A/55/305

UNSCR (2014) UN Security Council Resolution 2147 (2014). UN Doc S/RES/2147

US Congressional Resolution Introduced Backing India's UN Security Council Bid (2016) Press Trust of India (16 June 2016). https://search.proquest.com/docview/1797038354?rfr_id=info%3Axri%2Fsid%3Aprimo. Accessed 3 July 2017

US Department of State (2012) Assessing US policy on peacekeeping operations in Africa. 13 September. http://www.state.gov/p/af/rls/rm/2012/197773.htm. Accessed 13 Mar 2016

USA Says Rwanda Army the Most Capable World's Peacekeepers (2014) News of Rwanda (4 February 2014). http://www.newsofrwanda.com/featured1/22241/usa-says-rwanda. Accessed 12 July 2017

Waugh C (2004) Paul Kagame and Rwanda: power, genocide and the Rwandan patriotic front. McFarland and Co, London

Wedgwood R (2010) Paul Kagame and Rwanda's Faux Democracy. New Republic. https://newrepublic.com/article/76786/rwanda-kagame-faux-democracy. Accessed 28 June 2017

Weisskopf T (1981) Capitalism, underdevelopment and the future of the poor countries. In: Smith M, Little R, Shackleton M (eds) Perspectives on world politics. Croom Helm, London, pp 327–336

Wendt A (1992) Anarchy is what states make of it: the social construction of power politics. Int Organ 46(2):391–425

Wilen N (2012) A hybrid peace through locally owned and externally financed SSR-DDR in Rwanda. Third World Q 33(7):1323–1336

Williams P (2013) The United Kingdom. In: Bellamy AJ, Williams PD (eds) Providing peacekeepers: the politics, challenges and future of United Nations peacekeeping contributions. Oxford University Press, Oxford, pp 93–114

Wilson G, Shpall S (2016) Action. The Stanford encyclopedia of philosophy. Stanford University Press, Stanford

WSO (2005) World Summit Outcome (15 September 2005). UN Doc A/60/L.1

Yihdego Z, Desta M, Merso F (2016) Towards rebalancing the narrative of international law. In: Yihdego Z, Desta M, Merso F (eds) Ethiopian yearbook of international law 2016. Springer, Cham, pp 3–10

Youngers C, Rosin E (2005) Drugs and democracy in Latin America: the impact of US policy. Lynne Rienner Publishers, London

**Philip Roberts** holds an MSc in International Relations and International Law from the University of Aberdeen. He served as a police officer in Scotland for 30 years and has also held security management posts in the private sector.

# Part III
# Current Development

# The Kenya/Somalia Maritime Boundary Delimitation Dispute

**Fayokemi Olorundami**

**Abstract** Somalia and Kenya have a land boundary in East Africa but have been unable to agree on where their maritime boundary should lie in the Indian Ocean. This dispute, which began years ago, is currently before the ICJ for resolution. This paper considers the current developments in this maritime boundary dispute discussing the prospects of the case whilst situating this within the broader context of delimitation practice in Africa.

## 1 Introduction

Somalia and Kenya have a land boundary in East Africa but have been unable to agree on where their maritime boundary should lie in the Indian Ocean. This dispute, which began years ago, is currently before the ICJ for resolution. The disputed area is reputed to be rich in oil, contributing to the difficulty of reaching an agreement, a phenomenon that is not unique considering the importance of oil and gas to the economy of States and the fact that the purpose for the creation of extended maritime zones is the exploration and exploitation of the natural resources under the seas. Although Kenya and Somalia attempted to settle their boundary dispute through negotiations, they did not prove fruitful, hence the institution by Somalia of an action before the ICJ. This paper considers the current developments in this maritime boundary dispute discussing the prospects of the case whilst situating this within the broader context of delimitation practice in Africa.

F. Olorundami (✉)
University of Greenwich, London, UK
e-mail: f.olorundami@gre.ac.uk

## 2 The Dispute

Kenya's and Somalia's claims in the Indian Ocean overlap. The disputed area is also the subject of a number of production-sharing contracts awarded by Kenya to various international oil companies, including Total and Eni. In different letters to these companies, Somalia claims that parts of the areas awarded by Kenya fall within its exclusive economic zone, declaring the activities of oil companies in those areas to be illegal and purporting to impose a daily fine on them for violating its sovereignty.[1] Kenya and Somalia had met on numerous occasions to negotiate a resolution of the dispute, but when this did not result in an agreement, Somalia instituted proceedings before the ICJ. According to Somalia in its memorial, during the negotiations held in 2014, both parties advanced positions that were so at odds with each other that it seemed safe to conclude that the parties were not close to reaching an agreement. This was further complicated by the fact that a meeting organised for the 25th and 26th of August 2014 at the request of Kenya did not take place because Kenya did not attend the meeting or provide Somalia with any explanation regarding its non-attendance.[2]

Both Kenya and Somalia are parties to the 1982 United Nations Convention on the Law of the Sea (UNCLOS),[3] having ratified it in July and March 1989, respectively. Under Article 83(1) of this Convention, they are under an obligation to delimit their maritime boundaries by agreement on the basis of international law in order to achieve an equitable solution. Article 83(1) does not specify a method of delimitation. However, States seem to favour the use of the equidistance method of delimitation. The ICJ itself has developed its three-stage delimitation methodology that has equidistance at its core. When utilising this methodology, the Court begins by drawing a provisional equidistance line. Then it asks whether there are any relevant circumstances that justify the shifting or adjustment of this provisional equidistance line. Lastly, it conducts a disproportionality test by checking that the areas attributed to a State by virtue of the first two stages are not disproportionate to the length of its coast.[4] Whilst this methodology is standard and seems straightforward, its application is not free from controversy.[5] It is this methodology that Somalia argues should be applied to the resolution of the dispute.[6] According to Somalia's memorial, there are no relevant circumstances justifying the shifting of the provisional equidistance line.[7]

---

[1] *Dispute Concerning Maritime Delimitation in the Indian Ocean (Somalia v. Kenya)*, Memorial of Somalia, 13 July 2015, Annexes 74–78.
[2] Ibid, paras 30–32.
[3] (Adopted 10 December 1982, Entered into Force 16 November 1994) 1833 UNTS 3.
[4] ICJ, *Maritime Delimitation in the Black Sea (Romania v. Ukraine)*, Judgment, (2009) ICJ Rep 61, paras 115–22.
[5] Olorundami (2017).
[6] Somalia's Memorial, paras 33–34.
[7] Ibid, para 34.

It is difficult to articulate categorically what Kenya's claims in the Indian Ocean are. This is because, at the time of writing, although Kenya had filed its counter-memorial before the Court, this had not yet been made public by the ICJ. The delay in filing the counter-memorial resulted from Kenya's preliminary objections to the jurisdiction of the Court, which had the effect of suspending the proceedings on the merit until these objections were dealt with. Notwithstanding, documents annexed to the Somali memorial detailing the negotiations between the parties show that Kenya is unwilling to have the boundary determined by the use of the equidistance method (referred to as the median line by Kenya in these documents).[8] Kenya, instead, argued that UNCLOS does not provide for the use of the median line in the delimitation of the EEZ or the continental shelf and that the 'two States are at liberty to opt for a delimitation methodology that guarantees equitable solution'.[9] For Kenya, an '[e]quitable [s]olution amounts to the proportionate sharing of "relevant maritime area" based on ratio of "relevant lengths of the coasts"'.[10] It went further to assert that the methodology for achieving this equitable solution is a line drawn along a parallel of latitude. Kenya referred to two situations where latitudinal boundaries were drawn in order to remedy the inequity that would have occurred if a strict median line was drawn, calling this 'regional state practice'.[11] Support for this position may be found in the official press statement made by Kenya's Office of the Attorney General and Department of Justice shortly after the filing of the counter-memorial on 18th December 2017. In that statement, Kenya asserts that a line drawn along a parallel of latitude has existed as a boundary between Kenya and Somalia since 1979 and that this had been recognised by Somalia up until 2014.[12] This indicates that Kenya believes there is no boundary to actually be drawn as one already exists. If the delimitation line is drawn in the manner requested by Somalia, some areas already awarded by Kenya to certain international oil companies will belong to Somalia.

In 2009, Kenya and Somalia signed a Memorandum of Understanding[13] giving prior consent to the Commission on the Limits of the Continental Shelf to consider their submissions on the outer limits of their continental shelves beyond 200 nautical miles. Whilst the agreement provides that they will not object to each other's submission, they nevertheless agreed that the recommendations to be made by the CLCS shall be without prejudice to the delimitation of the continental shelf, including areas beyond 200 nautical miles. As the MOU states, it was necessary to enter into the agreement in order to satisfy the requirements of Article 4 of Annex II of

---

[8] Ibid, annex 31. In the *Black Sea* case, the Court noted that these terms are interchangeable 'since the method of delimitation is the same for both'. See para 116.

[9] Ibid.

[10] Ibid.

[11] Ibid.

[12] Office of the Attorney General and Department of Justice (2018).

[13] Memorandum of Understanding between the Government of the Republic of Kenya and the Transitional Federal Government of the Somali Republic to grant to each other No-Objection in respect of submissions on the Outer Limits of the Continental Shelf beyond 200 Nautical Miles to the Commission on the Limits of the Continental Shelf, 7 April 2009.

UNCLOS, which requires UNCLOS State Parties to submit preliminary information on the outer limits of their continental shelf to the CLCS within 10 years from the date of entry into force of the Convention for the particular State.[14] Notwithstanding this agreement, after Kenya made its submission to the CLCS in 2009, Somalia raised an objection to its consideration by the CLCS. Under paragraph 5(a), Annex I, of the CLCS Rules of Procedure, the CLCS shall not consider any submission made by a State when the area that is the subject of the submission is under dispute unless parties to the dispute give prior consent. In any case, any consideration of a submission is without prejudice to the delimitation of the continental shelf between disputing parties.[15] Somalia had, in October 2009, repudiated the MOU arguing that it had been rejected by the Transitional Federal Parliament of Somalia and requesting that the MOU be treated 'as non-actionable'. Although Somalia subsequently withdrew its objection to the consideration of Kenya's submission by the CLCS notwithstanding its stance that the MOU was void and of no effect,[16] in 2014 it instituted proceedings at the ICJ praying the Court to determine the boundary between Somalia and Kenya in the Indian Ocean by means of a single line delimiting the territorial sea, exclusive economic zone and continental shelf, including the part of the continental shelf beyond 200 nautical miles from the coast. The case has not been heard on the merits due to the preliminary objections raised by Kenya.

## 3 Kenya's Preliminary Objections

Kenya raised a preliminary objection to the jurisdiction of the Court to hear and determine the matter on the basis of validity of the MOU. Kenya argued that the MOU was not only valid but that it also provided a method by which the parties were to delimit their boundary, namely that the boundary was to be determined by agreement of the parties after the CLCS had made its recommendations on their respective submissions.[17] The presence of this agreement as to a delimitation method meant that the Court did not have jurisdiction to hear the matter. Alternatively, Kenya argued that if the dispute is eligible to be resolved through third-party adjudication, then the appropriate means of such resolution is not the ICJ but arbitration

---

[14] At the Eleventh meeting of State Parties to UNCLOS, it was decided that since States only became acquainted with the documents concerning submissions to the CLCS (in accordance with paragraph 8 of Article 76 of UNCLOS) on 13 May 1999, and in view of the fact that the CLCS itself only just adopted its Scientific and Technical Guidelines on 13 May 1999, then for States for which the Convention had already come into force, the stipulation of ten years in Article 4 of Annex II of UNCLOS would be taken to commence on 13 May 1999. See Meeting of State Parties (2001) para a.

[15] CLCS/40/Rev.1 (2008) Rules of Procedure of the Commission on the Limits of the Continental Shelf, para 5(b), Annex 1.

[16] ICJ, Maritime Delimitation in the Indian Ocean (Somalia v. Kenya) Preliminary Objections, Judgment, (2017) paras 18, 19, 20 and 26.

[17] Ibid, para 32.

as the default procedure under Article 287(3) of UNCLOS since neither party declared a preference for any of the compulsory methods for dispute resolution in Part XV of UNCLOS.[18]

In considering Kenya's objection, the Court decided that the MOU was a valid treaty between Kenya and Somalia. The Court rejected the arguments by Somalia that its Minister for National Planning and International Cooperation did not have full powers to sign the MOU on behalf of Somalia and that, in any event, the MOU was subject to ratification by the Somali Parliament. It rightly referred to Article 46 of the Vienna Convention on the Law of Treaties, which provides that a State shall not invoke its internal law for the purpose of challenging the validity of a treaty that it has entered into. The Court also rightly concluded from various pieces of evidence that Somalia intended to be bound by the terms of the MOU. One such piece of evidence was a document signed by the Prime Minister of the Transitional Federal Government of Somalia granting full powers to the Minister to sign the MOU.[19] Another piece of evidence was an email sent before the MOU, which was signed by the Norwegian diplomat assisting the parties in drafting the MOU informing Kenya that 'the President of the Somali Republic has now approved the signing of the Memorandum of Understanding'.[20]

Although the Court found that the MOU was a valid treaty, it did not agree with Kenya that the parties were bound to agree on where the boundaries should lie between each other only after recommendations had been received from the CLCS on their respective submissions and that this precluded resort to third-party adjudication. Basing its interpretation on the rules in Articles 31 and 32 of the VCLT, the Court found that the contentious paragraph 6[21] did not preclude resort to other means of delimiting the maritime boundary and, in fact, was almost identical to Articles 74(1) and 83(1) of UNCLOS, which require States to delimit their maritime boundaries by agreement on the basis of international law. '[T]he reference to delimitation being undertaken by agreement on the basis of international law, which is common to [paragraph 6 and Article 83(1)], is not prescriptive of the method of dispute settlement to be followed.'[22] Additionally, Kenya's conduct in participating in negotiations in the hope that they will end in the delimitation of the boundary indicated that Kenya did not believe that the recommendations to be advised by the CLCS were a prerequisite for the resolution of the maritime boundary dispute.[23]

---

[18] Ibid, para 33.

[19] Ibid, para 46.

[20] Ibid, para 41.

[21] The MOU is not numbered. However, the Court numbered the paragraphs for convenience. Paragraph 6 of the MOU provides that 'The delimitation of maritime boundaries in the areas under dispute, including the delimitation of the continental shelf beyond 200 nautical miles, shall be agreed between the two coastal States on the basis of international law after the Commission has concluded its examination of the separate submissions made by each of the two coastal States and made its recommendations to two coastal States concerning the establishment of the outer limits of the continental shelf beyond 200 nautical miles'.

[22] Somalia v. Kenya) Preliminary Objections, Judgment, para 91.

[23] Ibid, para 92.

Furthermore, the MOU provided that the recommendations of the CLCS were without prejudice to the delimitation of the continental shelf.[24] This led to the conclusion that paragraph 6 only sets out the expectation of the parties that in accordance with Article 83(1), they would negotiate their boundaries after they received the CLCS recommendations, this negotiation being the first step in the delimitation of boundaries and not mandating the parties to wait for the recommendations of the CLCS before negotiating or prescribing a delimitation method.[25] This conclusion was reached after considering the ordinary meaning of the terms used in their context and in light of the object and purpose of the MOU according to Article 31 of the VCLT. It was also confirmed on the basis of Article 32 of the VCLT, which provides for a supplementary means of interpretation, allowing a court to consider the preparatory work of a treaty and the circumstances of its conclusion in interpreting that treaty.

This writer agrees with the decision of the Court that the more plausible interpretation is that the parties hoped that their negotiations would lead to a settlement of the maritime boundary dispute when the CLCS makes its recommendations. Although the contentious paragraph 6 literally favours the argument by Kenya, applying the interpretation rule in Article 31 of the VCLT requires that all the 'elements of interpretation—ordinary meaning, context and object and purpose—are to be considered as a whole'.[26] By considering them as a whole, the argument of Kenya is not quite persuasive. This issue highlights the importance of considering the various meanings that a provision might have and taking steps to clarify the intended meaning.

In addition to considering the above, Kenya had also contended that the Court did not have jurisdiction to hear the case as it should have been submitted to arbitration as the default method of dispute resolution. This argument was hinged on two facts. The first was that Kenya had, in 1965, made an optional declaration accepting the ICJ's jurisdiction under Article 36(2) of the Statute of the ICJ but had added a reservation to its optional declaration. That reservation removed from the jurisdiction of the ICJ all '[d]isputes in regard to which the parties to the dispute have agreed or shall agree to have recourse to some other method or methods of settlement'. The second fact relied upon by Kenya was that neither it nor Somalia had accepted any of the dispute resolution methods set out in Part XV of UNCLOS, and UNCLOS provided that in such an event, both parties are deemed to have agreed to submit their dispute to arbitration. Kenya argued that its reservation placed special significance on agreements to resolve disputes that were *les specialis* and *les posterior*.[27] By this, Kenya was referring to UNCLOS (to which it is a party, as well as Somalia) as both *les specialis* and *les posterior*. The ICJ rejected this argument, noting that there was nothing in the reservation that distinguished between highly specific agreements to resolve a dispute or one that was a general agreement for the

---

[24] Ibid, para 96.

[25] Ibid, para 98.

[26] Ibid, para 64.

[27] Ibid, para 120.

peaceful resolution of disputes. Also, the reservation referred to prior and future agreements to settle dispute and not just to future agreements, so there was no need to give preference to agreements made after Kenya's optional declaration. The Court's task was therefore to look at the content of a particular agreement to determine whether it fell within Kenya's reservation and that 'this does not turn on the degree of specificity or the date of that agreement'.[28]

In determining that it had jurisdiction to hear the case, the Court considered 'whether the optional clause declarations of the Parties constitute an "agreement" to submit the dispute to a procedure that entails a binding decision within the meaning of Article 282'.[29] Article 282 of UNCLOS provides that whenever States choose a particular method of dispute resolution, such a method will operate in lieu of other dispute resolution methods provided in Part XV of the Convention. In interpreting this, the Court considered that Article 282 covers situations where parties have agreed that their disputes be submitted to a procedure that entails a binding decision whether through general, regional, bilateral agreements or otherwise. The use of the word 'otherwise' in Article 282 meant that such optional declarations were contemplated within that article, a fact confirmed from the *travaux preparatoires*. The Court thus held that when a party has agreed to the Court's jurisdiction through the optional clause declaration under Article 36(2) of the Statute of the ICJ, this agreement falls within the scope of Article 282 of UNCLOS and applies in lieu of the other procedures set out in Section 2 of Part XV of the Convention, 'even when such declarations contain a reservation to the same effect as that of Kenya'.[30] On the basis of this then, the Court held that it had jurisdiction to hear the case on the merits. The ICJ therefore ordered Kenya to submit its counter-memorial by the 18th of December 2017 so that the proceedings on the merits can commence.[31] With Kenya's counter-memorial now filed, time limits for a reply and rejoinder from Somalia and Kenya, respectively, have been fixed by the Court. Somalia's reply is to be filed by the 18th of June, 2019, whilst the rejoinder is to be filed by the 18th of December 2018.[32]

## 4 Prospects of the Case

Somalia argues that the three-stage methodology of delimitation (also commonly referred to as the equidistance/relevant circumstances method) should apply to the delimitation of a single maritime boundary between it and Kenya in the Indian Ocean. It is very likely that this is the methodology that would be applied by the Court in delimiting the boundaries unless the Court agrees with Kenya that a

---

[28] Ibid, para 120.
[29] Ibid, para 129.
[30] Ibid, para 130.
[31] ICJ, *Maritime Delimitation in the Indian Ocean (Somalia v. Kenya)* Order of 2 February 2017, 2.
[32] ICJ, *Maritime Delimitation in the Indian Ocean (Somalia v. Kenya)* Order of 2 February 2018, 2.

boundary (along a parallel of latitude) already exists between the parties. In the *Black Sea* case, the Court held that it would always apply the three-stage methodology unless there are 'compelling reasons' making the equidistance method unfeasible in the particular case.[33] By unfeasibility, the Court was referring to the impossibility of drawing an equidistance line.[34] This can be seen in the *Nicaragua v. Honduras* case, where the Court declined to apply the equidistance method. In this case, the mouth of the River Coco was unstable, and it was impossible to fix the base points from which the equidistance line would have been drawn.[35] Since[36] the *Black Sea* case, all decisions of the Court have been made based on the three-stage methodology apart from the *Nicaragua v. Honduras* case mentioned previously.[37] The imperativeness of following the equidistance/relevant circumstances rule is very clear from this statement made by Judge Guillaume to the Sixth Committee of the General Assembly of the United Nations in his capacity as the President of the ICJ at the time: 'In *all* cases, the Court … *must* first determine provisionally the equidistance line. It *must* then ask itself whether there are special or relevant circumstances requiring this line to be adjusted with a view to achieving equitable results.'[38] Other tribunals have also adopted the ICJ's three-stage methodology. As the International Tribunal for the Law of the Sea (ITLOS) stated in the *Bangladesh/ Myanmar* Arbitration, 'jurisprudence has developed in favour of the equidistance/ relevant circumstances method. This is the method adopted by international courts and tribunals in the majority of the delimitation cases that have come before them.'[39] In the most recent maritime delimitation case between Ghana and Cote D'Ivoire, ITLOS applied the three-stage methodology calling it the 'established approach'.[40] This implies that Kenya is unlikely to succeed if it argues for the drawing of the boundary line along parallels of latitude as this is at variance with the Court's jurisprudence. Kenya's reference to regional state practice is also questionable. In the tribunal award in the *Guinea/Guinea Bissau* case, delimitations already concluded

---

[33] Black Sea case, para 106.

[34] ICJ, *Maritime Dispute between Nicaragua and Honduras in the Caribbean Sea (Nicaragua v. Honduras)*, Judgment, (2007) ICJ Rep 659, para 277

[35] Ibid.

[36] Even before the *Black Sea* case, the Court began to apply the equidistance/relevant circumstances method. An example may be found in the decision in *Maritime Delimitation and Territorial Questions between Qatar and Bahrain (Qatar v. Bahrain)*, Judgment, (2001) ICJ Rep 40 and the *Land and Maritime Boundary between Cameroon and Nigeria (Cameroon v. Nigeria: Equatorial Guinea Intervening)*, Judgment, (2002) ICJ Rep 303.

[37] See the cases of *Territorial and Maritime Dispute (Nicaragua v. Colombia)*, Judgment, (2012) ICJ Rep 624 and *Maritime Dispute (Peru v. Chile)*, Judgment, (2014) ICJ Rep 3, 62.

[38] Guillaume (2001), p. 11.

[39] Dispute Concerning Delimitation of the Maritime Boundary between Bangladesh and Myanmar in the Bay of Bengal (Bangladesh/Myanmar), Judgment, (2012) para 238.

[40] ITLOS, Dispute Concerning Delimitation of the Maritime Boundary between Ghana and Côte D'Ivoire in the Atlantic Ocean (Ghana/Côte D'ivoire) Judgment, (2017) para 402.

or yet to be concluded by other West African States were taken into consideration.[41] However, as Fietta and Cleverly note, that award 'has not been widely adopted in subsequent cases'.[42]

Notwithstanding that the three-stage methodology is the standard methodology of the Court and tribunals, the results to be achieved from its application are not actually predictable. In the first stage, for example, the Court will choose the base points from which to draw the provisional equidistance line, and the choice of base points has an effect on the provisional equidistance line drawn. Also, the Court is not bound by the base points that the parties have chosen. It will choose what it considers to be the 'most appropriate' base points.[43] In the *Black Sea* case, the Court refused to place base points on Serpent's Island, a choice that was criticised by commentators as amounting to a refashioning of nature since a provisional equidistance line should be drawn using all available base points.[44] Since one cannot predict what the 'most appropriate' base points are, one cannot predict the exact location of the provisional equidistance line.

The same uncertainty found in this first stage of the methodology may also be seen in the second stage where the Court has to decide whether there are any relevant circumstances and what their effect should be in relation to adjusting or shifting the provisional equidistance line. It is not clear how the identification of relevant circumstances translates into the shifting or adjustment that the Court eventually does.[45]

In the third stage of the methodology, the Court determines whether the areas appertaining to a State after the application of the first two stages is disproportionate to the length of its coast. This determination has been held not to be based on mathematical calculations depending on a broad assessment of things by the Court. However, this stage is almost redundant as no recent case has seen the delimitation line shifted on this basis.

What this means for the Kenya/Somalia case is that the provisional equidistance line drawn by Somalia may be different from the one drawn by the Court. Also, the Court may indeed find that there are relevant circumstances that justify the shifting of the line contrary to the assertion by Somalia that there are no relevant circumstances. However, in the case of *Cameroon v. Nigeria*, the Court found that there were no relevant circumstances that justified the shifting of the provisional equidistance line.[46] In the recent *Ghana/Cote D'Ivoire* case, ITLOS also refused to adjust the provisional equidistance line for the same reason that there were no relevant circumstances.[47]

---

[41] *Delimitation of the Maritime Boundary between Guinea and Guinea-Bissau,* Award (1985) RIAA, 146.
[42] Fietta and Cleverly (2016), p. 279.
[43] *Nicaragua v. Colombia*, para 191.
[44] Schofield (2013), p. 238.
[45] Evans (1991), p. 16; Antunes (2003), p. 271.
[46] *Cameroon v Nigeria,* para 305-06.
[47] *Ghana/Cote D'Ivoire*, para 480.

## 5  The Dispute and Maritime Delimitation Practice in Africa

This case is evidence of the growing trend amongst African States to settle their maritime boundaries and pave the way for harnessing the resources of the sea. Walker describes this trend as the end of sea blindness, attributing it to the availability of technology that now makes these resources available.[48] It is indeed ironic that African States are only just catching up on the need to delimit their maritime boundaries when they, led by Kenya, played a major role in the creation of the exclusive economic zone.[49] However, some African States, particularly States in the Gulf of Guinea, have experience in maritime boundary issues. For example, Nigeria has not only gone through third-party adjudication to have its boundary with Cameroon delimited, it is also a party to a joint development agreement with Sao Tome and Principe designed to be in force for forty-five years from the date of its entry into force.[50] These two States acknowledged that the overlapping EEZ claims they had (and still have) was a factor that contributed to their entering into the joint development agreement.

Indeed, Nigeria's experience indicates that joint development is an arrangement that African States should consider when they cannot delimit their boundaries rather than resorting to third-party adjudication. Judge Mensah of ITLOS and Miyoshi note that joint development is an alternative to maritime boundary delimitation.[51] Gao also submits that States may decide to convert a provisional joint development agreement into a permanent boundary solution.[52] Again, joint development might be useful when, after a boundary has been established, oil reservoirs straddle the boundary line.[53]

With third-party adjudication, there is a winner and a loser as the job of the Court or tribunal is to apply the law. However, with joint development, the parties make concessions regarding their maritime delimitation positions and agree to jointly develop the resources in the disputed area in accordance with certain agreed proportions.[54] The area of overlapping claims is usually the area that is subject to joint development,[55] and these claims are based on what a State perceives to be its entitlement in the disputed area. When parties agree on joint development, they benefit from sharing resources, which is the main driver of the dispute in the first place. They also benefit from better diplomatic relations. Again, they enter into an agreement that they have negotiated themselves and that is acceptable to them. This

---

[48] Müller-Jung (2016).

[49] Dux (2011), p. 50.

[50] Art 51.1, Treaty between the Federal Republic of Nigeria and the Democratic Republic of Sao Tome and Principe on the Joint Development of Petroleum and other Resources, in respect of Areas of the Exclusive Economic Zone of the Two States, 2001.

[51] Mensah (2006), p. 150; Miyoshi (1999), p. 6.

[52] Gao (2008), p. 60.

[53] Miyoshi (1999), p. 6.

[54] British Institute of International and Comparative Law (1989), p. 45; Shihata and Onorato (1996), p. 303.

[55] MacLaren and James (2013), p. 144.

stands in contrast to third-party adjudication, where the decision is unpredictable. It may be in recognition of these advantages that Kenya notes in its press statement made after submitting its counter-memorial that 'Kenya maintains that a **negotiated solution** to the maritime dispute is the best way of addressing the complexities and sensitivities surrounding the boundary issue.'[56]

Notwithstanding the value of joint development arrangements, sometimes it is as difficult to enter into joint development agreements as it is to delimit final boundaries.[57] This is because delineation of the joint development area is also a product of negotiations, and as it might happen with delimitation negotiations, parties may be unwilling to compromise on their positions and therefore may not reach an agreement. Nevertheless, considering the fact that joint development agreements are provisional, present advantages and have been useful to many States[58] that have concluded them, it would be in the interest of disputing parties to make every effort to enter into them. Although the Somalia/Kenya dispute is now before the ICJ, the parties still have the opportunity to shelve their dispute and enter into a joint development agreement. Whilst a defined boundary is the optimum option, the uncertainties associated with third-party adjudication make joint development an attractive option.

## 6 Conclusion

This paper considered the maritime boundary dispute between Somalia and Kenya in the Indian Ocean. At the moment, only Somalia's claims can be stated with accuracy as although Kenya has filed its counter-memorial to Somalia's memorial, this is not yet publicly available from the ICJ. Somalia wants the delimitation to follow the standard three-stage delimitation methodology. This paper has noted that it is unlikely that the Court will depart from this methodology. However, it still cannot be predicted what factors the Court will take into account in drawing the final boundary line. Whilst the ICJ decision will provide a binding solution to the dispute, there is value in both parties considering the advantages of entering into a joint development agreement to manage the risks of uncertainty that attend third-party adjudication.

---

[56] Office of the Attorney General and Department of Justice (2018) (emphasis in the original)

[57] Gao (2008), p. 41; Ma (1984), p. 59.

[58] See for example, the Treaty between Australia and the Republic of Indonesia on the Zone of Cooperation in an Area between the Indonesian Province of East Timor and Northern Australia [Timor Gap Treaty], 1989 and the 1979 Memorandum of Understanding between Malaysia and The Kingdom of Thailand on the Establishment of the Joint Authority for the Exploitation of the Resources of the Sea Bed in a Defined Area of the Continental Shelf of the Two Countries in the Gulf of Thailand.

# References

1979 Memorandum of Understanding between Malaysia and The Kingdom of Thailand on the Establishment of the Joint Authority for the Exploitation of the Resources of the Sea Bed in a Defined Area of the Continental Shelf of the Two Countries in the Gulf of Thailand

Antunes N (2003) Towards the conceptualisation of maritime delimitation: legal and technical aspects of a political process. Martinus Nijhoff Publishers, Leiden

British Institute of International and Comparative Law (1989) In: Fox H (ed) Joint development of offshore oil and gas: a model agreement for states for joint development with explanatory commentary. British Institute of International and Comparative Law, London

CLCS/40/Rev.1 (2008) Rules of Procedure of the Commission on the Limits of the Continental Shelf

Dux T (2011) Specially protected marine areas in the exclusive economic zone (EEZ): the regime for the protection of specific areas of the EEZ for environmental reasons under international law. Lit Verlag, Berlin

Evans M (1991) Maritime delimitation and expanding categories of relevant circumstances. ICLQ 40:1–33

Fietta S, Cleverly R (2016) A practitioner's guide to maritime boundary delimitation. Oxford University Press, Oxford

Gao J (2008) Joint development in the East China Sea: not an easier challenge than delimitation. IJMCL 23:39–75

Guillaume G (2001) Speech by His Excellency Judge Gilbert Guillaume, President of the International Court of Justice, to the Sixth Committee of the General Assembly of the United Nations. http://www.icj-cij.org/files/press-releases/5/2995.pdf. Accessed 23 Oct 2017

ICJ, *Dispute Concerning Maritime Delimitation in the Indian Ocean (Somalia v. Kenya)*, Memorial of Somalia, 13 July 2015. http://www.icj-cij.org/files/case-related/161/19082.pdf. Accessed 25 Oct 2017

ICJ, *Land and Maritime Boundary between Cameroon and Nigeria (Cameroon v Nigeria: Equatorial Guinea intervening)* [2002] ICJ Rep 303

ICJ, *Maritime Delimitation and Territorial Questions between Qatar and Bahrain (Qatar v. Bahrain)* [2001] ICJ Rep 40

ICJ, *Maritime Delimitation in the Black Sea (Romania v. Ukraine)* [2009] ICJ Rep 61

ICJ, *Maritime Delimitation in the Black Sea (Romania v. Ukraine)*, Judgment, (2009) ICJ Rep 61

ICJ, *Maritime Delimitation in the Indian Ocean (Somalia v. Kenya)*, Memorial of Somalia. http://www.icj-cij.org/files/case-related/161/18362.pdf. Accessed 15 Oct 2017

ICJ, *Maritime Delimitation in the Indian Ocean (Somalia v. Kenya)* Order of 2 February 2017. http://www.icj-cij.org/files/case-related/161/19346.pdf. Accessed 20 Oct 2017

ICJ, *Maritime Delimitation in the Indian Ocean (Somalia v. Kenya)* Order of 2 February 2018, 2. http://www.icj-cij.org/files/case-related/161/161-20180202-ORD-01-00-EN.pdf. Accessed 20 May 2018

ICJ, *Maritime Delimitation in the Indian Ocean (Somalia v. Kenya) Preliminary Objections* Judgment, 2 February 2017. http://www.icj-cij.org/files/case-related/161/161-20170202-JUD-01-00-EN.pdf. Accessed 20 Oct 2017

ICJ, *Maritime Dispute between Nicaragua and Honduras in the Caribbean Sea (Nicaragua v. Honduras)*, Judgment, (2007) ICJ Rep 659

ICJ, *Territorial and Maritime Dispute (Nicaragua v. Colombia)*, Judgment, (2012) ICJ Rep 624

ITLOS, Dispute Concerning Delimitation of the Maritime Boundary between Bangladesh and Myanmar in the Bay of Bengal (Bangladesh/Myanmar), Judgment, (2012) para 238. https://www.itlos.org/fileadmin/itlos/documents/cases/case_no_16/C16_Judgment_14_03_2012_rev.pdf. Accessed 6 Oct 2017

ITLOS, *Dispute Concerning Delimitation of the Maritime Boundary between Ghana and Côte D'Ivoire in the Atlantic Ocean (Ghana/Côte D'Ivoire)* Judgment, (2017). https://www.itlos.

org/fileadmin/itlos/documents/cases/case_no.23_merits/C23_Judgment_23.09.2017_corr.pdf. Accessed 6 Oct 2017

Ma Y (1984) Legal problems of seabed boundary delimitation in the East China Sea Occasional Papers/Reprints Series in Contemporary Asian Studies 1984. Baltimore

MacLaren G, James R (2013) Negotiating joint development agreements. In: Beckman R et al (eds) Beyond territorial disputes in the South China Sea. Edward Elgar Publishing, pp 144–151

*Maritime Dispute (Peru v. Chile)*, Judgment, (2014) ICJ Rep 3

Meeting of State Parties (2001) Decision Regarding the Date of Commencement of the Ten-Year Period for Making Submissions to the Commission on the Limits of the Continental Shelf Set out in Article 4 of Annex II to the United Nations Convention on the Law of the Sea (29 May 2001). UN Doc SPLOS/72 (2001)

Memorandum of Understanding between the Government of the Republic of Kenya and the Transitional Federal Government of the Somali Republic to grant to each other No-Objection in respect of submissions on the Outer Limits of the Continental Shelf beyond 200 Nautical Miles to the Commission on the Limits of the Continental Shelf, 7 April 2009

Mensah T (2006) Joint development zone as an alternative dispute settlement in maritime delimitation. In: Lagoni R, Vignes D (eds) Maritime delimitation. Martinus Nijhoff Publishers, Leiden, pp 143–152

Miyoshi M (1999) The joint development of offshore oil and gas in relation to maritime boundary delimitation. In: Schofield C (ed) Maritime briefing 5(2). IBRU, Durham

Müller-Jung F (2016) Kenya or Somalia: who owns the sea and what lies beneath? DW (19 September 2016). http://www.dw.com/en/kenya-or-somalia-who-owns-the-sea-and-what-lies-beneath/a-19557277. Accessed 25 Oct 2017

Office of the Attorney General and Department of Justice (2018) Press Statement on the Status of Kenya-Somalia Maritime Boundary Dispute at the International Court of Justice, in The Hague, The Netherlands. http://www.statelaw.go.ke/press-statement-on-the-status-of-kenya-somaliamaritime-boundary-dispute-at-the-international-court-of-justice-in-the-hague-the-netherlands/. Accessed 20 May 2018

Olorundami F (2017) Objectivity versus subjectivity in the context of the ICJ's three-stage methodology of maritime boundary delimitation. IJMCL 32:36–53

Schofield C (2013) One step forwards, two steps back? Progress and challenges in the delimitation of maritime boundaries since the drafting of the United Nations Convention on the Law of the Sea. In: Xue G, White A (eds) 30 years of UNCLOS (1982–2012): progress and prospects. China University of Political Science Press, Beijing, pp 217–239

Shihata I, Onorato W (1996) The joint development of international petroleum resources in undefined and disputed areas. ICSID Rev 11:299–317

Treaty between Australia and the Republic of Indonesia on the Zone of Cooperation in an Area between the Indonesian Province of East Timor and Northern Australia [Timor Gap Treaty], 1989. http://www.austlii.edu.au/au/other/dfat/treaties/1991/9.html. Accessed 18 Oct 2017

Treaty between the Federal Republic of Nigeria and the Democratic Republic of Sao Tome and Principe on the Joint Development of Petroleum and other Resources, in respect of Areas of the Exclusive Economic Zone of the Two States, 2001

United Nations Convention on the Law of the Sea (UNCLOS) 1982

**Fayokemi Olorundami** is lecturer in law at the University of Greenwich, London, UK. She obtained her PhD from the University of Aberdeen; her doctoral thesis is titled: 'The Contested Waters of the East China Sea: Resolving the Dilemma of Entitlement and Delimitation'.

# The ICC and Africa: Should the Latter Remain Engaged?

### Makane Moïse Mbengue and Kirsten McClellan

**Abstract** The International Criminal Court (the 'ICC' or 'the Court' hereafter) and Africa have had a tumultuous relationship since the creation of the Court. Although there has never been unanimous support for the Court in Africa, African states were key to the development of the Court and engaged closely with it since its early years. Since 2005, however, there has been a growing discontent with the Court and deterioration in the relationship between the Court and the African Union. Despite this, a number of African states remain committed to the ICC. In 2017, the withdrawal notifications of South Africa and Gambia were retracted, whilst the 'mass withdrawal strategy' is in reality a list of proposed changes to the Court's mandate, as this piece will show. For the relationship between Africa and the ICC to continue to evolve, there needs to be more effective discourse between African states and the ICC. In the long term, it is necessary for African states to strengthen their national judiciaries; there is also an option of expanding the jurisdiction of the African Court of Justice and Human Rights to international crimes. However, the best way forward is to continue to engage with the ICC.

## 1 Introduction

Uniquely in international law, international criminal law concerns the liability of individuals rather than states. The creation of the International Criminal Court (ICC, the Court)—through the Rome Statute of the International Criminal Court in 2002[1]—signified a new era in international criminal justice. The Court is the first

---

[1] Rome Statute of the International Criminal Court. http://legal.un.org/icc/statute/romefra.htm. Accessed 12 January 2018.

M. M. Mbengue (✉)
Faculty of Law, University of Geneva, Geneva, Switzerland
e-mail: makanembengue@unige.ch

K. McClellan
The Geneva Academy of International Humanitarian Law and Human Rights, Geneva, Switzerland

permanent international criminal tribunal with jurisdiction over war crimes, genocide, crimes against humanity and the crime of aggression.[2]

Under Article 13 of the Rome Statute of the International Criminal Court (Rome Statute), the jurisdiction of the ICC can be exercised in three ways: firstly, through a referral by a state party; secondly, through a referral by the United Nations Security Council (UNSC); and, thirdly, by opening an investigation by the Prosecutor *proprio motu*. Referrals by a state party or investigations *proprio motu* are only available where alleged offences are committed on the territory of a state party or by the national of a state party. Referrals by the UNSC, however, can include non-state parties. Importantly, the ICC was designed to interact complementarily with national courts to form a new system of international criminal justice. This is embodied in Article 17, which provides that the Court will only have jurisdiction where a state is 'genuinely unable or unwilling' to prosecute.

At the time of writing, there are 123 states parties to the Rome Statute, and Africa remains the largest regional bloc with 33 states parties.[3]

The ICC and Africa have had a tumultuous relationship since the creation of the Court. Although there has never been a unanimous support for the Court in Africa, African states were key in the development of the Court and have engaged with it since its early years. Since 2005, however, there has been a growing discontent with the Court and a deterioration in the relationship between the Court and the African Union (AU). Discontent has also begun to coalesce into a regional African movement with the primary criticisms leveled at the Court: neocolonialism, excessive focus on Africa and selective justice.

The catalyst for this coalescence was the issuance of an arrest warrant issued against sitting President Al Bashir of Sudan. Subsequent handling by the UNSC of AU deferral requests and concerns resulted in the 2009 AU statement of non-cooperation with the ICC.[4] Tensions further increased following the Prosecutor's *proprio motu* investigation of Kenya in 2011 and the indictments of President Kenyatta and Deputy President Ruto.[5] The deterioration in the relationship between Africa and the Court culminated in the 2016 withdrawal notifications by three states—South Africa, Gambia and Burundi—and the 2017 AU resolution on 'mass

---

[2] International Criminal Court website. 'About'. https://www.icc-cpi.int/about. Accessed 12 January 2018.

[3] African states parties to the Rome Statute at the time of writing are: Benin, Botswana, Burkina Faso, Cabo Verde, Central African Republic, Chad, Comoros, Congo, Cote d'Ivoire, Democratic Republic of the Congo, Djibouti, Gabon, Gambia, Ghana, Guinea, Kenya, Lesotho, Liberia, Madagascar, Malawi, Mali, Mauritius, Namibia, Niger, Nigeria, Senegal, Seychelles, Sierra Leone, South Africa, Tunisia, Uganda, United Republic of Tanzania, and Zambia. https://asp.icc-cpi.int/en_menus/asp/states%20parties/pages/the%20states%20parties%20to%20the%20rome%20statute.aspx.

[4] Assembly of the African Union, Thirteenth Ordinary Session, 1–3 July 2009, 'Decision on the Meeting of African States Parties to the Rome Statute of the International Criminal Court (ICC)'.

[5] Arnould (2017); du Plessis (2013); Vilmer (2016), pp. 1319–1342.

withdrawal'.[6] In January 2018, at the conclusion of the 30th session of the African Union Summit of Heads of State and Government, a decision was adopted to seek an advisory opinion from the International Court of Justice (ICJ) regarding the immunity of heads of state and government officials.[7] The Decision—entitled 'Decision on the International Criminal Court'—requests as follows:

> The African Group in New York to immediately place on the agenda of the United Nations General Assembly a request to seek an advisory opinion from the International Court of Justice on the question of immunities of a Head of State and Government and other Senior Officials as it relates to the relationship between Articles 27 and 98 (of the Rome Statute) and the obligations of States Parties under International Law.[8]

The Decision expresses, *inter alia*, the following:

> Deep concern with the decision of the Pre-Trial Chamber II of the ICC on the legal obligation of the Republic of South Africa to arrest and surrender President Al Bashir of The Sudan, which is at variance with customary international law and CALLS on Member States of the African Union, particularly those that are also State Parties to the ICC, to oppose this line of interpretation of their legal obligations under the Rome Statute;
> The need for member states to strengthen national and continental judicial and legislative mechanisms to deal with impunity in order to ensure that justice is served in a fair manner…

It is hoped that the UN General Assembly will vote favourably to request such an advisory opinion from the ICJ and that the latter will clarify the legal issues that might help defuse the tension between the ICC and the AU.

Despite the spread of discontent, however, many African states have remained engaged with the ICC. For example, a number of African states did not support the AU's non-cooperation statements, several African states in the UNSC supported the referrals of Sudan and Libya, self-referrals to the ICC by African states (Mali in 2012, CAR in 2014, Gabon in 2016)[9] have continued, the 'mass withdrawal strategy' is in reality a submission of a list of proposed changes to the Court and the withdrawal notifications of South Africa and Gambia were themselves withdrawn in 2017. The AU Decision on the International Criminal Court also upheld the need for justice when international crimes are committed. However, it must be noted that the AU does not represent a united front of African States—there still exists some State support, and African civil society organisations remain committed to the ICC.

---

[6] Assembly of the Union, Twenty eighth ordinary session, 30–31 January 2017, 'Decision on the International Criminal Court Doc.EX.CL/1006(XXX)'; African Union, 'Draft 2. Withdrawal Strategy Document', 12 January 2017. https://www.hrw.org/sites/default/files/supporting_resources/icc_withdrawal_strategy_jan._2017.pdf. Accessed 7 August 2017.

[7] See also Coalition for the ICC website.

[8] The text of the decision was not yet public at the time of the writing of the present contribution but was on file with Makane M. Mbengue. Therefore there may be some minor language differences between the text that is quoted in the present contribution and the text that will be made public at a later stage.

[9] International Criminal Court website. 'Situations'. https://www.icc-cpi.int/#. Accessed 14 August 2017.

In this context, this current development piece examines some of the recent developments in the relationship between the ICC and Africa. Section 2 examines the changing prosecutorial policy towards Africa, Sect. 3 discusses the State withdrawals and the AU's collective withdrawal policy, Sect. 4 examines the recent developments in international criminal law as a result of cases arising from African situations and Sect. 5 considers the AU proposal for establishing an African continental criminal court. Some remarks are made at the end.

## 2 Prosecutorial Policy and the Perils of Selective Justice

As stated above, one of the primary criticisms leveled against the ICC has been that of selective justice in view of the prosecutorial policy of the Office of the Prosecutor (OTP). The OTP is an independent organ of the Court that is responsible for conducting investigations and prosecutions against individuals allegedly involved in genocide, crimes against humanity, war crimes and the crime of aggression.[10] For an effective ICC, the Prosecutor must be considered above reproach and independent from politicisation.

Under Article 13 of the Rome Statute, the OTP is able to instigate investigations *proprio motu*, which it has done in Kenya and more recently in Georgia. The OTP is also not obliged to pursue investigations in all state referrals, only those that meet its selection criteria. Equally, the OTP must make a decision on whether situations referred by the UNSC should be prosecuted.[11] This independence and discretion is key to the effective functioning of any prosecutorial body; however, it is this discretion, or lack thereof, that has resulted in a perceived bias against African states.

The first situations before the ICC were self-referrals from African states. The investigation and prosecution of these cases worked to the OTP's advantage as it allowed an opportunity to demonstrate the Court's relevance and establish the OTP's credentials whilst guaranteeing a degree of state support, which would not be as forthcoming in a non-self-referral situation.[12] Until January 2016, however, all ICC investigations concerned African states, despite evidence of human rights violations in a range of other states, including Palestine, Colombia, Iraq, Syria and Afghanistan. In a view espoused by a number of academics and politicians,[13] the only rationale

---

[10] International Criminal Court website. 'Office of the Prosecutor'. https://www.icc-cpi.int/about/otp. Accessed 12 January 2018.

[11] Babington-Ashaye (2014), pp. 381–398.

[12] Vilmer (2016) *op. cit.*

[13] For example: The prominent Canadian academic William Schabas' comments re Mr. Moreno-Ocampo in a Guardian interview: *"he avoided situations where he would be likely to step on the toes of permanent members of the UN Security Council, from Afghanistan to Gaza to Iraq to Columbia"*, in Smith (2012); Jean Ping, the former Chairperson of the African Union Commission: *"ICC always targets Africans. Does it mean that you have nothing on Gaza? Does it mean that you have nothing [in the] Caucasus? Does it mean that you have nothing on the militants in Colombia? There is nothing on Iraq? We are raising this type of question because we don't want a double standard"*, in Kimani (2009).

for the failure to open investigations in these areas is that the decision was motivated by political considerations. This is particularly the case in relation to Palestine,[14] where, despite a declaration of acceptance of jurisdiction in 2009, the Prosecutor took three years to issue a statement to the effect that Palestine is not a state and that as such Palestine was not able to request that the Prosecutor investigate a situation.[15] African situations or alleged crimes, meanwhile, were acted on comparatively quickly, perhaps under the perception that they would be relatively easy cases to prove with minimal political backlash.[16]

Accusations of selective justice were raised during the term of the first Prosecutor, Luis Moreno Ocampo of Argentina. Vocal criticism of the first Prosecutor was expressed by Jean Ping (then African Union Commission Chairman) at the African Union Summit in Ethiopia in 2011:

> We Africans and the African Union are not against the International Criminal Court. That should be clear…we are against Ocampo who is rendering justice with double standards.[17]

The appointment of Fatou Bensouda of Gambia as Prosecutor in 2012 has eased some of the concerns of selective justice.[18] Beyond her impeccable legal reputation, the appointment of an African prosecutor signaled a political message to African states that their concerns regarding selective justice on the part of the Prosecutor had been heard. Since her appointment, Ms. Bensouda has taken steps that may in the long term assist in rehabilitating the reputation of the OTP and has undertaken an outreach campaign to change the negative attitudes towards the Court.[19] She has also opened investigations in states outside Africa, with preliminary investigations having commenced in Palestine in 2015, in Iraq/UK, in Afghanistan and in Georgia in 2016.

In September 2016, a new OTP Policy Paper on Case Selection and Prioritisation was released.[20] The Policy Paper reiterates the independence, objectivity and impartiality of the OTP. It also details the standards that the OTP will apply to prioritising cases. Although the Policy Paper does not directly address concerns regarding current investigations, such as the focus on Africa, the Policy Paper makes the workings of the OTP more transparent, which may help ease some of the AU's criticisms.[21] One notable development in the new Policy Paper is that it provides that

---

[14] It is interesting to note that an investigation into the situation in Palestine may be forthcoming, as in 2012 Palestine was granted the status of a 'non-member observer state' at the UN, and in 2015 was accepted as a party to the Rome Statute.

[15] Dugard (2013), pp. 563–570.

[16] Arnould (2017) *op. cit.*

[17] Richard Lough, 'African Union accuses ICC prosecutor of bias', *Reuters*, 29 January 2011, available at: http://www.reuters.com/article/africa-icc-idAFLDE70S09L20110129 (last accessed on 15 August 2017).

[18] Olugbo (2014), pp. 351–379.

[19] Labuda (2015), pp. 289–321.

[20] International Criminal Court, Office of the Prosecutor, 'Policy Paper on Case Selection and Prioritisation', 15 September 2016.

[21] du Plessis and Maunganidze (2016).

the impact of the crimes may be assessed in light of, inter alia, the increased vulnerability of victims, the terror subsequently instilled, or the social, economic and environmental damage inflicted on the affected communities. In this context, the Office will give particular consideration to prosecuting Rome Statute crimes that are committed by means of, or that result in, inter alia, the destruction of the environment, the illegal exploitation of natural resources or the illegal dispossession of land.[22]

Further, the Policy Paper states that

in relation to cases not selected for investigation or prosecution...the Office will also seek to cooperate and provide assistance to States, upon request, with respect to conduct which constitutes a serious crime under national law, such as the illegal exploitation of natural resources, arms trafficking, terrorism, financial crimes, land grabbing or the destruction of the environment. Finally, the Office recalls that it fully endorses the role that can be played by truth seeking mechanisms, reparations programs, institutional reform and traditional justice mechanisms as part of a broader comprehensive strategy.[23]

This expansion of considerations is comparable to the proposed expansion of the African Court on Human and People's Rights under the 2014 Malabo Protocol (discussed in more detail later). As such, it is indicative of a responsiveness to African complaints regarding the biased focus of the Court on offences that concern the West and the exclusion of offences important to Africa.

These recent developments—the appointment of an African Prosecutor, the new Prosecutorial Policy Paper and opening investigations outside of Africa—will hopefully address the concern of selective justice expressed by many African states and result in continued engagement with the ICC.

## 3 The Threats of Withdrawals: From a Negative to a Positive Impact?

The perceived bias of the Court in general and its prosecutorial policy and record have resulted in many African states campaigning for a coordinated withdrawal *en masse* from the Rome Statute and the notice of intention to withdraw by a number of individual states.

Withdrawal from the Rome Statute is governed by Article 127, paragraph 1, which provides as follows:

A State Party may, by written notification addressed to the Secretary-General of the United Nations, withdraw from this Statute. The withdrawal shall take effect one year after the date of receipt of the notification, unless the notification is withdrawn.

In October and November 2016, three African states parties, South Africa, Burundi and Gambia, notified the UN Secretary General of their intention to

---

[22] International Criminal Court, Office of the Prosecutor, 'Policy Paper on Case Selection and Prioritisation', 15 September 2016; article 41.

[23] International Criminal Court, Office of the Prosecutor, 'Policy Paper on Case Selection and Prioritisation', 15 September 2016; article 9.

withdraw under Article 127(1) of the Rome Statute. These withdrawal notifications were supported by the AU in its 'collective withdrawal strategy'[24] but triggered criticisms from a number of African states that have since reaffirmed their commitment to the Court.[25]

Two of these countries—South Africa and Gambia—have since reconsidered their positions and retracted their notifications of withdrawal. As such, they remain states parties to the Rome Statute (Gambia retracted its withdrawal notification following a regime change, whilst South Africa did so following a decision of the South African Court, which found the withdrawal notice '"unconstitutional and invalid" because it had not passed through parliament'.[26]

The withdrawal notifications of Gambia and Burundi appear to have been motivated by the perceived need to protect government officials from potential ICC investigations.[27] In Gambia, then President Jammeh had seized power in a coup in 1994, and during the course of his presidency, the government frequently committed acts that, if proven, could come within the jurisdiction of the Court. Just prior to then President Jammeh losing the election in December 2016, Gambia submitted its intention to withdraw from the Rome Statute. In January 2017, power was transferred peacefully to President Barrow, who, in February 2017, notified the UN Secretary General of Gambia's decision to rescind the withdrawal notification with immediate effect.

In relation to Burundi, allegations that state agents and groups launched widespread attacks against members of the civilian population who opposed the desire of President Pierre Nkurunzuza to run for a third term in office. This resulted in the OTP opening an investigation into the situation concerning the period 26 April 2015–26 October 2017. On 27 October 2017, the withdrawal of Burundi from the ICC came into effect. Unlike in Gambia, there has not been a regime change in Burundi, and as such it is perhaps unsurprising that Burundi proceeded with its withdrawal from the ICC.[28] The effective withdrawal of Burundi from the ICC will not, however, affect the ability of the OTP to investigate and prosecute for offences allegedly committed before the withdrawal came into effect, i.e. 27 October 2017. Per Article 127(2) of the Rome Statute, the Court will continue to have jurisdiction over Burundian officials for this period and the state will remain obliged to cooperate with any ongoing investigations. The January 2018 AU Decision takes note of

> The sovereign decision made by the Republic of Burundi to withdraw from the ICC effective October 27th, 2017, and condemns the decision by the ICC to open an investigation in

---

[24] African Union, 'Draft 2. Withdrawal Strategy Document'. 12 January 2017. https://www.hrw.org/sites/default/files/supporting_resources/icc_withdrawal_strategy_jan._2017.pdf. Accessed 7 August 2017.

[25] Lansky (2017).

[26] Reuters. February 22, 2017. 'South African Court blocks government's ICC withdrawal bid'. https://www.reuters.com/article/us-safrica-icc/south-african-court-blocks-governments-icc-withdrawal-bid-idUSKBN1610RS. Accessed 12 January 2018.

[27] Ssenyonjo (2017), pp. 1–57.

[28] Ssenyonjo (2017) *op. cit.*

the situation prevailing in the Republic of Burundi as it is prejudicial to the dialogue process under the auspices of the East African Community, and … constitutes both a violation of the sovereignty of Burundi and is a move aimed at destabilising that country.

South Africa was the only state to provide detailed reasons for its intended withdrawal from the Rome Statute.[29] These reasons included were the loss of credibility of the ICC due to its relationship with the UNSC and its focus on Africa, the ICC's performance and budget, the UNSC's refusal to consider Article 16 deferrals and conflicting international law obligations in respect of immunities.[30]

The position of South Africa should be considered more closely as its relationship with the ICC is reflective of the continent's relationship with the ICC. South Africa ratified the Rome Statute in 2000 and was the first African state to pass domestic legislation implementing the Statute. Further, South Africa refused to sign USA's bilateral immunity agreement (BIA). These agreements sought to protect USA nationals from prosecution by the ICC by providing that states would not be permitted to hand over 'current or former government officials, employees (including contractors), or military personnel or nationals' to the ICC.[31] In the case of a refusal to sign the agreement, the USA could, in accordance with its (then) new domestic legislation, suspend aid transfers and military assistance to the refusing State—in effect attempting to force compliance through economic sanctions.[32] This was not an empty threat; in refusing to sign the BIA, South Africa did lose USA's aid.

It was only after the 2009 ICC arrest warrant for President Al Bashir of Sudan that South Africa supported AU resolutions seeking the deferral of the investigation and the decision of non-cooperation. During the AU summit in 2013, South Africa voted against the Kenyan proposal for a mass withdrawal from the ICC. Initially, South Africa had tacitly avoided Al Bashir's entering South Africa, but on 13 June 2015 he entered the country to attend the AU Summit. During this visit, the ICC requested that South Africa arrest Al Bashir pursuant to its obligations as a state party to the Statute. The South African High Court ordered the government to prevent Al Bashir from leaving the country, but he was able to leave South Africa prior to the arrest warrant being served. It was in this context that the South African President notified the ICC of the intention to withdraw. This withdrawal then had to be rescinded as it had been issued without undergoing parliamentary approval.[33] It

---

[29] Akande (2016).

[30] Ssenyonjo (2017) *op. cit.*

[31] *See* 'Agreement Concerning the surrender of persons to the International Criminal Court between the Government of the United States of America and the Government of the Republic of Senegal' concluded 19 June 2003. http://guides.ll.georgetown.edu/c.php?g=363527&p=2456099. Accessed 15 August 2017.

[32] *American Service Members Protection Act 2002* (particularly Section 2007(a) which prohibited military assistance to governments of countries that are parties to the Rome Statute); Nooruddin and Lockwood Payton (2010), pp. 711–721; Jalloh (2009), pp. 445–499.

[33] For more detailed discussion see: Woolaver (2016, 2017).

remains to be seen whether South Africa will re-submit a statement of intention to withdraw from the Statute if proper domestic procedure is adhered to.

In January 2017, the AU Summit issued a resolution titled 'Collective Withdrawal Strategy'.[34] The title is inflammatory and is a misnomer. In reality, the strategy lists AU grievances with the Court and contains a number of possible reforms, most of which relate to the relationship between the ICC and the UNSC. The resolution is also non-binding and merely *calls on Member States to consider implementing its recommendations*.[35]

Furthermore, the AU does not represent a united front of African states. It is effective in bringing regional concerns to the attention of the international community but is incapable of representing the position of each of its member states individually. A number of states did not support the collective withdrawal strategy and eight issued reservations (Nigeria, Senegal, Cape Verde, Liberia, Malawi, Tanzania, Tunisia and Zambia).[36] This lack of consensus is strongly indicative of the disagreements between African states as to the best way to proceed and their relationship with the ICC.[37]

The retraction of the withdrawals of Gambia and South Africa and the reality of the 'Mass Withdrawal Strategy' as a list of reform recommendations indicate that the majority of African states remain supportive of the ICC. The ICC has also continued to enjoy the support of African NGOs and civil society[38] even when their states have officially adopted an anti-ICC position. Equally, the efforts of the ICC to accommodate African concerns (for example in the recent developments in the OTP) indicate that the Court values the continued support of Africa and wishes to remain engaged with the continent. The relationship between the ICC and Africa is important for both sides: it has given African states access to a permanent international tribunal dealing with offences they themselves may not be able to prosecute, and African engagement gave the Court much-needed early support and has allowed the development and refinement of principles of international criminal law.

---

[34] Assembly of the Union, Twenty eighth ordinary session, 30–31 January 2017, 'Decision on the International Criminal Court Doc.EX.CL/1006(XXX)'; African Union, 'Draft 2. Withdrawal Strategy Document', 12 January 2017. https://www.hrw.org/sites/default/files/supporting_resources/icc_withdrawal_strategy_jan._2017.pdf. Accessed 7 August 2017.

[35] African Union, 'Draft 2. Withdrawal Strategy Document', 12 January 2017, para. 8, https://www.hrw.org/sites/default/files/supporting_resources/icc_withdrawal_strategy_jan._2017.pdf. Accessed 7 August 2017.

[36] Kersten (2017).

[37] Ngari (2017).

[38] 'South Africa: Continent wide outcry at ICC withdrawal. Victims' advocates urge reconsideration, support for Court'. Human Rights Watch. 22 October 2016. https://www.hrw.org/news/2016/10/22/south-africa-continent-wide-outcry-icc-withdrawal. Accessed 5 August 2017.

## 4 Africa's Contribution to the Development of International Criminal Law

Given the focus of ICC investigations, many Africans fear that the continent has been used as a testing ground for new concepts of international criminal law. As the *ad hoc* tribunals have shown, the early cases of any judicial body invariably involve some experimentation and settling of principles; however, this only increases their importance in the development of an effective system. Without first cases, there can be no development of the law. The early cases from Africa have allowed the Court to establish new rules of international criminal law and to clarify existing principles across a range of areas, including the application of the principle of complementarity, fair trial process, modes of liability and the scope of liability.

The application of Article 17 of the Rome Statute (complementarity) was addressed in *Lubanga*,[39] where the Court and Prosecutor considered that there was no issue of admissibility as the situation had been a self-referral. Article 17 was further considered in *Bemba Gombo*,[40] where it was argued that proceedings at a national level precluded the prosecution of individuals before the ICC. The Court determined that the dismissal of charges at a state level amounted to a decision not to prosecute, which would make the case inadmissible before the ICC. Similarly, in *Katanga*,[41] it was argued that Katanga could not be prosecuted as he had already been investigated by the DRC and that the ICC could not exercise jurisdiction simply because it prefers to prosecute the case. The Appeals Chamber held:

> In the case of inaction, the question of unwillingness or inability does not arise; inaction on the part of a State having jurisdiction (that is, the fact that a State is not investigating or prosecuting, or has not done so) renders a case admissible before the Court, subject to article 17(1)(d) of the Statute.[42]

This may create difficulties if the state is attempting to address international crimes by non-prosecutorial means or by novel prosecutorial processes, which are proving slow to set up. The test is not that a member state is doing nothing at all; it is that the state is not investigating or prosecuting.

---

[39] ICC Pre Trial Chamber I, *Prosecutor v. Lubanga*, Decision Concerning Pre-Trial Chamber I's Decision of 10 February 2006 and the Incorporation of Documents into the Record of the Case against Mr Thomas Lubanga Dyilo, ICC-01/04-01/06-8-24, 24 February 2006.

[40] ICC Appeals Chamber, *Prosecutor v Jean-Pierre Bemba Gombo (Judgment on the Appeal Against Admissibility)*, 19 October 2010; A*merican Society of International Law, 'International Law in Brief'*, 2 November 2010, http://asil.org/files/2010/ilib/ilib101101pdf.pdf.

[41] ICC Appeals Chamber, Judgment on the Appeal of Mr. Germain Katanga against the Oral Decision of Trial Chamber II of 12 June 2009 on the Admissibility of the Case, 25 September 2009.

[42] ICC Appeals Chamber, Judgment on the Appeal of Mr. Germain Katanga against the Oral Decision of Trial Chamber II of 12 June 2009 on the Admissibility of the Case, 25 September 2009, para. 78.

Disclosure of information arose in *Lubanga*,⁴³ where the OTP had promised confidentiality to informants and that the information they provided would never be disclosed outside of the OTP; as such, 207 potentially relevant documents were not disclosed to the defence. This policy was held by the Trial Chamber to have jeopardised Lubanga's right to a fair trial and issued a stay of proceedings. The trial was only able to continue once the OTP had renegotiated the agreements with its sources so that the material could be disclosed. The issue of disclosure arose again in *Lubanga*⁴⁴ on account of the OTP's use of intermediaries to gather evidence. The defence alleged that that some of the intermediaries had procured or attempted to procure false evidence. In response, the OTP maintained its refusal to disclose the identity of a particular intermediary, meaning that they could not give evidence. The Trial Chamber held that the Prosecutor's actions constituted an abuse of process and ordered a stay. Although overturning the stay, the Appeals Chamber held that the Prosecutor should have complied with the Trial Chamber's order and that such compliance was 'the fundamental criterion for any trial to be fair'.⁴⁵

The mode of liability was controversially charged in *Katanga*,⁴⁶ when it was re-characterised by the Trial Chamber after the close of the evidence from co-perpetration (Article 25(3)(a)) to contribution to a crime committed by a group (Article 25(3)(d)). This re-characterisation resulted in a conviction and has raised questions as to whether it was consistent with the rights of the defendant given that this basis of liability was not addressed by either the prosecution or defence at trial.

The required evidentiary standard for the confirmation of charges has been addressed by the ICC in *Lubanga*,⁴⁷ where it was held that the standard required was 'sufficient evidence' to 'establish substantial grounds'. This standard is higher than that required for an arrest warrant, but lower than that required for conviction, and was designed to protect defendants from 'wrongful' and 'wholly unfounded' charges.

The use of circumstantial evidence in ICC trials is an important issue that was also raised in *Lubanga*.⁴⁸ The Trial Chamber held at paragraph 111 that 'when, based on the evidence there is only one reasonable conclusion to be drawn from particular facts, the Chamber has concluded that they have been established beyond reasonable doubt'.

---

[43] ICC Trial Chamber I, *Prosecutor v Thomas Lubanga Dyilo, Decision on the consequences of non-disclosure of exculpatory materials covered by Article 54(3)(e) agreements*, 13 June 2008, para. 73.

[44] ICC Appeals Chamber, *Prosecutor v Thomas Lubanga Dyilo, Appeal on the Disclosure of the Identity of Intermediary 143*, 8 October 2010.

[45] ICC Appeals Chamber, *Prosecutor v Thomas Lubanga Dyilo, Appeal on the Disclosure of the Identity of Intermediary 143*, 8 October 2010.

[46] ICC Trial Chamber, *The Prosecutor v Germain Katanga*, 7 March 2014.

[47] ICC Pre Trial Chamber I, *The Prosecutor v. Thomas Lubanga Dyilo*, Decision on the confirmation of charges, 7 February 2007.

[48] ICC Trial Chamber, Situation in the Democratic Republic of the Congo, *Prosecutor v Lubanga*, Judgment pursuant to Article 74 of the Statute, 14 March 2012.

The scope of principal liability and individual criminal responsibility has also been developing at the ICC as a direct result of African cases. At present, there are two conflicting approaches regarding the interpretation of Article 25(3) of the Rome Statute, which concerns individual criminal responsibility. In *Lubanga*,[49] the Court adopted a wide interpretation for the elements in which liability as a principal is grounded. This resulted in the expansion of the scope of criminal liability. Under this interpretation, three possible forms of common purpose arose: co-perpetration (where two or more people act together), indirect perpetration (where one person is acting through another agent) and indirect co-perpetration (where two or more people act together to bring about their criminal plan by using other persons as their agents). In the majority opinion, great reliance was also placed on 'general principles of law' derived from national legal systems, as opposed to plain reading of the Statute. In *Katanga*,[50] the Court held that the distinction between perpetrators and accomplices is grounded in the autonomous or vicarious character of their contribution to the offence. In essence, this approach seeks to apportion culpability by determining which party was in the driving seat and which party was merely a passenger along for the ride. There have not yet been enough cases before the Court to determine which approach, *Lubanga* or *Katanga*, it will ultimately favour. It is a process—over time greater precedent—that will provide more certainty for those working in and appearing before the Court.

Beyond the further development of existing principles, a number of landmark ICC decisions have also arisen from situations in Africa. The September 2016 conviction of *Al Mahdi*[51] for the war crime of intentionally directing attacks against religious and historic buildings in Mali was such a landmark decision. Arising out of a guilty plea, it was the first time that a conviction was recorded in an international criminal tribunal for the destruction of cultural sites and demonstrated the symbolic importance of protecting cultural heritage.[52]

The first ICC reparation order was also issued in *Katanga*[53] in March 2017. The requirement to pay reparations is hoped to assist in effecting reconciliation and represents a shift in the emphasis of criminal justice from being solely on the perpetrator(s) to focusing on the victims as well. The issuance of the first reparations order by the ICC demonstrates that it is not an empty principle but one that the Court is willing to apply.

During the early development of any legal system, somewhat experimental cases need to be heard by a court of law. In this regard, Africa and the cases it has raised

---

[49] ICC Trial Chamber, Situation in the Democratic Republic of the Congo, *Prosecutor v Lubanga*, Judgment pursuant to Article 74 of the Statute, 14 March 2012, paras. 976–1018.

[50] *Prosecutor v. Germain Katanga*, ICC Pre-Trial Chamber Judgment, 2008.

[51] Trial Chamber VIII, Situation in the Republic of Mali, Case of *The Prosecutor v. Ahmad Al Faqi Al* Mahdi, Judgment and Sentence, 27 September 2016.

[52] Aksenova (2013).

[53] ICC Press Release, 'Katanga case: ICC Trial Chamber II awards victims individual and collective reparations'. 24 March 2017. https://www.icc-cpi.int/legalAidConsultations?name=pr1288. Accessed 27 July 2017.

have been an essential catalyst for the development of international criminal law. The precedents set in such groundbreaking cases contributed to the effectiveness of the field and carved out international law's powers to provide protection to those in need of the law and its mechanisms. The principles established and refined from these cases will impact not only the ICC but potentially the African Court of Justice and Human Rights with extended jurisdiction to core international crimes.

## 5 Tailoring an Alternative/or a Parallel Criminal Justice in Africa?

In 2008, the AU adopted the Protocol on the Statute of the African Court of Justice and Human Rights (Merger Protocol),[54] which concerned the merger of the African Court of Justice (ACJ) and the African Court of Human and Peoples' Rights (AfCHPR) to form the African Court of Justice and Human Rights (AFCJHR). This Protocol has not yet come into force as it has not received the required 15 ratifications.

In June 2014, the AU adopted the Protocol on Amendments to the Protocol on the Statute of the African Court of Justice and Human Rights[55] (Malabo Protocol). Although adopted by the AU, the Protocol does not enjoy unanimous support and will not enter into force until it has been ratified by 15 states (at the time of writing, the Protocol has been signed by 10 AU member states but has not been ratified by any member state[56]). The Protocol is intended to expand the jurisdiction of the African Court of Justice and Human Rights (AFCJHR), and the following are noteworthy:

- it proposes to include offences currently covered by the ICC (crimes against humanity, genocide, war crimes);
- it proposes to add offences of terrorism, mercenarism, trafficking, illicit exploitation of natural resources and the unconstitutional change of government, which are not found in the Rome Statute and are of great concern to African states as they underpin many of the continent's conflicts; and
- it provides for immunity for heads of state. However, it does not follow that the implementation of such an immunity in a regional court would deter offenders;

---

[54] African Union (2008) 'Protocol on the Statute of the African Court of Justice and Human Rights'. https://au.int/sites/default/files/treaties/7792-treaty-0035_-_protocol_on_the_statute_of_the_african_court_of_justice_and_human_rights_e.pdf. Accessed 8 January 2018.

[55] African Union (2014) 'Protocol on amendments to the protocol on the Statute of the African Court of Justice and Human Rights'. June 2014. https://au.int/en/treaties/protocol-amendments-protocol-statute-african-court-justice-and-human-rights. Accessed 2 August 2017.

[56] African Union website. 'Protocol on Amendments to the Protocol on the Statute of the African Court of Justice and Human Rights' 'Status list'. https://au.int/sites/default/files/treaties/7804-sl-protocol_on_amendments_to_the_protocol_on_the_statute_of_the_african_court_of_justice_and_human_rights.pdf. Accessed 12 January 2018.

indeed, it could potentially cause leaders to retain power at any cost. It must also be noted that the immunity provided by the African Court may not prevent the ICC from investigating and prosecuting the African Court's members. For example, if the Malabo Protocol were to be implemented and the implementing states had been parties to the Rome Statute but had withdrawn their membership, they could still be investigated and prosecuted for offences committed during their ICC membership period under Article 127(2). Equally, for any states that were members of both the ICC and the African criminal court, Article 17 could potentially allow the ICC to investigate heads of state as an immunity in the regional court could be argued to make that court 'unable' to prosecute and as such leave open the option for the ICC to do so.[57]

There are pros and cons to this proposed expansion of jurisdiction.[58] On the one hand, it would enable African states to prosecute serious offences themselves without forced recourse to the ICC; it would allow greater consideration of African priorities, such as the exploitation of resources; it would involve the creation of additional organs of the Court, i.e. a Defence Office and a Victims Office; and it would allow alternative justice measures, such as truth commissions, to be included. On the other hand, the expansion of jurisdiction as proposed by the Malabo Protocol is not realistic as the proposed mandate is over-ambitious[59] and economically unfeasible. African states do not have the ability to finance such expanded continental judicial activities, as well as their national judicial systems. The cost of the Court would need to be largely borne by the AU, which is itself underfunded and which, further, does not represent a unified position of all its member states.

There could also be a difficulty in staffing the Court. The Protocol states that there would be a total of 16 judges: five with experience in international law, five with experience in international human rights law and six with experience in international criminal law. As the Court would consist of three chambers (pre-trial, trial and appeals), either there would not be enough specialist judges or cases would be heard by judges without specialisation in the area. In order for each case to be heard by a judge with specialisation in the relevant area, more judges are required, which would in turn increase the financial demands of the Court.[60]

Perhaps the greatest difficulty that any African continental court with criminal jurisdiction would face is the lack of political will. Without genuine commitment from all governments involved, no court can function effectively, particularly when that court professes to investigate and prosecute high-ranking officials. Unfortunately,

---

[57] du Plessis (2012).

[58] For an interesting discussion see (2016) 'Seeking Justice or Shielding Suspects? An analysis of the Malabo Protocol on the African Court'. African Centre for Open Governance. http://kptj.africog.org/wp-content/uploads/2016/11/Malabo-Report.pdf. Accessed 8 January 2018.

[59] Gaeta and Labuda (2017).

[60] (2016) 'Seeking Justice or Shielding Suspects? An analysis of the Malabo Protocol on the African Court'. African Centre for Open Governance. http://kptj.africog.org/wp-content/uploads/2016/11/Malabo-Report.pdf. Accessed 8 January 2018.

the extent of real support can only be known when a state is being investigated, and one of the real difficulties of international courts is that cooperation cannot be forced. It is also an important consideration that by dealing with these offences at regional, as opposed to international, level, states would not be engaging fully in the international community, including ensuring that the ICC is a truly international court.

At present, it appears that the realistic option is to enable African states to strengthen their national (or regional) judicial systems over the long term, as well as engaging with the ICC. The January 2018 AU decision referred to earlier is an example of African states' willingness to engage with international criminal justice. Equally, the ICC needs to improve on its perception problem so that it is seen as a legitimate forum for the investigation and prosecution of international crimes. This can only be done by broadening its focus from Africa and engaging in a dialogue with African states about their concerns.

## 6 Conclusion

The primary concerns raised by African states with respect to their relationship with the ICC include fears of neocolonialism, prosecutorial focus on Africa, the close relationship between the ICC and the UNSC, the issue of immunities for heads of state and the peace versus justice debate remaining, even though a number of African states remain committed to the ICC. As a result, and in spite of the sometimes strained relationship, African states have been central to the development of international criminal law. The early cases from Africa have allowed the Court to clarify such important principles as fair trial rights before the ICC, the protection of cultural sites and the use of reparations as a remedy under the ICC. The relationship between African states and the ICC was at its most tense in 2016 when three states (South Africa, Gambia and Burundi) notified the ICC of their intention to withdraw, followed by the 2017 AU resolution on 'mass withdrawal'. However, a number of African states remain committed to the ICC, and in 2017 the withdrawal notifications of South Africa and Gambia were retracted. The February 2018 decision by the AU to seek an advisory opinion from the ICJ regarding the issue of immunities suggests that African states want to remain engaged with international courts and tribunals. In short, African states should strengthen their national judiciaries; the option of extending the jurisdiction of the African Court of Justice and Human Rights to international crimes may also be among the solutions. However, the best way forward is to continue to engage with the ICC.

# References

Akande D (2016) South African withdrawal from the International Criminal Court – does the ICC Statute lead to violations of other international obligations? EJIL Talk. 22 October 2016. https://www.ejiltalk.org/south-african-withdrawal-from-the-international-criminal-court/. Accessed 16 Aug 2017

Aksenova M (2013) The Al Mahdi judgment and sentence at the ICC: a source of cautious optimism for international criminal justice. EJIL Talk. 13 October 2013. https://www.ejiltalk.org/the-al-mahdi-judgment-and-sentence-at-the-icc-a-source-of-cautious-optimism-for-international-criminal-justice/. Accessed 17 Aug 2017

Arnould V (2017) A court in crisis? The ICC in Africa, and beyond. Egmont Paper 93

Babington-Ashaye A (2014) Politicising the International Criminal Court: redefining the role of the United Nations Security Council in the age of accountability. ASIL Proc 2014:381–398

Coalition for the ICC, 'Challenging ICC, AU seeks opinion on head of state immunities from top UN Court'. http://www.coalitionfortheicc.org/news/20180201/globaljustice-weekly-au-seeks-icj-opinion-head-state-immunities-witnesses-take-stand. Accessed 7 Feb 2018

du Plessis M (2012) Implications of the AU decision to give the African Court jurisdiction over international crimes. Institute for Security Studies Paper No 235

du Plessis M (2013) Universalising international criminal law. The ICC, Africa, and the problem of political perceptions. Institute for Security Studies Paper No. 249

du Plessis M, Maunganidze OA (2016) ICC Prosecutor's policy on case selection: timely, but is it enough? Institute for Security Studies. https://issafrica.org/iss-today/icc-prosecutors-policy-on-case-selection-timely-but-is-it-enough. Accessed 26 July 2017

Dugard J (2013) Palestine and the International Criminal Court. Institutional failure or bias? J Int Crim Just 11:563–570

Gaeta P, Labuda P (2017) Trying sitting heads of state: the African Union v the ICC in the Al-Basjir and Kenyatta cases. In: Abbas, Bantekas, Jalloh (eds) Africa and the International Criminal Court. Oxford University Press

Jalloh C (2009) Regionalizing international criminal law? Int Crim Law Rev 9:445–499

Kersten M (2017) Not all it's cracked up to be – the African Union's "ICC Withdrawal Strategy". Justice in Conflict blog. 6 February 2017. https://justiceinconflict.org/2017/02/06/not-all-its-cracked-up-to-be-the-african-unions-icc-withdrawal-strategy. Accessed 25 July 2017

Kimani M (2009) Pursuit of Justice or Western plot? Africa Renewal. http://www.un.org/africarenewal/magazine/october-2009/pursuit-justice-or-western-plot. Accessed 15 Aug 2017

Labuda P (2015) The International Criminal Court and perceptions of sovereignty, colonialism, and Pan-African solidarity. Afr Yearb Int Law:289–321

Lansky SR (2017) Africans speak out against ICC withdrawal. Governments signal continued support for Court. Human Rights Watch. https://www.hrw.org/news/2016/11/02/africans-speak-out-against-icc-withdrawal. Accessed 1 Aug 2017

Ngari A (2017) The AU's (other) ICC Strategy. Institute for Security Studies. 14 February 2017. https://issafrica.org/iss-today/the-aus-other-icc-strategy. Accessed 25 July 2017

Nooruddin I, Lockwood Payton A (2010) Dynamics of influence in international politics: the ICC, BIAs, and economic sanctions. J Peace Res 47:711–721

Olugbo B (2014) The African Union, the United Nations Security Council, and the politicisation of international criminal justice in Africa. Afr J Leg Stud 7(3):351–379

Smith D (2012) International Criminal Court to deliver its first judgment. The Guardian. https://www.theguardian.com/law/2012/mar/13/international-criminal-court-first-judgment. Accessed 30 July 2017

Ssenyonjo M (2017) State withdrawal notification from the Rome statute of the International Criminal Court: South Africa, Burundi, and the Gambia. M Crim Law Forum:1–57

Vilmer J (2016) The African Union and the International Criminal Court: counteracting the crisis. Int Aff 92(6):1319–1342

Woolaver H (2016) International and domestic implications of South Africa's withdrawal from the ICC. EJIL Talk. 24 October 2016. https://www.ejiltalk.org/international-and-domestic-implications-of-south-africas-withdrawal-from-the-icc/. Accessed 16 Aug 2017

Woolaver H (2017) Unconstitutional and invalid: South Africa's withdrawal from the ICC barred (for now). EJIL Talk. 27 February 2017. https://www.ejiltalk.org/unconstitutional-and-invalid-south-africas-withdrawal-from-the-icc-barred-for-now/. Accessed 16 Aug 2017

(2016) Seeking justice or shielding suspects? An analysis of the Malabo Protocol on the African Court. African Centre for Open Governance. http://kptj.africog.org/wp-content/uploads/2016/11/Malabo-Report.pdf. Accessed 8 Jan 2018


**Makane Moïse Mbengue** is Professor of International Law at the Faculty of Law of the University of Geneva and Affiliated Professor at Sciences Po Paris (School of Law). He was the Lead Expert for the negotiations and drafting of the Pan-African Investment Code (PAIC) in the context of the African Union. Prof. Mbengue acts as counsel in disputes before international courts and tribunals and as advisor for governments in several fields of international law, in particular investment negotiations. He is the author of several publications in the field of international law.

**Kirsten McClellan** [BA (University of Sydney); LLB (University of Sydney); LLM specialising in Human Rights Law (University of London)] is a criminal law solicitor admitted to practice before the Supreme Court of New South Wales, and the High Court of Australia. She has worked in criminal defence law in Australia, the UK, and the USA.

# Part IV
# Case Report

# Case Note on *PetroTrans Company Ltd. v. Ministry of Mines of the Federal Democratic Republic of Ethiopia*

Thomas R. Snider and Jackson Shaw Kern

## 1 Introduction

In January 2016, an international arbitral tribunal seated in Switzerland and comprised of three members from Switzerland, France, and the United States rendered its final award in the case of *PetroTrans Company Ltd. v. Ministry of Mines of the Federal Democratic Republic of Ethiopia*.[1] PetroTrans commenced the arbitration in late 2012 under the auspices of the International Chamber of Commerce (ICC) after the Ministry terminated five petroleum production sharing agreements (PSAs) that had been awarded in 2011 to explore and develop petroleum resources in southeastern Ethiopia. PetroTrans accepted several time-sensitive obligations under the PSAs, including an obligation to provide or arrange a loan for the Ethiopian government to be repaid from the government's share of proceeds under the PSAs.[2] After PetroTrans failed to obtain the loan and to fulfill other obligations, the Ministry terminated all five PSAs.

PetroTrans initiated the arbitration under the terms of the PSAs and sought an order that the Ministry be bound to specific performance of the contracts or, in the alternative, to pay nearly US$1.5 billion in damages. The Ministry responded and counterclaimed, seeking damages. After several rounds of written pleadings, the tribunal held an evidentiary hearing and subsequently issued an award dismissing all claims and counterclaims.

---

[1] Solomon (2016) and Jones (2016).
[2] Bekele (2016).

T. R. Snider (✉) · J. S. Kern
Al Tamimi & Company, Dubai, United Arab Emirates

Addis Law Group LLP, Addis Ababa, Ethiopia
e-mail: T.Snider@tamimi.com

## 2 Background to the Dispute

The Ogaden Basin in southeastern Ethiopia was first identified as holding potential for hydrocarbons in the 1930s.[3] Petroleum exploration commenced in earnest in the 1950s, and, in the early 1970s, an American company named Tenneco discovered natural gas deposits at Calub and Hilala, deep in the basin, some 1200 km southeast of Addis Ababa.[4] Further wells were drilled by the Soviet Petroleum Exploration Expedition (SPEE) in the 1980s, whose efforts better delineated the gas resources, estimated in 2015 to be some 4.7 trillion cubic feet.[5] Additional evaluative work was undertaken in the 1990s, and in the 2000s, the Malaysian oil company Petronas secured the rights to further explore and develop the areas known as Blocks 3 and 4, 11 and 15, 12 and 16, and 17 and 20, as well as the Calub and Hilala fields.[6] These territories capture some 93,000 km$^2$, encompassing a large swath of the Ogaden Basin.

In 2010, Petronas decided to withdraw from Ethiopia, and in July 2011, the Ministry awarded these territories to PetroTrans, a Samoan-incorporated entity with offices in Hong Kong, following an international tender.

Under the PSAs, which were governed by Ethiopian law, PetroTrans obtained the rights to explore, develop, and ultimately participate in any resulting production of petroleum resources from these territories provided that it undertake numerous investments embodied in a highly specified work program. PetroTrans accepted several time-sensitive obligations, including an obligation to provide or arrange for a loan for the Ethiopian government, to be repaid from production proceeds. At various stages of negotiation for the PSAs, PetroTrans represented that it was working with two large Chinese state-owned oil companies to ensure the capacity and expertise required to undertake the work program.

By mid-2012, the loan was not forthcoming, and neither of the larger companies had joined the venture. The Ministry was also unsatisfied with PetroTrans's progress on the work program. In the face of numerous notices, PetroTrans maintained that it was analyzing and interpreting geological data collected by SPEE and Petronas, that it had commissioned other technical studies, and that it was preparing to commence fieldwork. Citing the inability to obtain the loan or advance the work program, the Ministry terminated all five PSAs in July 2012, 1 year after the time of contract signing.

In November 2013, the Ministry signed five PSAs with Poly-GCL Petroleum Investment Ltd., a Chinese company, over the same contractual territories.[7]

---

[3] Abebe (2013).
[4] Abebe (2013).
[5] Maasho (2015).
[6] Abebe (2013).
[7] Solomon (2016).

## 3 The Arbitration

In December 2012, PetroTrans initiated an arbitration against the Ministry administered under the Rules of Arbitration of the ICC pursuant to the terms of an arbitration agreement featuring in all five PSAs. These terms designated Geneva, Switzerland, as the legal place of arbitration, with the matter to be decided by three arbitrators. PetroTrans nominated Mr. Philippe Pinsolle, a partner in the Paris office of the law firm of Quinn Emanuel Urquhart & Sullivan LLP, as its party-appointed arbitrator.[8] The Ministry nominated Professor David Caron, who, at the time, was a dean and professor of international law at the Dickson Poon School of Law, King's College, London, and later a judge in the Iran-United States Claims Tribunal in The Hague.[9] (Professor Caron passed away in early-2018.) The ICC accepted both nominations and subsequently appointed Ms. Gabrielle Nater-Bass, a partner with the law firm of Homburger AG in Zurich, as the presiding arbitrator.[10]

PetroTrans was initially represented in the arbitration by Mr. Pierre Bienvenu, Mr. Martin Valasek, Ms. Alison Fitzgerald, and Ms. Michelle Lutfy of the Montreal and Ottawa offices of the law firm Norton Rose Fulbright.[11] In 2014, Ms. Domitille Baizeau, Dr. Marc Veit, Ms. Lorraine de Germiny, Ms. Juliette Richard, and Mr. David Bonifacio of the Geneva and Zurich offices of the law firm Lalive took over representation of PetroTrans.[12] Mr. Tadesse Kiros, based in Addis Ababa, was co-counsel with both firms to PetroTrans.[13]

The Ministry was represented by Dr. Zewdineh Beyene Haile, Professor Won Kidane, Mr. Jackson Shaw Kern, Ms. Aseel Barghuthi, and Ms. Erica Young of the Addis Law Group LLP and Mr. Thomas R. Snider, who then was a shareholder with Greenberg Traurig LLP in Washington, DC, and is now a partner and the Head of Arbitration at Al Tamimi & Company in Dubai.[14]

In the alternative to its claim for specific performance, PetroTrans sought nearly US$1.5 billion in damages—an amount thought to be among the largest ever asserted against an African state in international arbitration. The Ministry responded by filing counterclaims for damages sustained as a result of PetroTrans's failure to perform the work program under the PSAs.

After several rounds of written pleadings, the arbitral tribunal held a two-week evidentiary hearing in Zurich in March 2015. (While the arbitration maintained its legal seat in Geneva, the hearing was held in Zurich for practical reasons.) The hearing was conducted in English pursuant to the terms of the arbitration agreement in the PSAs.

---

[8] Jones (2016).
[9] Ibid.
[10] Ibid.
[11] Ibid.
[12] Ibid.
[13] Ibid.
[14] Jones (2016).

In an award dated December 31, 2015, and delivered to the parties in January 2016, the tribunal rejected all of PetroTrans's claims against the Ministry, concluding that the Ministry had validly terminated the PSAs for failure of performance. The tribunal also dismissed the Ministry's counterclaims.

## 4 The Arbitral Jurisprudence of Petroleum in Ethiopia

The *PetroTrans* case is reminiscent of an earlier matter faced by Ethiopia in the waning days of the Empire. Under a contract entered into in 1966, the U.S. oil-and-gas firm Baruch Foster Corporation was granted a northern concession to explore for and exploit petroleum resources. Ethiopia terminated the contract in 1970 on the ground that Baruch Foster had not discharged minimum obligations to drill within a stipulated time.

Baruch Foster initiated arbitration under the terms of the concession agreement, which provided for arbitration of "all disputes, disagreements and controversies which shall hereafter arise between the parties thereto during the term of this Agreement and which are related to the execution, interpretation or performance thereof, any alleged breach hereof, or the alleged non-recognition or violation of any rights or privileges herein expressed."[15]

In February 1974, a three-member tribunal seated in Geneva and chaired by the late René David, a draftsman of Ethiopia's Civil Code of 1960, dismissed all the claimant's claims.[16]

Baruch Foster first claimed that the contractual time limit for its performance should be extended on grounds of *force majeure* and that if it were not reinstated in its concession, it was owed compensation by Ethiopia. The governing law of the contract was established as follows:

> Wherever in this Agreement specific provision is made for the application of Ethiopian law, such shall ... govern; otherwise, this Agreement shall in all respects be governed by and interpreted in accordance with generally recognised principles of international law.[17]

In seeking to establish an incident of *force majeure*, Baruch Foster first cited "the committed schedules of the contractors which we have selected to conduct our planned geophysical and drilling programme."

In rejecting this finding, the tribunal wrote that

---

[15] Award in the Matter of an Arbitration between Baruch-Foster Corporation and the Imperial Ethiopian Government, dated 15 February 1974.

[16] In a notable historical irony, Ethiopia was represented by Lalive & Budin of Geneva, including personal representation by Jean-Flavien Lalive. This firm, now known only as Lalive, would later represent PetroTrans Company Limited. Baruch Foster Corporation was represented by the then-firm Davies, Richberg, Tydings, Landa & Duff of Washington.

[17] Award in the Matter of an Arbitration between Baruch-Foster Corporation and the Imperial Ethiopian Government, dated 15 February 1974.

[i]t is not enough for an event to constitute force majeure that it should have been beyond the reasonable control of the party affected by it. The very concept of force majeure is based on the assumption that the event alleged should not have been reasonably predictable. This principle is to be found in all national laws and in particular in the Law of Ethiopia and the Common Law of the U.S.A.[18]

Baruch Foster further cited difficulties encountered in engaging a contractor with adequate drilling equipment. In response, the tribunal wrote that "[c]onsiderations similar to those given above compel the Tribunal to reject this argument since it again concerns a difficulty in carrying out the contract where the risks of encountering difficulty had been accepted by [Baruch Foster Corporation] as its own responsibility."[19]

Finally, with regard to a cited 1969 blowout in a neighboring concession operated by Mobil, the tribunal found as follows:

> It has not been established that the blow-out was unavoidable and still less has been established the danger that such a blow-out might happen again in another site chosen by [Baruch Foster Corporation]. Additionally, it does not seem that such another site had ever been localised nor that the necessary arrangements for the drilling of a first well had ever been made.[20]

The tribunal further rejected Baruch Foster's argument that Ethiopia had waived any right of termination by receiving various payments from it after the time at which the termination right first arose.

Ethiopia asserted a counterclaim. Noting the broad arbitration agreement, the tribunal first rejected Baruch Foster's submission that the counterclaim fell outside of its jurisdiction. The tribunal then ordered compensation under force of a liquidated-damages-type clause in the contract that expressly bound Baruch Foster to a minimum expenditure of US$800,000 and rendered any shortfall in this amount payable to the state.

The tribunal rejected Ethiopia's claim that Baruch Foster's non-performance was premeditated and the result of fraud on the latter's part and thus declined to award any damages on that basis.

---

[18] Ibid. *Force majeure* is established in Ethiopian law at Article 1792 of the Civil Code of 1960 ("(1) Force majeure results from an occurrence which the debtor could normally not foresee and which prevents him absolutely from performing his obligations. (2) Force majeure shall not exist where the occurrence could normally have been foreseen by the debtor or where it renders more onerous the performance by the debtor of his obligations").

[19] Ibid.

[20] Ibid.

## 5 Conclusion

While more than 40 years elapsed between the rendering of the awards in the *Baruch Foster* and *PetroTrans* matters, these two cases remain the most prominent to which Ethiopia has been a party in the extractives sector to date.

## References

Abebe B (2013) Ministry of Mines signs agreement with Chinese firm for Ogaden gas reserves. Fortune
Bekele K (2016) PetroTrans' claims for compensation turns out dry. The Ethiopian Reporter
Jones T (2016) Ethiopia defeats claim by Chinese energy investor. Global Arbitration Review
Maasho A (2015) Ethiopia eyes gas production, exports by 2017 – PM. Reuters
Solomon T (2016) International court rules in favour of Ethiopia in exploration suit. The Africa Report

**Thomas R. Snider** is a Partner and the Head of Arbitration at Al Tamimi & Co. in Dubai. He has represented corporate entities and sovereign states in a wide range of matters involving international arbitration and other forms of cross-border dispute resolution, including state-to-state arbitration, international commercial arbitration, international investment disputes, and U.S. court litigation. From 2001 to 2009, he was a member of the legal team representing the Government of Ethiopia before the Eritrea-Ethiopia Claims Commission, an international arbitral tribunal that adjudicated claims for loss, damage, and injury arising during an international armed conflict. Mr. Snider frequently speaks and writes on topics involving international law and dispute resolution. Before relocating to Dubai, he was a Professorial Lecturer in Law at the George Washington University Law School in Washington, D.C.

**Jackson Shaw Kern** is a Counsel with the Addis Law Group. Jackson has acted as counsel across Africa, Asia, Europe, and the Americas, where he represents sovereign States, State entities, and State enterprises as well as private interests in a wide range of contentious matters. Jackson is a past visiting fellow of the Lauterpacht Centre for International Law, University of Cambridge, and a frequent guest lecturer at institutions including the Peking University School of Transnational Law. In co-authorship with Jose Daniel Amado of the Catholic University of Peru and Martin Doe Rodriguez of the Permanent Court of Arbitration, Jackson has recently completed a book to propose reforms in international investment law, entitled Arbitrating the Conduct of International Investors, the book is forthcoming in 2018 from Cambridge University Press.

# Part V
# Book Review

# Zeray Yihdego, Alistair Rieu-Clarke and Ana Elisa Cascão (Eds.): The Grand Ethiopian Renaissance Dam and the Nile Basin—Implications for Transboundary Water Cooperation

## Earthscan Studies in Water Resource Management, Routledge 2018, 226 Pages

Götz Reichert

It was in June 2013 when the wider international public became fully aware of the dramatic changes currently transforming the hydropolitics of the Nile: a high-level meeting of Egyptian politicians, chaired by then President Mohammed Mursi, discussing strategies to prevent Ethiopia from building a major dam upstream on the Blue Nile. The deliberations ranged from building international pressure on Ethiopia to even bombing the building site of the 'Grand Ethiopian Renaissance Dam' (GERD) itself. The discussion, which became public since it was unintentionally aired live on television, revealed both the deep concerns in Egypt regarding potentially harmful impacts of the infrastructure project on its lifeline, the Nile, and the helplessness of Egypt's political elite, which was confronted with an entirely new situation. Since ancient times, Egypt has used a major share of the Nile's water resources and persistently rejected claims for increased water uses by upstream riparians by invoking 'historic rights'. While the distribution of the Nile waters between the riparians has always been a matter of fierce controversy, it is obvious that the building of the GERD is about to change the respective power constellations in the Nile Basin profoundly.

The Nile is the world's longest river, running for almost 6700 km from the Equatorial Plateau of East Africa in the south to its estuary into the Mediterranean Sea in the north. Its main tributaries are the White Nile, fed by its headwaters in Burundi and in Rwanda, and the Blue Nile, originating in the Ethiopian highlands. While the White Nile is the river's longest feeding stream, the Blue Nile contributes up to 60% of its annual flow. Additional waters that stem from the Tekeze/Atbara

---

G. Reichert (✉)
Center for European Policy, Freiburg, Germany

© Springer International Publishing AG, part of Springer Nature 2018
Z. Yihdego et al. (eds.), *Ethiopian Yearbook of International Law 2017*,
Ethiopian Yearbook of International Law 2017,
https://doi.org/10.1007/978-3-319-90887-8_10

and Baro Akobo rivers of Ethiopia flow into the Nile, which makes the total water contribution of Ethiopian rivers to the Nile up to 85% of the total Nile annual flow. The Nile Basin is shared by eleven riparian countries: Tanzania, Uganda, Rwanda, Burundi, the Democratic Republic of the Congo, Kenya, Ethiopia, Eritrea, South Sudan, Sudan and Egypt. Today, approximately 257 million people live within the basin, with the biggest population in Egypt (85.8 million), followed by Ethiopia (37.6 million), Uganda (33.6 million) and Sudan (31.4 million). While the geographical, hydrological, ecological, socio-economic and political conditions vary considerably between the riparians, they share the experience that the river has played a pivotal role in their development since ancient times. Even today, agriculture is the dominant economic sector in most riparian countries. The basin's population is expected to grow significantly within the coming decades, thereby further exacerbating the challenges to the management of the Nile's water resources.

The GERD is a hydropower project under construction on the Blue Nile in Ethiopia close to the Sudanese border since 2011. On completion, the GERD will be Africa's largest dam—with a height of 155 m, a length of 1.8 km, a storage capacity of 74 km$^3$ and an electricity generation capacity of 6450 MW. Given the dependency of the riparians on the Nile's water resources, it is evident that the opportunities provided, and the risks posed, by such a major dam are of utmost importance, especially for Ethiopia, Sudan and Egypt. In this respect, their perceived interests differ significantly owing to varying circumstances, which are to a large extent determined by their respective position either as upstream (Ethiopia) or as downstream riparians (Sudan, Egypt). Consequently, the potential impacts of the GERD in these countries—opportunities and risks alike—raise a variety of distinct and yet closely intertwined questions, which cannot be analysed and answered by one discipline alone. There is indeed an urgent need for a comprehensive analysis of this watershed development in the making. Therefore, the multidisciplinary volume 'The Grand Ethiopian Renaissance Dam and the Nile Basin—Implications for Transboundary Water Cooperation' is published at the right time to take a closer look at the impacts of the GERD on the Nile and its riparians from the perspectives of law, political science, economics and hydrology.

Three chapters of the volume explore the legal questions raised by the construction of the GERD regarding the international relations of the Nile's riparian countries: in Chapter 2 (The Nile Basin Cooperative Framework Agreement: Disentangling the Gordian Knot), Salman M. A. Salman locates the legal relevance of the GERD within the overall framework of international water law pertaining to the Nile. Against the geographical, political and historical background of sharing the Nile's water resources, Salman outlines the controversies relating to colonial and post-colonial legal arrangements regulating the Nile, most notably the 1902 and 1959 Nile treaties. Against this background, he explores the attempts to promote transboundary cooperation particularly through the Nile Basin Cooperative Framework Agreement (CFA), which was signed by five Nile riparians in May 2010 but vehemently opposed by Egypt and Sudan. While Salman highlights that the controversy over historic or acquired versus equitable rights had dominated the negotiations of the CFA, he considers the CFA's adoption as a watershed event in the development of international water law within the Nile Basin. On this basis, in

Chapter 3 (Agreement on Declaration of Principles on the GERD: Levelling the Nile Basin Playing Field), Salman takes a closer look at the Declaration of Principles (DoPs) on the GERD of March 2015, which endorsed established principles of international water law and cooperative mechanisms and set out an agreement on the sharing of benefits and the prevention of negative impacts of the dam. Salman describes the negotiation process that led to the DoPs and the December 2015 Khartoum Document, which endorsed the decision to commission a French company to conduct an external impact assessment on the GERD. Salman argues that the DoPs and the Khartoum Document have created 'a new legal order' that has replaced the 1902 and 1959 Nile treaties—a legal order that is based upon contemporary principles of international water law, thereby levelling 'the playing fields of the Nile Basin'. He highlights that this paradigm shift opens new opportunities for cooperation for sustainable and optimal utilisation of the Nile. In Chapter 4 (International Water Law Developments on the Sharing of the Blue Nile Waters: A Fairness Perspective), Zeray Yihdego and Alistair Rieu-Clarke examine how the fairness principle—as formulated by Thomas M. Franck—helps explain the strengths and weaknesses of the Nile legal framework. Based on a discussion of the principles of equitable utilisation, which is well established in modern international water law, Yihdego and Rieu-Clarke conclude that, while the old Nile treaty regime fails the fairness test, the post-1990 Nile Basin initiatives and legal developments are more aligned with Franck's notion of fairness. They argue that a basin-wide or regional approach to cooperation, particularly if it includes the participation of non-state actors, helps to rectify imbalances in power among riparians and to ensure fairness.

The next two chapters employ a political science perspective to the GERD. In Chapter 5, Ana Elisa Cascão and Alan Nicol take a closer look at the 'Changing Cooperation Dynamics in the Nile Basin and the Role of the GERD'. They provide a detailed analysis of the achievements, pitfalls and challenges within the Nile Basin Initiative and the negotiation of the CFA. The authors argue that the GERD and related norms and processes are partly the result of changes in the transboundary relations among the riparian countries since the mid-1990s. They also consider the GERD as a catalyst for future cooperation, in terms of its capacity to create shared benefits, including trade in energy, and as an opportunity to expand regional development and integration in the Eastern Nile Basin region. In Chapter 6 (GERD and Hydropolitics in the Eastern Nile: From Water-Sharing to Benefit-Sharing?), Rawia Tawfik and Ines Dombrowsky highlight, on the one hand, the dam's potential benefits for all riparians—ranging from economic development for Ethiopia to electricity provision to Egypt and Sudan. On the other hand, the authors caution that the GERD's downstream impacts will depend on the respective filling and operating modes. They conclude that while the GERD has the potential for benefit sharing, this depends on the conclusion of an agreement on water sharing as a prerequisite.

The next two chapters take a closer look at the economic implications of the GERD for both downstream and upstream Eastern Nile Basin countries, especially with regard to different options for the filling of the dam's reservoir. In Chapter 7 (Analysing the Economy-Wide Impacts on Egypt of Alternative GERD Filling

Options), Brent Boehlert, Kenneth M. Strzepek and Sherman Robinson analyse three dam filling scenarios to understand the economic impacts of the GERD on Egypt: (1) an 'unconstrained scenario' that assumes that the dam will be filled swiftly depending on available water flow from the Blue Nile, (2) a three-year filling period and (3) a 10-year filling period. Each of these scenarios considers three release requirements while the GERD is filling: no minimum release and a 15 billion cubic metre (BCM) and 30 BCM minimum releases each year, respectively. The authors conclude that even the worst-case scenario impacts of unconstrained filling of the GERD on Egypt's economy are modest; Egypt's economy would not be significantly affected by the filling of the GERD regardless of the option that is chosen. Furthermore, they maintain that the higher short-term gains to the Ethiopian economy suggest that a more rapid filling policy would have higher Nile-wide economic benefits. In Chapter 8, Tewodros Negash Kahsay, Onno Kuik, Roy Brouwer and Pieter van der Zaag undertake an 'Economic Impact Assessment of the Grand Ethiopian Renaissance Dam Under Different Climate and Hydrological Conditions'. On the one hand, the authors identify substantial basin-wide economic benefits from the GERD. On the other hand, they suggest that to avoid adverse effects on the Egyptian economy during the dam's filling period, the impounding period of the dam should be extended during dry years. Furthermore, the authors recommend the institution of a basin-wide energy trade scheme that allows Egypt to buy electricity from the GERD. Finally, they identify a need for further studies on the potential impact of climate change on transboundary economic impacts of the GERD.

The last two chapters of this volume deal with the hydrological aspects of the GERD regarding not only the initial filling options but also the long-term operation of the river system. In Chapter 9 (From Projecting Hydroclimate Variability to Filling the GERD: Upstream Hydropower Generation and Downstream Releases), Ying Zhang, Solomon Tassew Erkyihun and Paul Block analyse three different reservoir-filling strategies and associated impacts on upstream and downstream countries and consider questions over who bears the risks associated with natural streamflow variability. Against this background, the authors call for closer cooperation among Ethiopia, Sudan and Egypt regarding the reservoir filling and the management of the water resources for purposes of fostering development and regional integration. In Chapter 10 (Managing Risks While Filling the Grand Ethiopian Renaissance Dam), Kevin G. Wheeler presents a new modelling framework for the simulation of complex multi-objective reservoir operations throughout the Eastern Nile Basin. The framework can accurately simulate the operational decisions of a managed river system and is capable of supporting negotiations between the riparians. Wheeler demonstrates the framework's application by analysing potential coordination and adaptation strategies among the agencies administering the dams of Ethiopia, Sudan and Egypt during the initial filling of the GERD reservoir. He warns that a rapid non-cooperative filling of the reservoir would pose significant risks to downstream riparians. Such risks to downstream riparians during the filling period could only be minimised with an explicit coordination plan. The author concludes that risks to Egypt could be substantially minimised by a basic level of coordination with an agreed annual release. Wheeler highlights that such coordination must be built on the transparent sharing of information.

This overview of the legal, political, economic and hydrological implications of the building of the GERD for the Eastern Nile Basin illustrates the variety, complexity and urgency of the questions raised and to be answered by the relevant riparian countries. It is a great achievement of this multidisciplinary endeavour of leading experts not only to provide up-to-date analyses of the highest standards in their respective fields but also to look at often closely interlinked aspects of the subject matter from different angles. In this respect, Chapters 2, 3 and 4 on the legal aspects, in conjunction with Chapters 5 and 6 on the hydro-political dynamics in the Eastern Nile Basin make the archetypical upstream-downstream constellation, which has dominated riparian relations for centuries, most transparent. Given Egypt's persistent claim of 'historic rights' to the Nile waters, it would have been an additional asset if an outspoken proponent of this position would be represented in the volume. Nevertheless, the authors master the delicate task of giving a comprehensive and balanced account of the different interests of Ethiopia, Sudan and Egypt; the respective legal claims derived therefrom; and the resulting hydropolitical dynamics. The reader is provided with excellent analyses of the historic development, current status and potential future of the legal framework governing the Nile. It becomes apparent that the riparians will only succeed in resolving their differences in a sustainable manner if they overcome the perceived dichotomy of the main principles of international water law by abandoning an antagonistic understanding of the no-harm rule and the principle of equitable utilisation. In other regions of the world, e.g. Europe, such a shift from a paradigm of mere coexistence to one of active cooperation has already fostered the development of governance regimes for the successful management of transboundary freshwater resources for the mutual benefit of all riparians involved. To enable such a paradigm shift, the authors take a fresh look at the legal relevance of the fairness concept and the hydropolitical preconditions for the sharing of benefits, which are potentially opened up by the building of the GERD. It is one of the outstanding strengths of this interdisciplinary compilation that these legal and hydropolitical reflections, which provide general guidance to the riparians on viable options for the future design of their transboundary relations, are complemented by detailed analyses of the economic (Chapters 7 and 8) and hydrological implications (Chapters 9 and 10) of specific options for the initial filling of the dam reservoir and the long-term management of the river system. In this respect, the different and sometimes differing views compiled in this volume show the complexity of the task to find solutions that will satisfy the justified interests of upstream and downstream riparians alike. Only on the basis of such a comprehensive assessment and honest discussion of the pros and cons of the various options for the operation of the GERD and the overall management of the waters of the Eastern Nile Basin can a fruitful cooperation for the mutual benefit of all riparians be possible.

As a *conditio sine qua non*, the willingness to start a conversation in good faith is required from Ethiopia, Sudan and Egypt. In this respect, the book 'The Grand Ethiopian Renaissance Dam and the Nile Basin—Implications for Transboundary

Water Cooperation' serves as an initial platform for the urgently needed analysis and discussion of pertinent problems and potential solutions for transboundary water cooperation in the Eastern Nile Basin at a crucial point in time. By providing ample space for varying views within and between disciplines, it makes a valuable contribution to the future resolution of conflicts and the fostering of cooperation on the sharing of the Nile waters in the future. After all, bombing the GERD is clearly not an option.

**Götz Reichert** is Head of the Department on Environment, Energy, Climate and Transport at the Center for European Policy, Freiburg, Germany, and formerly legal consultant for the World Bank.

# Won L. Kidane: The Culture of International Arbitration

## Oxford University Press 2017, 336 Pages

**Makane Moïse Mbengue and Elise Ruggeri Abonnat**

Besides the issue of arbitrators' appointment rules, not much has been written about the topic of diversity in international arbitration and "the scholarly discourses have largely downplayed the possibility that this deficit may impact arbitration outcomes."[1] Going against the current of conventional thinking, Kidane's book entitled *The Culture of International Arbitration* remedies this reality by questioning the "establishment" or epistemic community of international arbitration.

The choice of chapters' titles, and their combination, is particularly evocative as the reader is taken on a journey through a critical examination of the international arbitration field (including investment and commercial arbitration), as viewed through the prism of diversity, culture, and legal traditions. After an introduction on the meaning of legal culture in international arbitration and its relevance to any critique of the field (Introduction and Chapter 2, "Defining Legal Culture"), the following chapters of part I entitled "Culture and the Legal Framework and Theoretical Pillars of International Arbitration" examine "The Political and Cultural History of International Arbitration in Various Legal Traditions" (Chapter 3), as well as the dominant contemporary legal theories (Chapter 4, "The Theories and Theoreticians of International Arbitration") before turning to "The Evolving Justifications of International Arbitration" (Chapter 5). Against this background, the author explains in Chapter 6 the "Culture and the Legal Infrastructure of Commercial Arbitration" and in Chapter 7 the "Culture and the Legal Infrastructure of Investment Arbitration". Specifically, the reader sees how a culture of its own has developed in each arbitration field, although they "suffer from the same problem of stranger justice."[2] The first two chapters of the second part entitled "Deconstructing the Mythology of

---

[1] P. 135.
[2] P. 176.

M. M. Mbengue (✉) · E. R. Abonnat
University of Geneva, Geneva, Switzerland
e-mail: Makane.Mbengue@unige.ch

Specialized Knowledge in International Arbitration" (Chapter 8) discuss how the rules of procedure and evidence used in international arbitration combine different legal traditions, which "often masks the invisible cultural barriers" (Chapter 9, "Fact-Finding and Cultural Diversity in International Arbitration"). The remaining chapters successively turn to the arbitrators' appointment and challenge rules (Chapter 10, "The Typical Process for Selection and Challenge of Arbitrators") questioning "The Mythology of Specialized Knowledge" (Chapter 11). Finally, Chapter 12 (Conversations on the Role of Culture in International Arbitration) reports conversations between Kidane and international judges and arbitrators on the relevance and effects of cultural diversity in international dispute settlement.

Using a thought-provocative ton and well-documented research, Kidane invites us to think outside the box and cast a different eye on the arbitration system and identify the far-reaching consequences attached to the existence of a "close-knit epistemic community of largely European arbitrators with common aspirations."[3] Instead of denouncing and focusing on the quasi-monopoly held by a core group of jurists, the author endeavors to question and deconstruct the pillars of international arbitration as we think it is. Thus, Kidane's book offers a multidimensional approach to (non)diversity in arbitration, from both theoretical and practical angles.

In part I, Kidane challenges biases and stereotypes with history and facts. In chapter 3 (The Political and Cultural History of International Arbitration in Various Legal Traditions), in particular, he recalls the preeminent and leading role played by Africa since the very beginning of the ICSID Convention. Not only were the very first 15 ratifying states of the Washington Convention African—prompting the reminder that "without Africa, there would have been no ICSID"[4]—but African states were also pioneers in shaping the practice of investment arbitration. Indeed, we are reminded that the three founding Lybian oil cases "set the ideological tone that generations of students of international arbitration were incubated with."[5]

This historical African footprint also resulted in the creation of persisting stereotypes such as "identif(ying) all of the newly independent African states as cousins of Muammar Gaddafi."[6] Some stereotypes, Kidane explains, are apparent in arbitral awards. For instance, outcomes such as the *Salini* award[7] are "an excellent demonstration of Africa's worst nightmare"[8] since arbitrators using "their theoretical and intellectual power to defend a set of indefensible principles and decisions"[9] outrooted the dispute from Africa to Paris, against the very terms of the binding agreement.

---

[3] P. 83.
[4] P. 28.
[5] P. 30.
[6] P. 31.
[7] *Salini Construttori S.p.A (Claimant) v. The Federal Democratic Republic of Ethiopia, Addis Ababa Water and Sewerage Authority (Ethiopia) (Respondent)*, ICC Arbitration No. +=&23/AER/ACS, Award regarding suspension of the Proceedings and Jurisdiction, December 7th 2001.
[8] P. 61.
[9] P. 50.

Although today the suspicions toward international arbitration are said to come from the "developing world," the reader may be surprised/interested to know that the prevalent dubious feeling toward arbitration was initially rooted in both civil and common law traditions. Indeed, when reading chapter 3, it seems that the relationship between western domestic jurisdictions and international arbitration was one of "jealousy," "competition," and "hostility."[10] For instance, American courts' tolerance for international arbitration was rather limited until the adoption of the Federal Arbitration Act (FAA) in 1925, which marked the "triumph" of arbitration over domestic courts.

Chinese and African legal traditions, on the other hand, have shown, at early stages, openness toward mediation and conciliation techniques. For instance, African societies used alternative dispute settlement methods before the era of colonization and have used them in their judicial processes. Likewise, Kidane explains that a distinguishing feature of Chinese arbitration law consists in the application of equitable principles.

In chapter 4, entitled "The Theories and Theoreticians of International Arbitration," Kidane focuses on legal writings relating to the alleged existence of a supranational arbitral legal order. He describes the issue of sharing powers among international tribunals and domestic courts and how the latter have gradually set the parameters of their tolerance toward a supranational adjudicative framework. There exist, however, several positions to describe the relationship between domestic courts and international tribunals. This debate has been widely shaped by members of a "prosperous epistemic community" (i.e., Emmanuel Gaillard, Jan Paulsson, Catherine Rogers, Gary Born, Subdaresh Menon), and the author openly tackles each of them. For instance, Paulsson's position that "arbitration (…) functions routinely without judicial assistance" is, as Kidane points out, extravagant and reflects a "utopian notion of self-governance."[11] Whether it is an autonomous or transnational legal order, international arbitration "is indeed an 'ethical no-man's land.'"[12]

In the following chapters (Chapter 5, "The Evolving Justification of International Arbitration," and Chapter 7, "Culture and the Legal Infrastructure of Investment Arbitration"), Kidane continues to tackle stereotypes. His demonstration consists in showing that the justifications of international arbitration (i.e., neutrality, enforceability, flexibility, expertise, and confidentiality) are based on a biased archetype that multinational business "want(s) to stay out of what it consider(s) inhospitable, biased and ignorant local courts."[13] Kidane seeks an answer to the common assumption that local courts are biased and corrupted and perhaps provocatively wonders what "superior mechanism does the arbitral system have to avoid that?" He observes in this regard that although international arbitration may minimize jurisdictional problems (personal or subject matter jurisdiction), it is not protected against parallel

---

[10] P. 33.
[11] P. 80.
[12] P. 84.
[13] P. 91.

litigation. He denounces the conventional thinking behind the notion of neutrality and calls the reader to think about the true meaning of neutrality from an African state perspective when involved in a dispute with a western multinational company, concluding that from this standpoint "neutrality (…) is difficult to achieve, at least in the current [state???] of North-South economic hierarchy."[14]

As described in Chapter 7 (Culture and the Legal Infrastructure of Investment Arbitration), the challenges raised from the lack of diversity are more apparent in this field than in commercial arbitration. The author offers observations about the empirical studies aimed at analyzing whether or not the ICSID system shows signs of bias in favor of developed countries or, more accurately, whether the risk of bias from arbitrators is proportional to the level of development of a given country (the less developed the more biased).[15] In this last chapter of the first part, it is recalled that many empirical studies avoid "the most fundamental question of the impact of the diversity deficit on the outcome."[16]

In the second part, entitled "Deconstructing the Mythology of Specialized Knowledge in International Arbitration," Kidane asks, what is the most important legal qualification that is required for international arbitration? It should be the familiarity with the applicable law to a dispute, in his view. In-depth knowledge of an applicable law would most likely enable an arbitrator to understand the facts. However, as Kidane explains in his second part, the "elitist approach" consisting in selecting arbitrators from the same legal traditions significantly contrasts with this objective.

The chapters of the second part are based on the assumptions that "facts are probably more culturally sensitive than law – to the extent that the two could be readily separated."[17] The absence of diversity may therefore equally affect the proper application of the law as the determination of facts, which in turn influence the outcome of an award.

In Chapter 8, entitled "Diversity in the Epistemology of Judicial Fact-Finding in the Major Legal Traditions of the World," Kidane exemplifies the diversity of fact-finding in major legal traditions (common law, civil law, Chinese legal tradition, and Islamic legal traditions) of the world and describes it as a source of cultural misunderstanding among arbitrators. We learn, for instance, that the Chinese civil procedure is less confrontational than the common law system and favors a conciliatory approach. Although international arbitration has endowed itself with common sets of rules such as the IBA Rules on the Taking of Evidence, Kidane concludes that "they often mask the invisible cultural barriers."[18]

Interesting observations are made in Chapter 10 about the application of the rules of procedure and evidence (such as the International Chamber of Commerce Rules

---

[14] P. 104.
[15] P. 142.
[16] P. 146.
[17] P. 179.
[18] P. 212.

of Arbitration—"ICC Rules," the United Nations Commission on International Trade Law Model Law—"UNCITRAL Model Law," and the International Bar Association Rules on the Taking of Evidence in International Arbitration—"IBA Rules of Evidence"), on the difficulty to strike the right balance between fairness and economy of the process. The review leads to the thought-provoking conclusion that when it comes to fact-finding, "arbitrators are judges with limited checks and almost unlimited procedural powers."[19]

For a book denouncing cultural miscommunications and diverging perspectives, it should come as no surprise that the last chapter, "Conversations on the Role of Culture in International Arbitration," offers anecdotal account and first-hand knowledge of what goes on in the arbitral room. Judges of the International Court of Justice (Judge Yusuf, Judge Xue, Judge Sebutine) and arbitrators, who are, after all, part of the epistemic arbitral community, report their experience and observations on the role of culture in international arbitration.

Answering questions from the author, Judge Yusuf, for instance, explains that the manifestations of cultural differences are principally procedural. According to him, the most important factor in fact assessment is the legal tradition of the judge. Judge Yusuf explained that when a country decides to be represented by its own legal advisers and not by the dominant lawyers retaining the lion's share of ICJ cases, it adds some credibility to the position they are defending.

Whether one considers international arbitration as a system or as a framework would necessarily change the lens through which one could apprehend the issue of diversity in this field. Without hiding his preference, the author instructively explains why international arbitration should be seen as a framework. This book finds an absence of diversity in this field. Kidane's analysis is a legitimate reminder that the *status quo* is not an option as well as a prompt reminder of a well-known legal maxim that "Not only must *Justice* be done; it must also be *seen to be done*."

# Reference

Salini Construttori S.p.A (Claimant) v. The Federal Democratic Republic of Ethiopia, Addis Ababa Water and Sewerage Authority (Ethiopia) (Respondent), ICC Arbitration No. +=&23/AER/ACS, Award regarding suspension of the Proceedings and Jurisdiction, December 7th 2001

---

[19] P. 237.

# Part VI
# UN Document with Commentary

# UN Security Council Resolution 2378 (2017) and the Progressive Peacekeeping Agenda: A Commentary

## Christian Henderson

UN Security Council Resolution 2378, which was unanimously adopted[1] on September 20, 2017, is a notable resolution, bringing together, while attempting to drive forward, various ideas and reform proposals that have emerged in recent years in connection with United Nations peacekeeping operations. The fact that it was proposed by Ethiopia,[2] deliberated in Addis Ababa, and adopted during Ethiopia's presidency of the Security Council are testaments to the central role that this state has played, and continues to play, in UN peacekeeping, perhaps most notably through its position as the leading troop-contributing country to such operations.[3] In this respect, it is notable that the resolution "*[u]nderscor*[es] the importance of peacekeeping as the most effective tools [sic] available to the United Nations in the promotion and maintenance of international peace and security"[4] while also "[r]*eaffirming* [the Security Council's] resolve to strengthen the central role of the

---

[1] For fully supportive statements of Council members and the unanimous vote on the resolution see Security Council 8051st meeting Wednesday, 20 September 2017 (UN Doc S/PV.8051), pp. 1–35 at https://digitallibrary.un.org/record/1304967/files/S_PV-8051-EN.pdf.

[2] See *Letter dated 22 August 2017 from the Permanent Representative of Ethiopia to the United Nations addressed to the Secretary-General* (S/2017/766) at https://digitallibrary.un.org/record/1304967?ln=en.

[3] See http://www.providingforpeacekeeping.org/2014/04/03/contributor-profile-ethiopia/. During the adoption of resolution 2378, his Excellency Secretary-General António Guterres, thanked 'this month's presidency of the Security Council, Ethiopia, for being such a steadfast contributor to peacekeeping. Its personnel are on the front lines in some of our most challenging missions, and we are extremely grateful for that commitment'. See Security Council 8051st meeting Wednesday, 20 September 2017, UN Doc S/PV.8051, p. 2.

[4] UNSC Resolution 2378 (2017), preamble.

C. Henderson (✉)
University of Sussex, Sussex, UK
e-mail: c.m.henderson@sussex.ac.uk

United Nations in peacekeeping and to ensure the effective functioning of the collective security system established by the Charter of the United Nations."[5]

Following on from both the 2015 report of the High-Level Panel on Peace Operations, *Uniting Our Strengths for Peace*,[6] and the follow-up report of the UN Secretary General, *The Future of United Nations Peace Operations*,[7] as well as the "Leader's Summit on Peacekeeping" held in New York in September 2015, where new commitments were pledged by over 50 states,[8] the five-page resolution, *inter alia*,

- reaffirms the need for the peaceful resolution of disputes, in particular through the utilization of the good offices of the Secretary General[9];
- affirms the importance of political solutions in the design and deployment of United Nations peacekeeping operations[10];
- emphasizes the need for more thorough planning of peacekeeping missions and better training and equipping of their personnel[11];
- reaffirms its commitment to greater coordination with regional and subregional organizations, in particular the African Union[12];
- urges greater care in devising achievable mandates that can be met[13];
- stresses the need to fill the persistent capacity and capability gaps[14];
- recognizes the importance of improving the accountability, transparency, efficiency, and effectiveness of peacekeeping operations through consideration of the 2015 report and the recommendations of the UN Secretary General,[15] as well as ensuring a zero-tolerance policy toward sexual exploitation or abuse[16];
- furthermore, and in keeping alive debate regarding the controversial "Responsibility to Protect" concept, the resolution is clear that "States bear the primary responsibility for protection of civilians throughout their whole territory while mindful of the important role United Nations peacekeeping operations play in this regard."[17]

---

[5] Ibid.

[6] Report of the Independent High-level Panel on Peace Operations: *Uniting our Strengths for Peace: Politics, Partnership and People*, UN Doc. A/70/95-S/2015/446, 17 June 2015.

[7] Secretary-General's Report, *The future of United Nations peace operations: implementation of the High-level Independent Panel on Peace Operations*, UN Doc. S/2015/682, 2 September 2015.

[8] 'Leaders' Summit on Peacekeeping', September 2015 (New York) (Leaders' Summit on UN Peace Operations – 28 September 2015).

[9] UNSC Resolution 2378 (2017), para. 4.

[10] Ibid., preamble and para. 1.

[11] Ibid., preamble.

[12] Ibid., preamble, para. 14, para. 15.

[13] Ibid., preamble.

[14] Ibid., preamble, para. 11 and para. 17.

[15] Ibid., para. 5, para. 6, para. 11, para. 12, para. 13 and para. 17.

[16] Ibid., preamble and para 19.

[17] Ibid., preamble.

The UN Security Council also welcomed in the resolution the intention of Secretary General António Guterres to introduce peacekeeping reform,[18] which sits within the plans of the Secretary General for broader reform of the UN, and "[r]*equests* the Secretary-General to provide a comprehensive annual briefing to the Security Council on reform of United Nations peacekeeping every twelve months to be followed by a debate."[19] In this respect, it also "[u]*nderlines* the importance of adequate implementation and follow-up of United Nations peacekeeping reform" and "*requests* its Working Group [established in 2001] to review reform initiatives" in cooperation with Member States, in particular those that contribute troops and host countries.[20] While reform proposals have been made previously, the efforts of the resolution in ensuring continuous reporting and review of reform is not only welcome but also necessary to maintain the momentum of the reform agenda.

The focus of many of the criticisms targeted toward peacekeeping—as well as initiatives at reforming it—has been the overly ambitious nature of the mandates provided to operations. While this tendency can be traced back to the United Nations Operation in the Congo (ONUC) in the 1960s,[21] the post-Cold War era has witnessed the expansion of peacekeeping operations in terms of them often taking on a multidimensional approach in securing the transition from conflict to stable government, such as the operations within Mali and the Central African Republic, but also, and significantly, in terms of the "robustness" of the mandates that they have been provided with and the extent to which they are permitted to use force in self-defense and to achieve their mandates. In particular, the authorization to the United Nations Organization Stabilization Mission in the Democratic Republic of the Congo (MONUSCO)[22] in 2013 to take "all necessary measures" to conduct "targeted offensive operations" through an "Intervention Brigade," which were intended "to prevent the expansion of all armed groups, neutralize these groups, and to disarm them,"[23] was controversial for obvious reasons and even labeled by the Security Council itself as "exceptional."[24]

It is noticeable, in this respect, that the resolution does not specifically mention or proffer any response to developments and controversies in these areas. While the resolution reaffirms "the basic principles of peacekeeping, including consent of the parties, impartiality, and non-use of force, except in self-defence and defence of the mandate,"[25] it does not elaborate upon these and the way they have been, or should be, implemented. Given that the resolution picks up upon many of the other key elements of the 2015 High-Level Panel report and the follow-up report of the UN

---

[18] Ibid., para. 7, and para. 8.
[19] Ibid., para. 10.
[20] Ibid., para. 9.
[21] Boulden (2015).
[22] For details see https://monusco.unmissions.org/en.
[23] UNSC Resolution 2098 (2013), para 12(b).
[24] Ibid., para. 9.
[25] UNSC Resolution 2378 (2017), preamble.

Secretary General, the fact that it apparently sidestepped this issue may be viewed as a notable omission. While the resolution's contribution on this issue may have been implicitly tied in with its overarching theme of "efficiency and effectiveness," the 2015 High-Level Panel report was, in particular, keen to stress that while peacekeeping operations may take a liberal view of their right to defend their mandate—something that the report claims always allows for the proactive protection of civilians—enforcement action and counterterrorism operations were to be left to others, in particular regional organizations and *ad hoc* coalitions of Member States. In this respect, while Resolution 2378 (2017) is in many ways a progressive contribution to peacekeeping doctrine, building upon, or at least acknowledging, the 2015 High-Level Panel report's call for clarity on the use of force would have been a welcome addition to what was already a commendable resolution.

To date, it has been both nonpermanent Member States of the Security Council and developing states within the UN that have ensured that peacekeeping operations have sufficient manpower to operate, as well as acting as the drivers of progressive change in regard to peacekeeping operations in general. Ultimately, Ethiopia should be commended for using its presidency of the Security Council to maintain and push forward the agenda of peacekeeping reform, particularly given the momentum that it has been provided with in the last few years. Resolution 2378 (2017) is a manifestation of its clear priorities in this respect.

## Resolution 2378 (2017) on Peacekeeping Reform[26]

Adopted by the Security Council at its 8051st meeting, on 20 September 2017

*The Security Council,*

*Recalling* the purposes and principles of the Charter of the United Nations, and reaffirming its primary responsibility for the maintenance of international peace and security,

*Recalling* its resolutions 1325 (2000), 1809 (2007), 2033 (2012), 2167 (2014), 2171 (2014), 2242 (2015) and 2320 (2016); as well as the statements of its President of 16 December 2014 (PRST/2014/27), 25 November 2015 (S/PRST/2015/22) and 31 December 2015 (S/PRST/2015/26),

*Affirming* that lasting peace is not achieved nor sustained by military and technical engagements alone, but through political solutions, and strongly convinced that they should guide the design and deployment of United Nations peacekeeping operations,

---

[26] https://www.un.org/press/en/2017/sc12996.doc.htm. Accessed 22 September, 2017, Reprinted with the permission of the United Nations.

*Underscoring* the importance of peacekeeping as the most effective tools available to the United Nations in the promotion and maintenance of international peace and security,

*Reaffirming* its resolve to strengthen the central role of the United Nations in peacekeeping and to ensure the effective functioning of the collective security system established by the Charter of the United Nations,

*Further reaffirming* the basic principles of peacekeeping, including consent of the parties, impartiality and non-use of force, except in self-defence and defence of the mandate, and recognizing that the mandate of each peacekeeping mission is specific to the need and situation of the country concerned, and that the Security Council expects full delivery of the mandates it authorizes,

*Underscoring* the importance it places on the safety and security of peacekeepers in the field and the need for the Secretary-General and troop- and police-contributing countries, respectively, to work together to ensure that all peacekeepers in the field are willing, capable and equipped to effectively and safely implement their mandate,

*Recognizing* the pledges made by a number of Member States to help meet persistent capacity gaps and improve the performance and capabilities of uniformed and civilian personnel made at various multilateral meetings held in 2015 and 2016, including the "Leaders' Summit on Peacekeeping" held in New York in September 2015, the "UN Peacekeeping Defence Ministerial" held in London in September 2016 and the "Ministerial Conference on Peacekeeping in the Francophone Area" held in Paris in October 2016, and *underscoring* the need to fulfil these pledges in order to contribute to improving the overall effectiveness and efficiency of United Nations peacekeeping,

*Recalling* the Secretary-General's report entitled "The Future of United Nations Peace Operations: Implementation of the Recommendations of the High-Level Independent Panel on Peace Operations" (A/70/357-S/2015/682) and the recommendations of the report of the High-Level Independent Panel on Peace Operations (A/70/95-S/2015/446), which became the basis for further decisions of the Member States in the Security Council, and Fourth and Fifth Committees of the General Assembly, as well as the Special Committee on Peacekeeping Operations,

*Recognizing* that cooperation with regional and subregional organizations in matters relating to the maintenance of peace and security, and consistent with Chapter VIII of the Charter of the United Nations, can improve collective security,

*Reaffirming* that States bear the primary responsibility for protection of civilians throughout their whole territory, while mindful of the important role United Nations peacekeeping operations play in this regard and further recognizing the role that regional and subregional organizations can play in the protection of civilians, and in particular women and children affected by armed conflict, as well as in the prevention of and response to sexual and gender-based violence in armed conflicts and post-conflict situations,

*Recognizing* the indispensable role of women in United Nations peacekeeping, including supporting the critical role that women play in all peace and security efforts, including those to prevent and resolve conflict and mitigate its impact, *welcoming* efforts to incentivize greater numbers of women in military and police deployed in United Nations peacekeeping operations and *recalling* its resolution 2242 (2015) and its aspiration to increase the number of women in military and police contingents of United Nations peacekeeping operations,

*Reaffirming* its support for the United Nations zero-tolerance policy on all forms of sexual exploitation and abuse, welcoming the Secretary-General's continued efforts to implement and reinforce this policy,

*Noting* the signing, on 19 April 2017, of the Joint United Nations-African Union Framework for enhanced partnership between the United Nations Secretariat and the African Union Commission for peace and security in the African continent,

*Taking note* of the ongoing efforts of the African Union and the subregional organizations, within the framework of the African Peace and Security Architecture (APSA), to strengthen their capacity and undertake peace support operations in the continent, in accordance with Chapter VIII of the Charter of the United Nations, particularly the African Standby Force and its Rapid Deployment Capability,

*Further taking note* of the Secretary-General's report on options for authorization and support for African Union Peace Support Operations pursuant to Security Council resolution 2320 (2016), including the financing models as well as the joint planning and consultative decision-making and oversight proposal presented in that report, and noting the need to further develop this work, in consultation with the African Union,

*Recalling further* its encouragement for the African Union to finalize its human rights and Conduct and Discipline Compliance frameworks for African Union peace support operations, to achieve greater accountability, transparency, and compliance with international human rights law and international humanitarian law, as applicable, and with United Nations conduct and discipline standards, and *underscoring* the importance of these commitments as well as the requirement for oversight by the Security Council of operations authorized by the Security Council and under the Security Council's authority consistent with Chapter VIII of the Charter,

*Recalling* the commitment made by the Assembly of the African Union in January 2015, at its 24th Ordinary Session to fund 25% of the cost of its peace and security efforts, including peace support operations to be phased in over a 5-year period, as reaffirmed at the 25th Ordinary Session in Johannesburg in July 2015, *re-emphasizing* that consultative analysis and joint planning with the United Nation is critical to developing joint recommendations on the scope and resource implications of potential peace support operations, assessing action and undertaking missions where appropriate, and regularly reporting on such actions when taken and stressing the importance of full compliance with African Union and United Nations human rights and conduct and discipline policies and arrangements,

*Taking into account* its key role in strengthening United Nations peacekeeping and reaffirming its commitment to continue to consider the relevant recommendations of the Secretary-General's report (A/70/357-S/2015/682) as well as their implementation, as necessary,

1. *Stresses* that the primacy of politics should be the hallmark of the approach of the United Nations to the resolution of conflict, including through mediation, the monitoring of ceasefires, assistance to the implementation of peace accords;

2. *Further stresses* that prevention of conflicts remains a primary responsibility of States and actions undertaken within the framework of conflict prevention by the United Nations should support and complement, as appropriate, the conflict prevention roles of national Governments;

3. *Reaffirms* the duty of all States to settle their international disputes by peaceful means, inter alia through negotiation, enquiry, good offices, mediation, conciliation, arbitration and judicial settlement, or other peaceful means of their own choice;

4. *Recognizes* that good offices of the Secretary-General can help resolve conflicts, and *encourages* the Secretary-General to continue to use mediation to help resolve conflicts peacefully, working in coordination and closely with the relevant regional and subregional organizations, including the African Union, as appropriate;

5. *Further recognizes* the critical importance of improving accountability, transparency, efficiency and effectiveness in the performance of United Nations peacekeeping operations including through further consideration of the relevant recommendations of the report of the High-Level Independent Panel on Peace Operations (A/70/95-S/2015/446) and the relevant recommendations of the Secretary-General's report (A/70/357-S/2015/682), in accordance with existing purviews and procedures;

6. *Emphasizes* the importance of ensuring agile and flexible field support by promoting innovation for better delivery and results with a view to enhancing the overall effectiveness of peacekeeping operations;

7. *Welcomes* the intention of the Secretary-General to introduce peacekeeping reform within the Secretariat as well as on the ground and *underscores* the need to continue to engage and seek the support of Member States to ensure transparency;

8. *Takes note* of the Secretary-General's initiatives to pursue structural reform of the Secretariat to reinforce the United Nations peace and security architecture; *encourages* the Secretary-General to continue to engage with the Security Council and the General Assembly and relevant Committees on his initiatives;

9. *Underlines* the importance of adequate implementation and follow-up of United Nations peacekeeping reform in accordance with existing mandates and procedures; *requests* its Working Group established in accordance with the presidential statement of 31 January 2001 (S/PRST/2001/3), to review reform initiatives in close cooperation with other Member States, including troop- and police-contributing countries and host countries;

10. *Requests* the Secretary-General to provide a comprehensive annual briefing to the Security Council on reform of United Nations peacekeeping every 12 months to be followed by a debate, *further requests* the Secretary-General to provide updates to the Security Council, as part of his comprehensive briefing, on the continuous efforts made in filling the existing gaps in terms of force generation and capabilities as well as other relevant aspects necessary for peacekeeping to effectively and appropriately respond to peace and security challenges; and *further*

*requests* the Secretary-General to provide recommendations to the Security Council within 90 days of the adoption of this resolution on a mechanism to fill these gaps including through more effective and efficient training and capacity-building;

11. *Underscores* the need to enhance the overall effectiveness and efficiency of United Nations peacekeeping by improving mission planning, increasing the number of relevant pledges of capabilities, including niche capabilities, enablers, engineering, medical and rapid deployment units, as well as reinforcing peacekeeping performance through training and to fulfil the pledges made by a number of Member States at the various multilateral meetings held in 2015 and 2016;

12. *Reaffirms* its determination to pursue more prioritization when evaluating, mandating and reviewing United Nations peacekeeping operations, including through strengthening triangular consultations with troop- and police-contributing countries and the Secretariat, strengthening existing formal mechanisms, and underlining the shared responsibility for meaningful, inclusive, active and dynamic consultations, as well as enhancing its dialogue with host countries, with the aim of fully and successfully implementing peacekeeping mandates;

13. *Further reaffirms* its ongoing efforts to review peacekeeping operations to ensure maximum effectiveness and efficiency on the ground, and to deepen these efforts in partnership with troop- and police-contributing countries and other relevant stakeholders, and requests the Secretary-General to ensure data streams related to the effectiveness of peacekeeping operations, including peacekeeping performance data, are centralized to improve analytics and evaluation of mission operations, based on clear and well identified benchmarks;

14. *Further reaffirms* its commitment to the cooperation between the United Nations and regional and subregional organizations and arrangements in matters relating to the maintenance of international peace and security, and consistent with Chapter VIII of the Charter of the United Nations, which can improve collective security;

15. *Reiterates* its determination to take effective steps to further enhance the relationship between the United Nations and regional organizations, in particular the African Union, in accordance with Chapter VIII of the United Nations Charter;

16. *Underlines* the importance of accelerating the operationalization of the African Standby Force and *calls upon* the United Nations and Member States to continue to support within the existing means the strengthening of the African Standby Force's readiness as the overarching framework for African peace support operations, and *requests* the Secretary-General to report on the progress achieved in this regard in his next Report on Strengthening the Partnership between the United Nations and the African Union on Issues of Peace and Security in Africa, including the Work of the United Nations Office to the African Union (UNOAU), and *encourages* the UN Secretariat and the AUC to collaborate towards strengthening the APSA by supporting the APSA road map and silencing the guns master roadmap and their respective work plans;

17. *Reiterates* that regional organizations have the responsibility to secure human, financial, logistical and other resources for their organizations and *recognizes* that ad hoc and unpredictable financing arrangements for African Union led

peace support operations authorized by the Security Council and consistent with Chapter VIII of the Charter may impact the effectiveness of these peace support operations;

18. *Expresses its intention* to give further consideration to practical steps that can be taken, and the conditions necessary, to establish the mechanism through which African Union led peace support operations authorized by the Security Council and under the Security Council's authority under Chapter VIII of the Charter could be partly financed through United Nations assessed contributions, on a case by case basis, in compliance with relevant agreed standards and mechanisms to ensure strategic and financial oversight and accountability, and taking into account the work undertaken by the United Nations Secretariat and the African Union Commission in this regard, acknowledging the development of operations mandated or authorized by the AU;

19. *Reiterates* its request to the Secretary-General, where applicable, to continue to take steps to enhance measures in United Nations peacekeeping operations against all forms of abuse and exploitation of civilians by any member of the United Nations peacekeeping operations, *urges* troop- and police-contributing countries to take preventive and disciplinary action to ensure that such acts are properly investigated and punished in cases involving their personnel; *reiterates* its call for all non-United Nations forces authorized under a Security Council mandate to take adequate measures to prevent and combat impunity for sexual exploitation and abuse, hold perpetrators accountable and repatriate units when there is credible evidence of widespread or systematic sexual exploitation and abuse by those units;

20. *Requests* the Secretary-General, in coordination with the African Union, to present in his next Report on Strengthening the Partnership between the United Nations and the African Union on Issues of Peace and Security in Africa, including the Work of the United Nations Office to the African Union (UNOAU), a reporting framework which would establish clear, consistent and predictable reporting channels, including fiduciary and mandate delivery, between the Secretariat, the Commission and the two Councils, as well as standardized reporting requirements;

21. *Decides* to remain seized of the matter.

## References

Boulden J(2015-07-09) United Nations Operation in the Congo (ONUC). In: The Oxford Handbook of United Nations Peacekeeping Operations. Oxford University Press. Retrieved 12 Nov. 2017, from http://www.oxfordhandbooks.com/view/10.1093/oxfordhb/9780199686049.001.0001/oxfordhb-9780199686049-e-21. Accessed 27 Oct 2017

http://www.providingforpeacekeeping.org/2014/04/03/contributor-profile-ethiopia/. Accessed 20 Oct 2017

https://monusco.unmissions.org/en

'Leaders' Summit on Peacekeeping', September 2015 (New York) (Leaders' Summit on UN Peace Operations – 28 September 2015)

*Letter dated 22 August 2017 from the Permanent Representative of Ethiopia to the United Nations addressed to the Secretary-General* (S/2017/766) at https://digitallibrary.un.org/record/1304967?ln=en. Accessed 20 Oct 2017

Report of the Independent High-level Panel on Peace Operations: *Uniting our Strengths for Peace: Politics, Partnership and People*, UN Doc. A/70/95-S/2015/446, 17 June 2015

Secretary-General's Report, *The future of United Nations peace operations: implementation of the High-level Independent Panel on Peace Operations*, UN Doc. S/2015/682, 2 September 2015

Security Council 8051st meeting Wednesday, 20 September 2017 (UN Doc S/PV.8051), pp. 1–35 at https://digitallibrary.un.org/record/1304967/files/S_PV-8051-EN.pdf. Accessed 25 Oct 2017

UNSC Resolution 2098 (2013)

UNSC Resolution 2378 (2017)

**Christian Henderson** is Professor of International Law, University of Sussex, UK.

CPSIA information can be obtained
at www.ICGtesting.com
Printed in the USA
LVHW06*2102040818
585977LV00006B/119/P